THE TUDOR BOOKS
OF
PRIVATE DEVOTION

✠The Tudor Books of Private Devotion

By Helen C. White

THE UNIVERSITY OF WISCONSIN PRESS

PRINTED IN THE UNITED STATES OF AMERICA
BY THE VAIL-BALLOU PRESS, INCORPORATED

To

JOHN

with my thanks

ACKNOWLEDGMENT

My thanks are due, first of all, to the Henry E. Huntington Library and Art Gallery for the fellowship that made it possible for me to begin the basic research for this book at the Huntington Library in 1939–1940, and then to the University of Wisconsin for a semester's leave for research in 1947 that enabled me to push on the work already begun, and finally to the American Association of University Women for the Achievement Award of 1949, that helped me to complete it. I wish to express, too, my warm appreciation of the courtesy and helpfulness of the authorities of the Huntington Library, the Widener and Houghton Libraries of Harvard University, the Boston Public Library, the Folger Shakespeare Library, the Library of Congress, the British Museum, the Bodleian Library, the Library of Cambridge University, and the Libraries of the University of Wisconsin and the State Historical Society of Wisconsin.

In the references to sixteenth-century texts, titles have been given in as brief a form as possible, with the spelling and, as far as practicable, the punctuation of the original, but with the type and the capitalization standardized. In quotations the original spelling and punctuation have been kept with these exceptions: all contractions have been extended, merely typographical peculiarities of sixteenth-century printing disregarded, and the varieties of type reduced to two, roman and italic, with the italic reserved for special purposes.

H.C.W.

The University of Wisconsin
September 1, 1950

CONTENTS

LIST OF ILLUSTRATIONS

THE TUDOR BOOKS
OF
PRIVATE DEVOTION

I

INTRODUCTION

THE fact that a very considerable degree of continuity persisted throughout the revolutionary changes of sixteenth-century English life is pretty generally appreciated. Nowhere is this continuity better illustrated than in the collections of prayers for private devotion which were so popular a feature of the religious publication of the time. But, so far, on the whole, these collections have not received anything like the attention which they deserve.

Probably the main reason for this neglect is the obvious one. They have simply been overshadowed by the official books for public and common prayer. There is no question of the greater historic significance of these latter for charting the development of the new order which finally took shape in the Elizabethan Settlement. Nor is there any doubt that the official books remain the most certain source of information for over-all devotional influences. For, with the exception of certain privileged foreigners, everyone had to come in contact with the public prayer books as with the public services. That contact, however, might be and doubtless was of all degrees of interest or indifference, of fervor or nominal conformity. So it may be doubted whether for all their general influence the official books reached the religious mind of the time so intimately or reflected it so fully as the manuals of private devotion.

These by the very circumstances of their publication had to appeal to personal conviction and taste in the most personal of spiritual undertakings, solitary prayer. For no one was likely even to consider using a manual of private devotion unless he desired a more intensive exploration of the resources of prayer than was immediately available in common pious practice. And when it came to the choice of his manual, we may be sure that he would take pains to find one which appealed to his own particular tastes and interests. So this field of private devotional literature may well be expected to afford a more direct and more dependable way to the understanding of the religious consciousness of much of sixteenth-century England than any other single avenue of approach now available to us.

And it may serve, too, to throw some light upon the important but still too obscure history of private devotion. For the large and dramatic part played in the history of religion by controversies over liturgy and public prayer has tended to obscure and do something less than justice to the relative importance of private prayer. By its very nature public prayer is more accessible to observation and more susceptible of analysis and definition, to say nothing of dispute. And the focal character of its relation to personal and community observance alike, and the extensiveness of its involvements of faith and feeling make the public religious service a natural testing-ground for rival theories and sentiments, and a rallying-point for loyalties and aspirations in a time of sharpening division. The part which arguments over the Prayer Book have played in the history of English religious life is but one especially striking example among many in the history of religious observance.

Yet there is every reason to believe that private prayer antedates public and may fairly be considered the root and source of the latter.[1] Even in the primitive tribal world, where consciousness was evidently less highly individuated than in more sophisticated societies,[2] there is no reason to suppose that the hunger and thirst of the mind and heart were any less private than those of the physical organism, nor the sudden impact of fear and awe and wonder any less personally insistent than with more self-conscious man. The outthrusting of the experimental tentacles of the slow-moving mass of the community consciousness must have been individual here as elsewhere, and the first tentatives of formulation the product of the individual craftsman in the realm of word and gesture as in other efforts to give external body to the gropings of the mind.

The great themes of common prayer—the recognition of the presence of the divine, the praise of the power and majesty of God, the confession of unworthiness, the begging of help for the averting of disaster, the prayer for enhancement of inner strength, both physical and moral, the intercession for the living and the dead, the giving of thanks, the asking of forgiveness and the endeavor to placate divine wrath, the submission to the will of Providence, and not least, love's yearning to find words for its rejoicing in the presence of the beloved—these are the themes, too, of private prayer. In some degree all men have known these impulses, and yet here as in other categories of human experience, there have been great differences in the capacities of men to enter into these experiences, and probably still greater differences in the ability to find fit words for them. But it should never be forgotten, either, that here, as in all human undertakings, the yearning for perfection is no less insistent a part of the data than the obvious fact of human limitation. For all his preoccupation with what passes within the confines of his own too finite hide, there is in the least gifted or advanced of men ever a yearning for the extension of his experience beyond his own capacity, indeed, for the transcending of the limitations of his capacity. Even in that most universal of the acknowledgments of human limitation, the unconscious and almost involuntary specialization of interest and taste, man yet retains some wistful interest in the field which the distribution of his talents has led him to forgo. Consequently, most men have a broader and more active range of capacity for appreciation than creation. All excellence of expression, therefore, has a very real measure of social value and significance. For the artist satisfies not only his own need but his inarticulate brother's as well.

And, conversely, even the most individual and exalted expression of private devotion has its social indebtedness. For the ground of the most independent and fearless of spiritual adventurings is still the faith of the group, of the tribe, of the community, of the church, or of the general and undefined currents of the religious thought and feeling of the time.[3] When one realizes the scope of prayer, wide and deep and complex as human life itself, it is not difficult to understand that no one human spirit, not even the most gifted or the most experienced, is adequate for all its undertakings. Here what is true of all the great creative fields of human activity is supremely true, that the greater the artist the greater his indebtedness to the common experience of his group and his time.

But there is in this field a special and distinctive reason for emphasizing the social aspects of the individual spirit's solitary adventuring. The goal of all prayer is communion with Reality, with Divinity.[4] In all traditions men have believed that in prayer man enters into the presence of God.[5] Consequently, the direction which his prayer takes cannot remain unaffected by that fact. Men's conceptions of God have varied, from man to man, and place to place, and time to time. But the most elementary notion of God still has implications of universal wisdom and power and love that dwarf all the usual discriminations of individual and social into insignificance. So in the presence of God the customary preoccupations of human egoism fall away abashed, and the spirit freed from itself soars into the largeness of divine understanding.

There is, then, no real opposition between public prayer and private. They are but different facets of the same whole. Public springs from private prayer, winnowed by group trial and choice. In that process it becomes impersonal, objective, universal. But it never loses some impress of the particular mould out of which it came. And its continuing vitality and efficacy depend in no small degree upon the richness and immediacy of appreciation with which it is appropriated by recurrent individual need and aspiration. In other words, as Guardini so well pointed out, the lofty majesty of liturgy must continually be warmed by the particular passion of private prayer.[6]

And what is true of this distinction of social and private is in varying degrees true of some other dichotomies often mooted in this field, such as that between the intellectual and the emotional, and the prophetic and the mystical elements. Unquestionably, some periods and schools of devotion are more disposed to the affective elements than others. In general, seventeenth-century French devotion is more emotional than eleventh-century Roman, and there is no question that Saint Bonaventura is tenderer than Saint Thomas Aquinas, though hardly more passionate. But prayer at its best does justice to both the affective and the intellectual elements, for it involves the whole man. The difference is often, too, a matter of occasion. A prayer of praise or thanksgiving may well give rein to emotion where a prayer of intercession or resolution of amendment of life will hew more straitly to the intellectual line. But the greatest of prayers will have something of both.

And so with the opposition of the prophetic and the mystical. Each has its place. The discovery of revelation and the joyous proclamation of its message is one of the great inspirations to prayer. So, also, is the rapt appreciation and penetration of contemplation and the mystic's aspiration to union with the object of his contemplation. Luther's prayer like Jeremiah's is likely to be prophetic, and Bernard of Clairvaux' mystical, but both elements are to be found in the prayer of Saint

Paul and Saint Augustine. Again, the factor of function should not be disregarded, for there are occasions that suggest one type of prayer, and occasions that quite as obviously require another. For both elements have their part in religious life, in the knowledge and experience of God, which is its goal.

From the point of view of the student of literature, however, private prayer has special claims to attention, precisely at those points where it most differs from public. The very individuality of private prayer gives it a personal color that is always of peculiar interest to the student of literature. For those differences of emphasis and focus in the universals of human nature that constitute the wonder of personality are in themselves of perennial fascination to the literary mind. The fullness of revelation of the inward life, implicit in private prayer, offers fresh material for the exploration of the human consciousness. These values are timeless, and so of enduring validity.

Yet there are others of hardly less interest. One may read the successive formulations of public prayer and learn much of the currents of thought of the time, and of the interests and aspirations of the particular men or groups of men who had a hand in the shaping of those devotional media. But in the private prayers of the time one learns more of the spontaneous impulse, of the contemporary ebb and flow of hope and aspiration, of the habits of thought and feeling that emerge from the sequence of those particular moments of consciousness that constitute the character of the time. For the student of the history of thought and feeling here is firsthand evidence for the picking up and tracing of the patterns of the inner life of, in this case, the sixteenth century.

The most abundant supply of this material is to be found in the books of private devotion of the time. In a sense, of course, they violate the sanctities of solitary prayer. Some of them represent, as we shall see presently, a quite conscious effort to direct and guide private devotion into the channels acceptable to the forces that were reshaping religious life in the sixteenth century. Some of these prayer books had official standing, and were, in intention and in effect, instruments of official propaganda. But even in these books there is apparent a genuine religious purpose to bring aid to the devotional efforts of the less expert out of the professional's gleanings.

The gathering of collections of favorite prayers has been one of the immemorial exercises of piety in all traditions, and it has by no means been confined to the amateur collector or limited to the lay reader. We have Augustine's witness in one of the most intimately poignant and moving passages of the *Confessions* to the comfort he received in his extreme need from a great prayer of Ambrose.[7] The man who was, after Saint Paul, the most original and gifted of the devotional masters of the Christian tradition did not hesitate here, as elsewhere, to express his indebtedness to the praying of others for help in his own prayer. From the earliest days the treasuring up of the devotions of the masters has been one of the classic forms of professional activity in the history of Christian devotion.

Likewise, the making current of such collections has been one of the great pastoral activities of official religious leaders. For, after all, the life of private prayer has been the goal toward which the spiritual guide has ever directed his labors with the souls of those committed to his charge. It is that to which all his teachings are directed, and yet, however carefully he may prepare and train his spiritual pupils, it is at that point of the undertaking of private prayer that he must give over his direction and watch them stagger off on their own. Nothing is more natural, then, than that pastoral solicitude should seek to afford the pupil some help that will stay with him when his teacher and guide is no longer available. For that reason, the collection of prayers for private lay use is a very old undertaking of Christian piety, limited in the Middle Ages, say, by the state of public education, but still more by the great costliness of books. It was an undertaking to which the invention of printing brought undreamed-of resources by making books that had hitherto been restricted to the prosperous few widely and relatively cheaply available to increasing numbers of at least the middle grades of the economic and social structure. Indeed, a very large percentage of the publication of the time, estimated as more than 40 per cent by some scholars, was religious in subject matter, if not always in spirit.[8] And of this a very considerable proportion was concerned with the provision of aids to private devotion.

Sixteenth-century England had, of course, inherited a good many books of private devotion from the Middle Ages. They were of a number of different types, of which the most influential for the general audience were the Psalter and its offshoot, the Primer. Of these two, the latter was the more important, for it constituted what Henry Littlehales very aptly described as "the lay folks' prayer book." [9] This book was the fruit of generations of tradition and accretion and selection. In the course of time it had developed certain fixtures that one might expect to find in any primer, but there was still a wide margin for choice and adaptation in the provision of prayers for special needs and occasions. Above all, it had a tradition of flexibility and adaptability.

It was admirably suited, therefore, to the purposes of those who wished to bring about changes in the religious life and spirit of the times. It had early been subjected to the critical scrutiny of the sixteenth-century reformers who had no thought of changing the basic premises of religious doctrine and life, but who were anxious to purge the practice of that doctrine and life of acknowledged abuses and corruptions and to screw up the relaxed and weakened spring of its spirit. The Primer also attracted, however, the attention of men who wished to bring about various degrees of change in fundamental doctrine and pattern of life. The very criticisms of the earlier reformers now made it easier for these more radical reformers to adapt the Primer to their purposes. The result is a very interesting series of editions of the traditional book which reflect admirably the development of various stages in the English Reformation.

Indeed, the Primer became one of the official instruments of the government for propagating approved attitudes and states of mind and feeling. The resulting series of books is a fascinating one to study, because it is not by any means always easy to draw the line between the religious man's desire to conserve what is of enduring value through all contemporary changes and the statesman's concern about the precise degree of change which naturally conservative popular taste will stand. Nowhere is the tension between the exhilaration of sweeping away the past and the solicitude for keeping the prestige of the accepted and time-authenticated that runs through all sixteenth-century religious literature more apparent than here.

There were other types of devotional books besides the Primer— manuals of instruction for prayer and meditation and collections of prayers and meditations, as well as books of general spiritual direction of which portions at least were substantially devotional in character.[10] For many of these the old books of devotion were used rather freely, even as Scripture was, as a quarry out of which old prayers could be hewn in

whole or in part to be fitted into new contexts. And in still other cases
traditional prayers inspired imitations or what might be termed functional substitutes, which still bore recognizable relations to their ancient
originals or prototypes. From the source-hunting point of view the
running-down of these resemblances is a baffling business because of the
very freedom with which these authors worked in an age that had more
respect for authorities than for footnotes, for scholarly adornment than
for documentation. Consequently, it is for the student of the spiritual
impulses of the age both a teasing and a rewarding field of study.

For in these changes one picks up the main lines of the development
of the forces that were transforming the religious life of the time, with
many an incidental revelation of their inner day-to-day ramifications.
One receives, too, not a little insight into the ways of mass psychological
change, both directed and spontaneous, conscious and unconscious, with
the very impressive degree of continuity to be discerned even in a
period of such profound transformations.

II

THE MEDIEVAL INHERITANCE

IT WAS characteristic of the Renaissance to talk as if the world had begun all over again the morning of that very day. This is one of the most engaging manifestations of a certain adolescent exuberance that was an important element in the temper of the time. The reformers were soberer in their emotional tone, but they were no less positive in their acclaim of the new age of light and deliverance out of the darkness of the past. This psychology of "the world's great age begins anew," as a later poet was to put it for a very different time, is always to be reckoned with in any study of sixteenth-century England, but it is not to be taken too literally.

True, a considerable proportion of the religious thinkers of the period were engaged in a return to what they conceived to be the primitive state of the Christian community, as regards church government, discipline, and worship. And the prestige of the return to the primitive was enormously reënforced by the scripturalism of the age, which sought in the Word of God the indispensable authority for theory and practice. But not even the most radical primitivist can leap completely out of his time. The most thorough-going rebel is still a child of his day, and the things he most fiercely repudiates yet have power to call the changes of his thoughts. One may scorn fifteen hundred years of corporate experience, and even forget it, but he cannot escape its influence. So even the most optimistic of the sixteenth-century primitivists found it impossible to start at scratch as if those fifteen hundred years had never been. And to do justice to the good sense of most Englishmen, it may be doubted if very many of them really wanted to.

Especially is this true of private devotion. For here the reformers of every school had the most urgent reason for doing all they could to encourage and aid the inner life of piety. And in this field they had an especially rich inheritance. From the very beginning the Christian community had encouraged private prayer, not only of a formal and set pattern but also of a very personal and immediate character with every consideration for individual circumstance and occasion. And from the earliest days, likewise, Christian piety had cherished and disseminated the private productions of the masters of prayer.[1]

In this they were but carrying out a pattern which had been laid down for them in the Gospel reports of the way of life of the Master himself. Christ in his public ministry had given the supreme example of a life in which participation in the public devotional exercises of the Temple and the Synagogue, and teaching and preaching and healing went hand in hand with private prayer, which indeed found its nourishment and sustenance in solitary prayer in the wilderness, on the mountain top, in the garden. That example was not lost on his followers.

Fortunately, in the light of succeeding discussions of the relations between the active and the contemplative life, Saint Paul, the great shaping influence in the life of the church after the death of its founder, was not only a man of remarkable theological and organizing powers, but he was, also, deeply and profoundly a man of prayer, even a mystic, with a singular gift for putting the impulses of piety into words and for suggesting the ineffable. And the man who after Saint Paul contributed most profoundly to the development of the intellectual and devotional life of the church, Saint Augustine,[2] was likewise not only a great theologian and preacher and controversialist but also a contemplative of the first rank with an extraordinary talent for literary expression and a very original gift of introspection. The author of the Epistles and the author of the *Confessions* alike knew how to find words for their own private venturings into the presence of God that would put the fruits of their superlative genius at the disposal of their less gifted fellows.

Consequently, their prayers and their exhortations to prayer were treasured and circulated and used. Some of them, indeed, found their way into the liturgy of the church, the standard and common and universal public prayer of the mounting centuries. And their teaching and their example inspired others among their gifted successors to try to find words for their experience, in turn, and to put them, too, at the service of their fellows. But most important of all, they winged the faltering and half-aware aspirations of their inarticulate brethren to unknown generations. From the very earliest days to the present this unceasing interaction between public prayer and private has been the mainspring of the devotional life of the church.[3]

This is the secret, too, of the otherwise paradoxical influence which the development of monachism was to have upon the devotional aspirations of ordinary laymen and laywomen living in the world. For the contemplative achievements of the monk were but an intenser, a more professional and concentrated development of the devotional undertakings of the average Christian. Moreover, the monk, for all that he had separated himself from a pagan and sinful world, had not cut himself off from the integral and organic life of the church. His secluded effort was, therefore, a part of the corporate effort of the church and so a significant factor in its life.[4] And when in the western world, which here for our study of the background and inheritance of sixteenth-century England especially concerns us, monasticism became under the leadership of Saint Benedict of Nursia a dynamic, and even at certain points and at certain times a determining, influence in the life of the church, the influence of this specialization in prayer became of the greatest importance for the development of Christian devotion.[5]

This is easy to understand when we remember that there was in monasticism itself a very considerable social element. The monk was no solitary, but a member of a social group organized for the performance of the worship of God, for the *Opus Dei,* a service which the monastic community performed to the honor and glory of God and the spiritual benefit of the whole Christian body.[6] It was a social group, moreover, which was supposed to realize in its daily pattern of life the basic ethical values of Christianity. Therefore the function of the monastic orders as the specially and even professionally praying wing of the corporate church body was explicitly recognized by all, and, as the terms of countless monastic gifts and endowments make clear, acknowledged to the full by the lay members of the Church Militant.

The desire of the lay world to participate in the devotional observances of the monasteries manifested itself in many ways as monasticism grew and expanded. Indeed, some of the best known and most disastrous of the later difficulties of monastic discipline arose from this very fact.[7] But it was, also, one of the sources of the very great influence for good which the monasteries exerted on the life of their time. And the desire of lay men and women with the necessary cultivation and leisure to emulate monastic devotion was undoubtedly one of the motivating forces in the development of various types of devotional exercises which we shall have occasion to notice presently in greater detail.[8] It was natural, too, that members of the monastic orders with pastoral responsibilities, or members who felt themselves called to the work of public education and reformation, should endeavor to make provision out of their experience for the devotional life of the layman. Indeed, there were seldom wanting those who, conscious of the high privilege of their calling, were anxious to share their spiritual treasure with the less fortunate living in the world without their opportunities for training and experience.

In short, this interaction of monastic and lay devotion is so important for the history of private devotion that it is necessary to have some notion of the growth and development of monastic devotion to understand the corresponding development of popular private devotion, which is our field of inquiry.

It is tempting to sum up the history of Christian devotion in a series of great personalities, because the personal element is so important in Christianity, and because a series of great leaders do play so dramatic a part in the shaping of western monasticism. The very nature of Christianity with its emphasis upon the supreme personal element of the God who became Man and the Gospel story of that divine-human life upon earth focused attention upon personality.[9] And this was reenforced by the history of the successive persecutions of the early church with the very great demands made upon human courage and fortitude and the resultant moral significance of the martyrs and confessors whose supreme daring and fortitude did so much to hearten and sustain ordinary humanity and to vindicate its faith in the validity of its cause.[10] Especially was this important for the great numbers of the poor and humble who constituted so much of the membership of the early church, men and women whom their circumstances in the caste-ridden ancient world had given very little chance to measure their own capacities of moral action beyond submission and endurance.

This personal element was reënforced by the circumstances of the development of monasticism. The great monastic orders grew out of the patterns of life drawn up by personalities who combined rare insight into the needs of their times and unusual independence and originality in devising ways of meeting those needs. The first of our great masters of devotion, Saint Augustine, was not the founder of the institution of canons, but rather the reformer and the law-giver. As such, however, his work was to prove of wide and enduring influence.[11] The pattern of life which he worked out for his canons was designed to give a firm spiritual background and foundation for the daily life of priests who must fare forth into the streets and market places and courts and schools of their time and there plunge head-on into the maelstrom of a violent and critical age.[12] It must be a firmly founded faith and a thoroughly established inner discipline that would enable a man to bring into such a day-to-day battle the light and the energy that would win the surrounding pagan and heretical world to the Christian way of life.

Saint Augustine, whose own personal history had brought him into intimate contact with many facets of the confused life of his day, and whose temperament, at once versatile and passionate, had made him aware of the pull of the conflicting attitudes and values of a world of violently clashing forces, personal and impersonal alike, appreciated as could few men in authority the temptations and the strains to which human frailty was exposed in the heroic undertakings of the priesthood in that world of transition between paganism and Christianity. He, who had felt so keenly the charm of Plato [13] and the magnetism of the Fathers of the Desert alike,[14] was able more than most men to perfect a technique for building a spiritual shelter at the heart of the tempest and whirlwind of his day.

It is not surprising, therefore, that the pattern of life which he perfected, and still more the example which he himself gave, should have gone far beyond the relatively small and unimportant seaport which the genius of its bishop alone made famous and should have inspired emulation over the Christian world. Nor is it to be wondered at that in succeeding generations that pattern of life has not only found followers but has been a contributing source of inspiration to a series of experiments in meeting the no less serious and complicated problems of succeeding ages.[15]

But for the purposes of this study it is the great African bishop's own work in the devotional field that is the most interesting of his achievements. This is most enduringly apparent in the large number of his prayers, meditations, and treatises which, in whole or in part, have found their way into the breviary,[16] and in what might be called the semi-liturgical position which some of his prayers still hold, say in the prayers for thanksgiving after the Mass which are often found in the missals and manuals of prayer for the laity.[17] But from the point of view of sixteenth-century devotion still more important are the collections of Saint Augustine's prayers (or prayers ascribed to him) which achieved wide circulation in the Middle Ages and survived the changes of the sixteenth century in the veneration of Protestant and Catholic alike.[18]

And perhaps most consequential of all is the way in which Saint Augustine's prayers were used over and over again in general collections of prayers compiled for personal use by scholars and clerics or published by zealous pastors for the use of laymen. Indeed, Saint Augustine continued throughout the Middle Ages to exercise an influence on devotion not only through his own prayers, but as one of the great sources of inspiration and stimulation to other composers of prayers and meditations.[19] Some of their works, indeed, were actually ascribed to him and were printed and widely circulated as his works in both Catholic and Protestant devotional circles of the sixteenth century.

The prayers of Saint Augustine bear the impress of his highly mystical yet profoundly philosophic piety, and they are redolent of that richness of imagination and warmth of feeling that are the distinctive marks of his literary endowment. To a singular degree they combine the majesty of Roman prayer as still apparent in the Catholic liturgy with a distinctive personal warmth and immediacy that make Saint Augustine of all the ancient fathers seem closest to our introspective generation. It is easy to understand why their author should have exercised the most profound and most widespread influence since Saint Paul on the shaping of Christian piety.

If one compares Saint Augustine's prayers with those of his successors, it is quite apparent that they do not by any means exhaust the possibilities of Christian devotion, or to put it in more positive terms, that they have their own characteristic limits of range and emphasis. To begin with, many of them are addressed to God without distinction of person, that is, they do not discriminate between the members of the Trinity. It is easy to detect Platonic influences in Augustine's conception of God, as revealed in the terms of some of his addresses to the Deity. God as the indwelling beauty of the world, God as the richness that answers the heart's thirst, God as the light of the world to be apprehended in the lowliest human spirit—these are the concepts through which Augustine approaches God. True, Augustine is one of the most explicit and abject of the world's penitents. The confessional and the penitential themes are congenial to his experience and his habit of thought, but there is nothing of despair or uncertainty in his approach to divine justice. For he has known the fullness of the divine mercy and the miracle of divine grace. He is the most triumphant, even exultant, of the world's penitents and converts.

For all his tenderness and warmth, there is something very tough-minded about Saint Augustine, as may be seen in the *Confessions*. That work may be the most candid, but it is certainly the least senti-mental of that difficult genre. For all its passionate exultation in the wonder of his deliverance, there is no trace of self-glorification in it. It is his God who is the theme and not himself. It is that basic objectivity of his that gives breadth and power to the sensitiveness of his intro-spection. And one feels that in all his prayers. They are centered in God and not in himself. If the very versatility and range of his theo-logical speculations have laid him open to possible charges of incon-sistency and ambiguity, at least so far as his thinking is mirrored in that of his most enthusiastic followers, there can be no doubt of the healthiness and the sanity of his influence as a devotional force. In the greatest of his prayers, one enters with him into the presence of the Most High, and more than that one can hardly say of any de-votional writer.

The intellectual and spiritual progeny of Saint Augustine proved in the centuries to come literally beyond number, but in all the fields in which his followers sought to emulate his titanic example, he still towered above their heads. That is not true, I think, of the next great mountain-top figure in the history of Christian devotion. The world into which Benedict of Nursia came about a century and a half later was a very different one from Augustine's. It may be doubted if any one person could then have made himself felt in the immediate scene as Saint Augustine had made himself felt. For the process of dissolution of the ancient world was a century and a half more advanced by Bene-dict's time. The integrity of background that one still feels even in the most bewildered of Saint Augustine's broodings over the fall of Rome has receded by Benedict's time, and what remains of the ancient civilization is not so much confused as degenerate and enfeebled. Something of the firmness of mind of Roman civilization is still to be discerned in Benedict's own habits of thinking and in his spirit, but one knows without being told that in these things he rises above his time. For all his steadiness and clarity, his is quite literally a solitary beacon raised above the surrounding darkness and inertia. Indeed, he had to flee his world to save it.[20]

And yet that was only one side of Saint Benedict, as it was only one side of the sixth century. From a sinking civilization he fled into the wilderness, but it was not an empty wilderness. There were pagans there and barbarians, both the new arrivals and those whom the ancient civilization, like all civilizations, had never reached. And he was not content to let the wilderness or the pagans and barbarians continue as they were. For Benedict was a pioneer, a reformer, an educator, who set himself to the redemption of what must have seemed an appalling situation. It was not an age in which, we may repeat, any man could hope to make the impression which Saint Augustine had made on his world. The process of dissolution, and the advance of chaos, had gone too far. But it was an age in which a man could plant the seeds of a harvest which men would reap long after he was gone from the scene. And this Saint Benedict did.

It has been said that any institution is but the lengthened shadow of one great man. That is a statement of very doubtful truth, but it comes as close to being true of Saint Benedict's foundation as of any man's. For in his great rule he developed a pattern of life that would make it possible for countless generations of men after him to function, surely one of the most creative things any man can do.[21] It is characteristic of Saint Benedict that we have from him directions for prayer, a philosophy of prayer, a framework and an orientation of life for prayer, but not much of his own prayer directly. And if we compare him with Saint Augustine, we have nothing like the sense of his personality, the look and the feel of the inward and outer man that we have with Saint Augustine.

And yet, if one tries to define the Benedictine contribution to the development of Christian devotion, there is nothing hazy or uncertain here. Rather one feels as if he were on that clear height on which Benedict built his great spiritual experiment station and powerhouse, of which the light still streams across the ages for all the devastations of the successive waves of violence that have dashed against those heights. There is something very clear, very steady, very serene, very luminous in the pages of the great Rule and in the record of everything Benedict ever did. And one perceives it in the influence of his children in the centuries to follow, for all who have attempted the contemplative life in a systematic and social fashion from his day to this are in some degree his children. The key to that spirit is to be found in the word which he took as his watchword, *Pax*.[22] *Pax* to Benedict was not something to be hugged timidly to the nonresistant breast. It was not a refusal to join the fray, nor a minimal rejection of detested violence.

It was, rather, something positive, the peace of mastered and ordered and transmuted passions. It was a balance of physical labor (and that in a world which despised physical labor and could not comprehend the free election of such self-abasement) and mental and spiritual labor. It was a new version of the age-old Greek ideal of the harmonious man, not designed for a small aristocracy at the top of a slave-supported society, but for men of all classes and talents in a pioneering world. The Benedictines were not always to keep that ideal in more prosperous ages, but the ideal was there for revival, and there have never been wanting sons of Saint Benedict to hold the torch of his original vision aloft. But impressive as the educational work of the Benedictines has proved, not that, but the corporate and community worship of God, the great *Opus Dei,* has been their central purpose.[23] In all Benedictine devotion there is to be discerned that central stability and firmness of orientation, that serene spirit, with its roots in the soil, burgeoning in the open sunlight of God's presence. There is something at once very simple, even homely, and something very sublime in Benedictine devotion.[24]

The response to Benedict's example is one of the heartening facts in the history of Christianity. But the succeeding centuries, which brought such glory of achievement and of influence to the order which Benedict founded, brought, also, the great liabilities of success. Fashion misleads men as to their vocation. Prosperity tempts to comfort, success to complacency. Perhaps for most men there was something precarious in that serene balance of Benedict. In the course of the centuries there is complaint, self-criticism, uneasiness. Zeal, always skittish before ease and impatient of calm, made its protest, and having been listened to too often with theoretical approbation and practical indifference, betook itself to more direct action.

Of all the reformed Benedictines, the greatest is doubtless the Cistercian, Bernard of Clairvaux.[25] In many ways he reminds one of Saint Augustine rather than of Saint Benedict. He has the same instinct for great affairs, the same insight into the currents of his time, the same magnetism for his fellows. But he is a more concentrated and a more austere type of man.[26] Of course, his was basically a very different problem from Saint Augustine's; it was not the recalcitrance of a pagan or heretical world that confronted him. Rather it was weakness and lack of enthusiasm within the lines. The salt had lost its savor. The task that engaged his extraordinary moral energy was the whetting of the zeal of the elect, the renewal of the strength of those in possession.

Saint Bernard is warier of beauty than Saint Augustine, though we have no reason to believe that its love had ever betrayed his singularly pure spirit as it had Saint Augustine's. But he has something of the same delicacy of self-awareness as the author of the *Confessions* and the same warmth of feeling. Only in him it is very straitly focused upon the object of his devotion. And here again, he differs markedly from Saint Augustine in his conception, or perhaps rather in the distribution of emphasis in his conception of the object of his devotion. For his devotion is not to the supreme indwelling spiritual reality of the universe, human and divine, but to the humanity of Christ, conceived of with great liveliness of imagination and apprehended with singular tenderness of affection.[27]

The penitential and the ascetic notes are strong in Bernard; after all, they are his profession. But this devotion to the humanity of Christ warms the austerity of his writing not only with tenderness for his master, but with a homely directness and fullness of sense realization that gives peculiar power and conviction to everything he touches.[28] It is as if in apprehending the glorified humanity of Christ he came to appreciate all the facets of human life more fully and richly. And not least is this apparent in his devotion to the Mother of Christ, for Bernard is one of the great sources of Marian devotion.[29] There is a very profound connection between the devotion to the humanity of Christ and to his mother, apparent both in the spreading of the two [30] and in the later attacks upon Marian devotion. The range and delicacy of the development of sentiment in Bernard's Marian prayers is one of the great influences for the development of a warmer and tenderer type of devotion throughout the twelfth century.[31] It mitigated the austerity of much of medieval devotion, with its preoccupation with death and judgment and retribution. And if there is some sacrifice of grandeur, of the terrible and beautiful sublimity of the *Dies Irae,* for instance, there is a more than compensating gain in the closer approach of heaven and earth, and in the warmer and more immediate apprehension of the day-to-day redemption of human life.

This process was carried a number of steps forward by the founder of the Franciscan order. Again, a new man of great originality and magnetism faced a new set of conditions, faced them not as something contemplated from afar, but as something discovered most intimately within his own spirit, much as Saint Augustine in his day had found his own soul the theatre of the vast conflicts of his age. For Francis of Assisi was no innocent contemplating from afar the wickedness of a barbarian and pagan world. What he faced was the growing materialism of the Christian world itself, not the attenuation of zeal in those who had undertaken special responsibilities, but the weakening of Christian ideals and values in the masses of supposedly Christian men, the spiritual corruption of a great civilization.[32]

The growing security and prosperity of Italy had provided the material basis for the cultural triumphs of the thirteenth century; the increasing refinement of manners and feelings and the growing appreciation of the charms of art and culture held the seeds of the great artistic achievements to come. But the Renaissance of the twelfth century had already suggested the dangers which were later to be realized in fact in the Renaissance of the sixteenth century, that the cultivation of the possibilities of human life on this earth might bog down in luxury and curiosity, that the indispensable third of the Platonic triad, goodness, might be lost sight of in the pursuit of an inadequate ideal of truth and beauty, and the immortal destiny of man forgotten in the pursuit of this world's delight.[33]

Francis, the son of a prosperous and ambitious and by no means entirely Philistine merchant, had known within his own ardent young spirit the lure of chivalric ambition, the imaginative appeal of luxury, and the charm of social intercourse. His warm, outgoing enthusiasm for congenial company had made him the leader of the pleasure-seeking youth of his town. In other words, he had, like Saint Augustine before him, felt within his own soul the power of the forces with which he now undertook to contend. His attack was characteristically more radical than Saint Augustine's in that he undertook to do battle with the powers which threatened the destruction of Christianity on the immediate ground where he found himself. For ambitious slavery to wealth and power he substituted the freedom of voluntary poverty's rejection of the appetites of greed and ambition, and for the sociable pursuit of pleasure he substituted love of all created things, human and nonhuman. And for the anxieties of the ambitious man he substituted joy, the joy of complete and spontaneous acceptance of God's will. These three substitutions are the most thoroughgoing and the most effective of the substitutions men have ever attempted even in the realm of the spirit.

But quite as important as the theoretical reorientation of Francis was the influence of the techniques which he chose for his work of reform. Unlike most reformers, Francis had apparently no taste for arraignment or for eradication. His desire rather was for transformation, for the moving of the existent to the potential. His talent was not so much that of the word as of the act. His impulse was dramatic.[34] And it was quite as much out of the instincts of his own nature as out of any intellectual diagnosis of the needs of the time that he found his great instrument of operation in imitation, the imitation of Christ.

And this imitation he undertook for the most part in the midst of men. There are a few solitary episodes, of which the most famous is the retreat on Mount Alvernia that culminated in the stigmatization. But most of his work of imitation was done in the fields and the market places and the barns and the little villages of his immediate Umbrian world. It was the most direct and immediate apostolate to the masses conceivable, even as had been the apostolate of Christ. In him contemplation had quite literally come down from the Benedictine heights into the lowly places of the earth, and walked the highroads and the fields very much as in Christ's day.

Francis composed but little, and most of what he said we know from the reports of others. But what he did and what he was caught the imaginations of men and inspired one of the most magnetic and persuasive of personal legends on record.[35] Particularly did the example of his prayer with its stress on the affective and imaginative elements of devotion inspire succeeding generations of his followers and, through their preaching and their composition and dissemination of prayers, the popular devotional life of the whole church.[36] And that devotion to the humanity of Christ which Saint Bernard had done so much to propagate took on a homelier and more specific character in Francis' endeavor to penetrate into the heart of Christ's life on earth by humble and loving emulation. The imitation of Christ was no devotional abstraction for Francis of Assisi but the most actual and constant undertaking of his life.

Saint Francis' was not, however, the only attempt to solve the problem of the thirteenth century, the actual Christianizing of the supposedly but still very imperfectly Christian masses of the people.[37] Dominic Guzman has never had the personal appeal for ordinary humanity that Francis still possesses. The preacher will probably never make the appeal of the jongleur, nor the theologian of the artist. The intellectual battleground can seldom claim the dramatic interest of the physical, even with life eternal at stake. And yet in the end the work of Saint Dominic served the cause of devotion well. For when the scholastics had won the victory and, as is the way of men, had pushed it too far, and in the ingenuities of their own minds threatened to lose their grip on reality, spiritual and intellectual, it was the Dominicans, especially in Germany, who found their way out of the aridities of too restricted a rationalism to the greener heights of a living and humane mysticism.[38] And with the wisdom learned in dealing with the stirring and challenging city life of the high Middle Ages they performed yeoman service in the vital task of making available the riches of contemplation to the quite unmystical masses of medieval men and women.

Dominican devotion is good in the bone, and that intellectual firmness and centrality was to prove of great value in the growing lushness and even, now and then, extravagance of late medieval piety. And still more important, in view of the increasing criticism and disillusionment of those times, was the Dominicans' resolution to keep up with the advancement of knowledge and to take their part in the battle of ideas.[39] And their respect for the unceasing labor of popular education led to a contribution of growing significance as the invention of printing made the appeal to popular understanding easier and more influential for good or ill.

This appeal to popular understanding played a large part, also, in the progress of that movement known as the "New Devotion," of which Gerhard Groot is the pioneer, but the author of the *Imitation of*

Christ, the chief luminary.[40] The work of the Brethren of the Common Life is difficult to assess, for much of its effectiveness as a reforming movement was overshadowed when reform went into revolution in the sixteenth century. It is a part of the by no means as yet fully clear or appreciated story of the Catholic Reformation. In the beginning the work of the Brethren of the Common Life included certain elements that are found in reforming groups of different points of view at this time, such as a desire for a more practical and direct expression of the devotional impulse and an interest in education. Certain later developments cast a shadow of ambiguity over what seem to have been thoroughly orthodox and loyal tentatives of reform.[41] There certainly can be no doubt of the orthodoxy of the *Imitation of Christ;* indeed, it was the Protestant reformers who found difficulty in the highly developed Eucharistic devotion of the fourth book. There is no question, however, that the increasing introspection and the tendency to systematization of the devotional life that are characteristic of the sixteenth century [42] had in Thomas à Kempis' work given their coloring to the old conception of the imitation of Christ.[43] And something, too, of the repetitious and lingering quality of popular contemplation was added to the monastic type.[44]

Indeed, highly individual as the *Imitation* is in its exquisite blending of tenderness and modest reserve, it may be said to sum up the development of Christian devotion to the eve of the Protestant Reformation. For it is characteristic of this history which we have been so summarily outlining that nothing is ever quite left behind. There is something snowball-like in the process, and something richly multifarious in the final effect. It would be hard, indeed, not to see here fresh evidence of the basic continuity of the inner life of man.

And yet, in spite of all the continuity in the tradition of monastic devotion, there is ever something that is changing, growing, and revealing fresh implications in ancient values, fresh possibilities in what one would have thought well-worn themes, new facets to oft-expressed emotions. For all the concentration of prayer, there is here something expansive, genuinely creative—"the working of the Spirit," these great pioneers of prayer would call it.

But, humanly speaking, one may note certain tendencies persistently recurrent under the surface of this development through the centuries. Always the leaders are men of great force and independence and originality of mind and character, but they are, also, men of unusual sensitiveness to the course of events around them. They are by no means solitary in their perceptions or their diagnosis, or even in the remedies they devise to meet circumstance, for as in the case of Saint Benedict, it is easy to mark out their indebtedness to other leaders and movements. But they are the masters of the event with a psychological sense of time and place that is in the best sense statesmanlike. Even if they had all renounced the world, they displayed singular insight in their assessment of its condition and magnificent tact and resourcefulness in their meeting of its needs.

Another common denominator that should be noted, especially in view of the events of the sixteenth century, is the constant endeavor for reform. Some of this is, of course, the logical consequence of the devout Christian's ceaseless struggle for self-perfection. A man engaged in that endless struggle will naturally look to the relations of means to ends, and that in a corporate as well as individual sense. And if he is living in a community or institution dedicated to the spiritual enterprise before all others, he will labor for the reform of the group with which his own spiritual life is so organically identified. It would seem that with the changes in orientation of the religious life in the thirteenth century the theatre of this regard widened from the religious community, and even the order, to the secular world around. This is not to imply that the Benedictine on his height was indifferent to the world below. The record of Benedictine achievement for that world is too clear for any such misunderstanding, but it was not the immediate environment of the Benedictine monk in the same sense that it was of the Franciscan or the Dominican living in his mid-city friary; it could hardly impinge so directly or so constantly on his day-to-day consciousness.

Finally, there is always apparent in the larger sequences of these centuries of devotional development what can only be described as an instinct for harmony and for balance, a constant process of slow, sometimes almost imperceptible but ultimately decisive, adjustment and readjustment. There is nothing regular or automatic about it, but it is there. It is to be seen very clearly and even dramatically when Benedict flees from a world of deepening chaos and anarchy and high above the confusion builds a lighthouse where men may find not peace and safety but a chance to build an ordered and constructive way of life.

Peace and beauty are the by-products of that endeavor, and men who love peace and beauty take refuge there. Perhaps too many in the succeeding centuries forgot that that was a by-product and not an objective, and still less a means. Saint Bernard sternly redressed that balance. But in its purity and its austerity the Cistercian ideal remains a little aloof, a little too lofty perhaps for most men. Saint Francis and Saint Dominic fashion another approach in the dirt and the turmoil of the medieval town. So it goes from age to age.

Something of the same process of warping a little nearer to a more perfect harmony is to be seen, too, in the prayers that result from these changing approaches to the enduring problems of human redemption. The early Christian centuries developed magnificently the glory of God, the awesomeness of the Judge and the majesty of the Redeemer, and pulled all the deep and solemn organ stops of the basic themes of fear and contrition and pleading for forgiveness. It was a very serene and majestic humanity that looked down from beneath the crown on the earliest crucifixes, say of the sixth and seventh centuries. Then in the twelfth century that figure began to come to life in the devout imagination, and in the next century the human body began to bare the signs of its anguish, and pity and compunction came into the sinner's heart, and compassion to the face of the crucified God-Man upon whom he looked.[45] And presently, a new tenderness had come into the heart once obsessed with its own sense of sin and its fear of justice too well deserved, and that tenderness warmed all the sinner's thinking of God until the Judge vanished in the tender and compassionate Redeemer. There is light and beauty in this, and it is to be seen not only in the prayers of Bernard's followers and imitators but on the cathedral walls and in the paintings of the succeeding generations. But, presently, it will be only too necessary to have the tides of sentiment dammed and channeled by the firm line of thought that informs the most glowing and tender of the prayers of Saint Dominic's greatest son, Saint Thomas Aquinas.

Christian devotion had had a good deal of experience by the sixteenth century and had tried and amended many things. The result was a very rich and diversified inheritance of prayer. Of this inheritance, the works of two men in particular were to show extraordinary powers of survival, or perhaps, to be more accurate in view of the large part which apocryphal works were to play in the survival of Saint Augus-

tine, works expressing their spirit and influence.[46] The history of these
works may be taken, therefore, as representative in varying degrees
of the fate of a considerable portion of the devotional inheritance we
have been surveying, and illustrative of a process of adaptation highly
revealing of the psychology of the time.

A whole series of devotional works, either written by the great
African Father himself, or composed under his influence and attributed
to him, were translated or edited afresh in the sixteenth century. They
enjoyed a wide popularity, as may be seen from their continuing
republication through this century and into the next, and from their
frequent inclusion, in whole or in part, in the general collections of
prayers of the time. For instance, R. Fletcher translated *An Introduction
to the Love of God* and published it in 1574.[47] It was republished again
about seven years later.[48] Even more successful was *The Glasse of Vaine-
glorie,* which W. Prid translated and published in 1585,[49] for three
more editions of that book still survive from the next twenty years.

But of all these survivals of the genuine and the supposititious Saint
Augustine, far and away the most popular were the *Meditations* and the
Prayers. The *Meditations* consisted of selections from the *Confessions*
and from other works either written by their author or ascribed to him.
The *Prayers* were, likewise, mixed in character, consisting of genuine
compositions of the Bishop of Hippo and of works composed under
his influence, for which the prestige of his name was pretty recklessly
claimed. Published under these two headings and in various forms,
this body of literature proved one of the important sources of devotional materials in sixteenth-century England. One collection, *Certaine Select Prayers gathered out of S. Austines Meditations, which He
calleth His Selfe Talke with God,* or *Saint Augustines Manuell,* as this
work was sometimes called, was published without any translator's name
by John Day in 1574,[50] and ran through at least five editions in the next
dozen years. Thomas Rogers, one of the most active translators of the
time, tried his hand with this material in *S. Augustines Manuel,* published in 1581,[51] and running through the classic four editions between
that date and 1604. Rogers, also, translated another collection, *A Right
Christian Treatise entituled S. Augustines Praiers,* which was published in 1581.[52] Of that work, four editions survive from the next
twenty-three years. But perhaps the most popular of these translations
from Saint Augustine was Rogers' version of *His Private Talke with*

God: A Pretious Booke of Heavenlie Meditations, published in 1581,[53] which continued to be published well into the next century. A half dozen editions by various printers still survive.

Finally, as we shall see presently, many compositions by both the real and the supposed Augustine found their way into the general prayer collections of the time. Thomas Becon, for instance, in the edition of his famous *Pomander of Prayer* which John Day published in 1561, included a group of meditations ascribed to Saint Augustine.[54] And the Day *Book of Christian Prayers* of 1578 included a number of prayers and meditations taken from various works of Saint Augustine, selected and arranged with a good deal of freedom.[55] These are but striking examples of a very common practice.

The other great example of a medieval devotional survival is the *Imitation of Christ,* attributed in those days to both John Gerson and Thomas à Kempis. Probably the most popular of all later medieval works of devotion, this great work was published in Latin some time between 1470 and 1475, and in whole or in part had run through some fifty Latin editions by the end of that century.[56] The first of the surviving English translations, that of the first three books by William Atkinson, was printed by Wynkyn de Worde in 1502 and by Pynson in 1503. To this was added in 1504 the translation of the fourth book by the Lady Margaret, grandmother of Henry VIII.[57] In this form the Atkinson translation ran through at least half a dozen editions in the first quarter of the century. But in or about 1530 appeared the translation of Richard Whitford, the famous monk of Syon, of whom we shall presently hear more, and soon ran into a series of editions, of which half a dozen still survive from the next twenty-five years.[58]

The years that immediately followed the last of Whitford's editions in 1556 were hardly favorable to the republication of medieval contemplative literature. Yet in 1567 came a new translation, that of Edward Hake, under unmistakably Protestant auspices,[59] and this was republished in the following year, and at least once in the three years thereafter. But of these later translations the most popular was unquestionably that of Thomas Rogers, which appeared in 1580 [60] and ran through at least eight editions in the next twenty years, and continued to be published well into the next century.

All of these works, of course, offered difficulties to the Elizabethan translator. Rogers in particular was quite explicit as to the problems

he met and the methods he adopted for their solution. For he explained
on the title page of *A Pretious Booke of Heavenlie Meditations* that his
original had been "not translated onlie, but purified also, and with most
ample and necessarie sentences of Holie Scripture adorned." And he
justified at some length certain omissions which he felt compelled to
make lest the work lead "to the destruction of some, or to the offence
of anie good Christian." [61] With the *Imitation*, the problem was even
more serious, for the fourth book of that work was devoted to the
Eucharist. Edward Hake got round the difficulty by tacitly omitting
the fourth book and, without any reference to it, in his second edition
(of 1568), joining to the first three books of the *Imitation* a very charm-
ing but quite unrelated treatise called *A Short and Pretie Treatise touching the Perpetuall Rejoyce of the Godly, even in This Lyfe.*[62] This
example of omission Rogers followed in his first surviving edition of
1580, printing only the first three books. But in what was at least the
seventh edition of his translation, that of 1592, he added to the first
three books a translation of the *Soliloquium Animae* under the title,
*The Sole-Talke of the Soule, or, A Spiritual and Heavenlie Dialogue
betwixt the Soule of Man and God.*[63] And, characteristically, he explained even on the title page that this work "for the great affinitie it
hath with other bookes of the Auctor published heeretofore in our native
tongue, is now entituled *The Fourth Booke of the Imitation of Christ."*

But this was not the only change. As he had in his version of the
pseudo-Augustinian meditations, so now in the three books which he
kept of the *Imitation* Rogers felt obliged to make certain changes in
his original, and these he proceeded to justify in a very candid address
to the Christian Reader (edition of 1592), in which he explained that
he had not changed the sense of his author except "where himselfe hath
varied from the truth of God." Then he went on to remind the reader
that the author himself "had wished to have some godlie corrector of
his faultes, and praied unto almightie God gratiouslie to reveale, such
thinges offensive, either unto himselfe, or unto some other." That prayer,
Rogers now triumphantly concluded, "God hath heard, and discovered
those things for thy benefit, and testification besides how Kempisius,
the Auctor, howsoever living in a Popish time, was yet in hart no
Papist, but would like well of that which is doon, as I trust thou wilt,
whose edifieing, and spirituall comforting, I have onlie aimed at." [64]

It is easy to smile at Rogers' confidence, but the fact remains that whatever the logical or historical shortcomings of his approach, it made possible the salvaging for the devout public of a considerable portion of the medieval inheritance of devotion. The story of how that was accomplished affords one of the most revealing of clues to the development of sixteenth-century religious thought and feeling, for in studying the changes involved, one learns much of what was most enduring in the Christian devotional tradition and what was most important in the sixteenth-century approach to that tradition. And nowhere could that better be studied than in England where the life of prayer had been cherished from the earliest Christian times, and where the great conflicts of the sixteenth century were to break so dramatically and with such decisive results.

III

THE PSALTER

*T*HE great men who inspired and directed the development of monastic devotion bear a very special relation to the art of private prayer. In every sense of the word they were men of distinctive genius and vocation. They devoted themselves to prayer, choosing a way of life that gave them the time, the training, the means, and the environment to realize the possibilities of systematic prayer. And they were men who had the talent and the will not only to make the most of the opportunities already available, but to strike out for themselves and create new ones. In short, they were the pioneers, the creators, and the leaders in the corporate enterprise of Christian devotion.

And yet they would be the first to acknowledge their indebtedness to the common treasury of their religious tradition, for they realized more than anybody else, the need of something beyond their own resources for the expression of even their most personal experience. Had not the author of the Lord's Prayer himself, in the supreme agony of the cross, turned to the words of the psalmist for the ultimate cry of his soul? [1] Surely none of his followers need be ashamed to follow that example, so moving and so august.

Their leaders certainly were not. They went to the same storehouse to which he had gone, the Psalms of David and others, upon which Hebrew devotion had drawn for centuries for public worship and for private solace and inspiration. The Psalms had formed the quarry out of which personal piety might supplement the prescribed prayers for the morning and evening devotions which Jewish tradition like most other religious traditions, ancient and modern, enjoined.[2] And we may be sure that literate and aspiring piety meditated the noble and varied themes of the Psalter in many an hour of solitary recollection. Indeed, the Gospels themselves are evidence of the thoroughness with which the very imagery and phrasing of the Psalms had permeated the consciousness not only of Christ but of his followers who reported his words. And the Psalms continued to be the great quarry of Christian devotion even after the new religious movement had left the synagogue. Fearful as they were of the seductive grace of the lyric poetry and song of the pagan world about them, the early Christians sang the Psalms of David with a clear conscience, and taking them for their models fashioned the first Christian hymns in a rough, unmetrical psalm form.[3]

Thus the Psalter not only furnished one of the basic service books of the church, but it became the Christian's earliest book of private devotion and source of fresh devotional creation. In the high Middle Ages its primacy was unchallenged,[4] but as we shall see presently, before the end of that period very formidable rivals for lay favor were to come out of its pages. Yet for all the expansion of the literature of private devotion since then, the Psalter has never ceased to this day to hold its position of basic importance.

But the very universality that has assured its continued use through the changing circumstances and attitudes of more than two millennia to some extent has impaired that immediate relevance to the moment's need and that specific availability that are essential to popular use of devotional materials. Various experts early sought to make the Psalter easier to use. One device was the heading for each psalm pointing out its main significance and so suggesting its specific usefulness for particular individual needs, an editorial device of ancient origin, and still a familiar feature of contemporary Bibles and psalters. A second device, of which we shall see more in sixteenth-century editions, was the analytical index to the Psalter, calling attention to the appropriateness of certain psalms for specific needs and occasions. Again, this is ancient, perhaps the most famous of these guides to the use of the Psalms is that ascribed to Saint Athanasius.[5] And, again, this device has continued to the present day, as illustrated in the famous guide of the Gideons' Bible, which, of course, extends beyond the Psalms to the Bible as a whole.

Still another device was to expand the Psalter with supplementary materials that would increase its availability for use by the layman. The Psalms are the most famous prayers in the Bible, but they are not the only ones. Moses' great song of victory in the fifteenth chapter of Exodus, *Cantabo Domino,* is an example of a psalm-like prayer; the praise of Tobias in the thirteenth chapter of the Book of Tobit, *Benedictus deus qui vivit in aeternum,* is another. There are a number of such prayers in the Old Testament which the old dispensation had not used in any special way for worship but which the church did take out under the name of "canticles." And to these were added three prayers of a similar nature from the New Testament, the Magnificat from Luke, the Canticle of Zachary, *Benedictus Dominus Deus Israel,* and the Canticle of Simeon, *Nunc dimittis,* also from Luke.[6] There is evidence to suggest that as early as the eighth century the addition of the Creed and the Lord's Prayer and other materials essential to the religious instruction of the laity made the Psalter a substantial prayer book for private use.[7] The well-known tendency of all liturgies to grow by accretion continued to operate here as elsewhere, however. A later stage of the process is well illustrated by the tenth-century Bosworth Psalter. This splendid and historic monument to Anglo-Saxon religious life contains not only the Latin Psalter, the canticles for lauds and the psalms in that office, and the Benedictus, Magnificat, etc., frequently annexed to psalters but a hymnal containing 101 hymns for the different canonical hours and seasons, the canticles for the third nocturn of the monastic office, with a later addition of a calendar, a short litany, the Preface and Canon of the Mass, and the Mass of the Blessed Trinity.[8] Such a book was, of course, designed not only for private devotion but to enable the owner, obviously a personage of considerable consequence, to follow the public recitation of the divine office, as well.[9]

But the process of growth did not by any means stop here. To these liturgical and semi-liturgical additions already noted were added in the course of time two other types of material. The first were nonscriptural prayers, often from the pens of the masters of devotion referred to in the preceding chapter, prayers designed to help the layman meet the day's exigencies, such as prayers for the morning and the evening, and prayers for various special needs of body and soul, and for recurring human emergencies. The second body of material was more directly pedagogical in character, consisting of tables and charts and treatises presenting information deemed essential for the daily living of the layman. In such a process of growth the Primer itself may be said to have taken shape within the covers of the Psalter. In the thirteenth century this process of development was so advanced that the Primer finally emerged from the Psalter as a separate book.[10] So it will be simpler to study these nonscriptural prayers of the Psalter in the total context of the Primer. But in spite of the separate development of the Primer and of its increasing popularity, the Psalter still continued to grow as a distinctive prayer book for the layman.

The language issue rose early in England, but, significantly in view of later agitations, apparently without extraneous complication. In fact, it was involved enough in itself, as will become apparent if we take a look at some of the important efforts at its solution that have survived the vicissitudes of more than a thousand years. What must be close to the earliest of these efforts goes back to the ninth century, and takes the very primitive form of an interlinear Anglo-Saxon gloss on a Latin text, the well-known Vespasian Psalter.[11] Such a gloss was clearly intended for a man who knew some Latin but whose grasp on the language was insecure. In that period and place, with literary interest pretty much confined to the clergy and with clerical learning in a generally low state, it is reasonable to conclude that this was in fact designed for the help of a cleric whose Latin was limited. And the fact that this gloss continued to be copied and to be used for a good many years after its original composition would certainly indicate that its service was appreciated.

A further step in the direction of a real translation is represented by the so-called Paris Psalter, a still very crude parallel-column version of Latin and Anglo-Saxon, belonging to the age of King Alfred. Indeed, the prose version of the first fifty psalms may be attributed if not to the pen of King Alfred then to his general educational influence. The remainder of the Psalms are in Anglo-Saxon verse.[12] Again, the very fact that this version was copied and circulated and used in the ensuing years in which linguistic difficulties were presently added to the circulation hazards of the manuscript age, speaks of appreciation of its usefulness for the purpose for which it was designed. In view of King Alfred's personal interests and example, it is certainly not unreasonable to guess that such a version might interest some at least of his immediate associates among the nobles of the time, and thus add to the imperfectly Latinate of the clergy some scarcely Latinate among the laity.

Something like that certainly happened after the Norman Conquest, for French came into the psalters of the late eleventh and twelfth centuries,[13] for the French-speaking nobility and gentry. It was only natural, therefore, that when in the fourteenth century, the makers of psalters undertook to reach the emerging middle classes of the period, they were forced to make provision for readers who did not use French.[14] It is in the first quarter of this century that the copy of the metrical version of the Psalter which the Surtees Society reprinted with its edition of the Vespasian Psalter, was transcribed, and probably not long before when it was composed, as may be judged from the first stanza of the first psalm, *Beatus vir*:

> "Seli bern, that noght is gan
> In the rede of wicked man;
> And in strete of sinfulle noght he stode,
> Ne sat in setel of storme um-gode." [15]

This stanza gives a very good notion of this metrical psalter, often lively enough, but still a pretty crude undertaking from the point of view of translation, and still cruder from that of poetry.

Of a very different order is a version made quite a few years farther into the fourteenth century, perhaps begun somewhere about 1338 and continued for some years thereafter, that of Richard Rolle, the famous hermit and contemplative writer of Hampole.[16] This work, quite apart from any question of the genius of the author, involves a much profounder type of approach. For what Rolle was aiming at was not a gloss or a readily apprehensible introduction to the Psalter but an understanding of its meaning and significance. The interpretation of the Psalms was an old enterprise of Christian scholarship, and there was a vast body of such interpretation, which the summarizing and abstracting enterprise of medieval scholarship had already made easily accessible to the scholar in a work like Peter the Lombard's famous *Commentaries on the Psalms and St. Paul.* To put this scholarship at the disposal of a friend who was not a scholar and presumably knew little Latin was one of the main objectives of Rolle's English Psalter.

But for a man of Rolle's temperament, there was more to it than interpretation. For the friend for whom he composed the work was a nun, Margaret Kirkeby, like himself committed to the labors of contemplation and obviously aspiring to rise to the heights of its opportunities, for she was enclosed as an anchoress in 1348.[17] The non-Latinate religious woman was an ancient source of inspiration for such efforts in the vernacular, as witness the *Ancren Riwle,* for even if her Latin could not be counted on, her interest and application could. She made a worthy if modest audience for the best work of interpretation of which her spiritual mentor was capable. In the present case, Rolle brought not only scholarly resources in the narrower sense but scholarly competence in a more specialized sense. Rolle had already written his Latin Psalter for the benefit of his fellow university scholars. Moreover, he had something beyond the scope of mere learning, a profound and sustained experience of spiritual life himself. What he could do for Margaret Kirkeby, therefore, was to share with her not only the scholar's understanding but the contemplative's experience of the Psalms.

And this was what he proceeded to do. His characteristic approach to the spiritual life is to be seen in the first sentence of the prologue which he prefixed to the work: "Grete habundans of gastly conforth and joy in God comes in the hertes of thaime that says or synges devotly the psalmes in lovynge of Jhesu Crist." [18] The technique which the author uses is a fairly systematic, and, in spite of the frequent elaborateness of the development, a basically simple, one. He takes up the Latin text of the Psalter, not only psalm by psalm but verse by verse. The Latin verse is followed by as direct and simple an English translation as Rolle can compass, and that in turn by an interpretation that is usually concerned in the main with the meaning and implications of the words of the Psalmist for the spiritual life of the Christian. The opening of Psalm 3 is a good example of his technique:

Domine quid multiplicati sunt qui tribulant me; multi insurgunt adversum me. "Lord, whartille ere thei manyfald that angers me? Many rises ogaynes me." The voyce of Cristenmans saule says til Crist, for persecucioun of gastly enmys and bodily, "Lord whartille", that es, whether til thaire schendeschipe or myne? If I overcome thaime it es til my coroun, if thai overcome me it es my dampnacioun. "Multiplyed ere that angers me", that es, vices and fleschely covaytys agaynes wham ilke a rightwise man feghtes alle his lyve here; il men feghtes noght bot ogaynes God. For til hym thai make thaime contrarie and acordes thaime til synne. "Many" that es, fendes and the fendes lyms, "rises ogaynes me" for to put me dowen and bring me oute of charite als thei ere.[19]

It is clear that Rolle had hopes of a wider audience than the one friend for whom he first composed the work, and the character of that audience is made clear in what he has to say of the language of his translation: "In this werk I seke no strange Inglis, bot lightest and comunest and swilke that es mast like unto the Latyn, so that thai that knawes noght Latyn, be the Inglis may cum tille many Latyn wordes." [20] The hopes which inspired such a sentence were more than realized. At least twenty manuscript copies of Rolle's English Psalter survive in all the main dialects of the period, and it is clear from them that the work was used not only by religious houses but by laymen, too. Indeed, it may be said to have become the closest to what those informal times knew as a standard English psalter, and in spite of the fact that the Lollards made their interpolations in it and used it for their purposes, it seems to have continued to enjoy that eminence until the eve of the Reformation. [21]

But Rolle's was not the only type of psalter that found popular favor in those years. There are a number of expanded psalters of the type we have met earlier that appeared in English toward the end of the fourteenth century and the beginning of the fifteenth. In these English psalters the instructional element is understandably even more important than in the earlier. One that has managed to weather the hazards of the intervening years provided an A.B.C., the Ten Commandments, and tables of the Seven Works of Bodily Mercy, the Five Bodily Wits, and the Seven Deadly Sins with the virtues opposed to them, etc. There is also a short "declaration" of the paternoster, and the twelve articles of the Creed, together with a number of Graces. Another psalter of the period includes the Parables of Solomon, the Book of Ecclesiastes, the Book of Sapience, and the Book of Ecclesiasticus. [22] In other words, the still-growing Psalter continued to provide the layman with not only a very rich and substantial devotional aid, but on the whole, a very practical one as well.

The Psalter in English was caught up, however, in the very complicated maelstrom of the agitations and disputes growing out of the Lollard movement. The long struggle over the Scriptures in the vernacular, involving not only basic differences with regard to religious authority but in all probability very important differences with regard to the nature of the Christian religion itself, to say nothing of different views of the relations of the layman and the professional, the educated and the uneducated, the privileged and the unprivileged, etc., is too large to more than allude to here. Suffice it to say that the church decree of 1408, forbidding the translation of any part of the Bible into English without formal episcopal permission, did restrict the development of the English Psalter. The Psalms were used, of course, quite freely for meditations or commentaries or prayer books, but the complete English Psalter fell under the suspicion of heresy. It is significant that so far as we know, no English psalter was printed until the anonymous English psalter of 1530 which we shall look at in some detail presently.[23]

It had been, of course, the hope of many of the Protestant reformers that the reading of the Word of the Lord alone would satisfy the hungry minds of men and wean them from dependence upon merely human compositions. And there is no question that for a good many Englishmen of the sixteenth century the treasures of Scripture, especially Scripture in their own tongue, did suffice. But the need for more specific help in prayer persisted, partly because of the nature of prayer, and partly because of the occasions of prayer. There was no question of the potency of Scripture for stimulating the imagination and inspiring resolution, but it was equally clear that the realization of these possibilities involved the adaptation of traditional materials to personal need and particular occasion. Clearly, if Scripture were to suffice, help was needed, such help as was already available in the traditional expanded Psalter.

But the publication of the Psalter in the sixteenth century was no longer a purely devotional matter. Like every other religious activity it ran head-on into the controversies of the time, for even what might have been regarded as a fairly routine editorial job could be used very effectively for purposes of propaganda on behalf of whatever position the editor supported on the points at issue.

The language problem, already so important in the history of the Psalter, is a good example. Here, as elsewhere, it appeared in two forms, the old one of availability to the man who knew no Latin, and the more recently mooted question of the relation of the text offered to other versions of Scripture.

We have already seen how the makers of psalters in the Middle Ages were forced when they undertook to reach the middle classes to make provision for readers who could read only English. The growing importance and self-consciousness of the same middle classes in the sixteenth century made the language issue an especially potent one for popular appeal, quite apart from the variety of religious and other issues involved in the question of the free circulation of the Scriptures in the vernacular.

And then there was still the complicated matter of the choice of text and the manner of its rendering. In an age of general agreement on basic religious acceptances, the problem could remain academic. But once argument over authenticity and meaning of text had broken into the public arena, then the textual problem became a highly controversial one with implications and involvements beyond the scope of a literary essay like this. The important thing for our study of the English devotional books of the sixteenth century is that the language issue in both forms was raised and played a large part in the successive editions of the Psalms that are so striking a feature of the religious publication of the time.

Apparently the first English psalter to be printed is one which, according to the colophon, Francis Foxe published at Argentine (or Strassburg) in 1530. That colophon has been challenged as fictitious, put forth in view of the English laws against unauthorized translation of Scripture into the vernacular, and Martin de Keyser (Martin Emperor) of Antwerp has been suggested as the real printer.[24] The translator (the Johan Aleph to whom the introductory epistle is ascribed is an obvious pseudonym) has not been identified. It has been suggested that he may be George Joye to whose activities in the field of the English books Thomas More had referred in a fashion that suggested that Joye had published a translation of the Psalter about this time.[25] But George Joye published a quite different version of the Psalms four years later in August of 1534, under his own name, and although no place is mentioned on the title page or in the colophon, Martin Emperor admitted in the latter that he printed it. The difference in version is not by any means conclusive, because in those days men who handled their Latin easily were accustomed to making pretty casual translations, and the same author might and often did use quite different versions for the same passage of Scripture. Moreover, George Joye seems to have been a man seriously interested in the matter of the English books at a time when the importance of the issue would not make the labor of two different complete translations by any means unthinkable.[26] But there is a great difference between the general atmosphere and effect of these two publications.

That of the acknowledged George Joye version is, aside from the fact of the English version, a curiously neutral affair. The title page itself suggests nothing out of the way: "Davids Psalter, diligently and faithfully translated by George Joye, with brief Arguments before every

Psalme, declaringe theffecte therof." The brief arguments are for once exactly that, as may be seen in the one prefixed to Psalm 46, "God is our refuge and strength": "The chirche is compared by an allegory unto a defensed Cite, cannot be hurte: because the lorde is present with it." [27] And there is no supplementary material in the volume.

Very different is the effect of the Psalter of 1530. To begin with, the very title page raises the language issue on both counts: "The Psalter of David in Englishe purely and faithfully translated aftir the texte of Feline: every Psalme havynge his argument before, declarynge brefly thentente and substance of the wholl Psalme." The text of Feline to which this description refers is, of course, the new Latin version which Martin Bucer, the famous German reformer, had recently made as a result of his study of the Hebrew text and published under the pen name of Aretius Felinus.[28] The same appeal on the language issue is underscored in the introductory epistle to the English nation already referred to, namely that this version comes closer to the Hebrew original than the usual Latin, and that it is in the vernacular.[29]

As for the headings, which are, as we have seen, an old device of the Psalter for the elucidation of the meaning and relevance of the text, these play a very conspicuous part in this book, for they afford a very practical instrument for the direction of attention to what seems to the editor important. Most of these comments are free of any direct reference to the controversies of the time, but there is one striking exception. The editor takes advantage of the heading for Psalm 16, *Conserva me domine,* to deliver a thrust against gifts to the monasteries very much in the manner of Simon Fish, claiming for the lay poor the traditional dues of holy poverty:

In this Psalme David desireth goddis helpe: affirminge that god hath no nede of his goodis, but that his goodis ought to serve his poore neghbors which he call sayntis and thei that bestowe their goodis of eny other thynge then profiteth theis sayntes, make Idols with them.[30]

But this is exceptional. For the most part the editor makes his contribution to the reforming cause by using these interpretive headings to suggest an attitude, a way of approaching one's world, that would nerve the reader to face the contemporary situation as this editor envisages it. It is, in substance, a psychology of crisis in which the embattled hosts of the righteous are seen as drawn up facing the ungodly. It is exactly the sort of psychology that would prove extremely effective for an age of revolutionary crisis. The introduction to Psalm 119, "Blessid are thei whiche live pure and innocently," is a case in point:

This Psalm declarethe in howe grete pryce and reverence, the sayntes or holy men have the lawes of god: howe ernestly they are occupied in them, howe they sorowe to se them broken and sayde ageinste of the ungodly: howe they praye to be taughte them of God, and to be accoynted and acostomed withe them, and (to be shorte) howe they desyer thois men to be destroyed (what so ever they be) which breke and saye ageinste them.[31]

It is easy to see how people who had been reading the Psalms in the light of such an introduction would be more easily stirred to battle on any one of a half-dozen crucial issues of the time.

This topical application of the Psalms extends to the selections from them that are so often included in sixteenth-century collections of prayers and meditations. It was, of course, as we have seen, an old habit of devotional writers to make selections of psalms or groups of psalms for some fresh devotional purpose. This is well illustrated in a collection which we shall presently have occasion to discuss in some detail, the *Praiers of Holi Fathers* which Richard Grafton printed somewhere about 1540. For a large section of that book is devoted to a collection of psalms headed "Certaine Psalmes picked forthe very mete for dayly prayers unto God." [32] The highly topical application of this selection is made clear in the headings attached to the individual psalms; for instance that for Psalm 79, "Oh God the heathen have invaded thyne herytage," is "Agaynste Antechrist pursuynge and kyllyng the holy ones of God and defilyng the misteries of Goddes woorde." [33] And another, a smaller section, is devoted to a selection headed, this time quite frankly, "Psalmes of David against tirauntes and persecutours of Goddes woorde." [34]

But there were even better missionary possibilities in the English Psalter. An edition which Rowland Hall printed at Geneva in 1559 realized some at least of them. For there is less stress on the language problem on the title page of this edition and more on the doctrinal:

The Boke of Psalmes, where in are conteined praiers, meditations, praises and thankesgiving to God for his benefites toward his Church: translated faithfully according to the Ebrewe. With brief and apt annotations in the margent, aswel for the declaracion of the mynde of the Prophet, as for the joyning together and continuance of the sentence: with two tables, the one conteyning the names of the Psalmes according to the ordre of the Alphabet, and the other concerning the chief pointes of our belief comprehended in common places.

The address to Queen Elizabeth on behalf of the English church at Geneva makes clear the general orientation of the undertaking with its reference to the persecution of the Church of England in the reign of Mary, and its commendation of the Psalms of David to Queen Elizabeth for her own spiritual needs.[35] The most interesting aspect of this book is, of course, the marginal comment promised in the title page. Its quality may be judged by a comment on Psalm 106 : 29: "Thus thei provoked *him* unto angre with their owne inventions, and the plague brake in upon them." This the marginal comment explains as "Signifiyng, that whatsoever man inventeth of him selfe to serve God by, is detestable and provoketh his angre," [36] an incidental but telling contribution to the contemporary dispute over ceremonies.

But it was not in keeping with the Psalter tradition that the Psalms should remain apart from other devotional materials, nor did they long remain so in the sixteenth century. Probably not more than a dozen years after the publication of the psalter of 1530, Edward Whitchurch published a new edition of the same version without hint of its provenience [37] but with the addition of "certayne godly prayers thorowe-oute the whole yere, commenly called collettes," [38] and, also, with the unheralded addition of four of the canticles, *Benedicite omnia opera, Magnificat, Benedictus dominus, Nunc dimittis,* and *Te deum laudamus* (Augustine and Ambrose) and *Quicunque vult* (the Creed of Athanasius).[39] This was certainly a noticeable move in the direction of the old expanded Psalter.

Another of a somewhat different type may be seen in the book which John Whyte published, probably in 1550, but without any indication of place or date, *The Psalter, or Boke of the Psalmes, wherunto are added Certayne Other Devout Prayers Taken out of the Byble.* A psalter with a similar title had already been published even more obscurely without even the printer's name about ten years before.[40] In view of the uncertainties of the religious picture at this time there is nothing remarkable in such discretion. What is worthy of note in Whyte's publication is the collection of "certayne other devout Prayers taken out of the Byble," which is appended to the Psalter.[41] We shall have occasion presently to look at these prayers in some detail, for they contain not only the usual occasional prayers from the Old Testament, but a number from the New as well. For the present, the important thing to note is that by the middle of the century the old expanded Psalter, now in English, is finding its way in varying degrees into print.

But the full possibilities of the Psalter for the daily use of the average man were not realized before 1562 when Sternhold and Hopkins completed their classic *Book of Psalms*. There was, as we have seen from the Surtees Psalter, nothing new in their effort to translate the Psalms into English verse. A number of later writers had been experimenting with such metrical versions, of whom the most notable were Sir Thomas Wyatt and the Earl of Surrey. And quite recently, in 1550, a selection by William Hunnis had been published. The terms in which Hunnis explained his selection suggest a good deal of contemporary activity in the field, for he declared in his address to the reader that he had picked out "these psalmes folowing which no late wryter hath hytherto touched."[42] The literary quality of the volume may be judged from the opening of Psalm 57, *Miserere mei deus:*

> Be mercyfull to me o god
> be mercyfull to me,
> My fleshe, and hart, my soule and minde
> putteth their truste in the.
>
> Under the shadowe of thy wynges
> there shall be my defence
> Untyl this time of tyraunye
> be paste away from hence.[43]

It is interesting to note, too, in view of the tendency to make available to the new age the expanded Psalter that even in this very small book room is found for some of the canticles and "The Complaynt of a Synner."[44]

But it was Thomas Sternhold's first publication of nineteen psalms in 1549 that marked the beginning of a work that was to prove enduringly popular. A new edition before the end of the year raised the number of psalms thus translated to forty-four, seven of them the work of John Hopkins, who was, also, to give his name to the corporate enterprise. In rapidly succeeding editions the number of psalms was increased with the aid of various other writers until the Psalter was complete by 1562.[45]

But the appeal of the English metrical versions was only part of the story. Tunes to which the Psalms could be sung had begun to be printed without harmony as early as 1556. In 1563 John Day published the harmony in four separate-part books. The settings for this edition were mainly the work of two distinguished composers of the time, Thomas Causton and W. Parsons. And their example was soon followed by other leading composers of the day who contributed to successive editions in the years that followed.[46]

The fact that the Psalms could be sung is probably the key to their phenomenal popularity, a popularity which the new religious leaders were not slow to turn to good account. As an early seventeenth-century Catholic writer was to complain:

There is nothing that hath drawne multitudes to be of their Sects so much, as the singing of their psalmes, in such variable and delightfull tunes: These the souldier singeth in warre, the artizans at their worke, wenches spinning and sewing, apprentises in their shoppes, and wayfaring men in their travaile, litle knowing (God wotte) what a serpent lyeth hidden under these sweete flowers.[47]

That the editors of the Sternhold and Hopkins volume were quite aware of this appeal may be seen from the title page of the edition which John Day published in 1567:

The whole booke of Psalmes, collected into Englishe Meter by Thomas Sternhold, John Hopkins and other, conferred with the Hebrue, with apt Notes to sing them withall. Newly set forth and allowed to be song in all Churches, of all the people together, before and after morning and evenyng prayer: as also before and after the Sermon, and moreover in private houses, for their godly solace and comfort, laying aparte all ungodly songes and ballades, which tend onely to the nourishyng of vice, and corrupting of youth.

But in spite of the emphasis of this title-page appeal, the editors of the volume offered a good deal more than a song book. In the form which their book finally assumed it was in fact the traditional expanded Psalter brought up to date, to fit the new orientation. This practical devotional objective of the undertaking is to be seen at once in the very beginning of the volume where the treatise of "Athanasius the great" is reprinted with its suggestions for special psalms for special needs.[48] In the terms in which many of these suggestions are couched there is both a fortitude and a sombre realism not unworthy of the great defender of the faith himself, as, for instance, in the following:

If thine acquaintaunce persecute thee, and many ryse agaynste thee, thou hast the third Psalme. . . .

If thou feelest the threatnings of God, and therby perceivest thy selfe to be dismayed, thou mayst say the 6. Psalme, and the 37. Psalme. . . .

If thou seest the wicked prosper in peace, be not so offended that thou be moved, but say the 73. Psalme.[49]

In short, Athanasius, or whoever first drew up this guide, recognized that this is a wicked world in which the righteous man may often find himself in unappreciative, not to say, hostile company, and provided comfort and reassurance accordingly.

But still the editors of this volume were clearly not satisfied. For they added "The Use of the Rest of the Psalmes not comprehended in the former Table of Athanasius." While the two lists are not entirely exclusive, the motive for this addendum seems to have been to make available psalms which Athanasius had neglected, and, still more, to provide for occasions which he could hardly have foreseen. One or two examples will give some idea of the nature of these occasions. The first of the additions imparts a patriotic tinge to pious thanksgiving: "If thou wouldest prayse God because hee hath geven us a good prince, which will and doth punishe the enemies of Christes religion, use the 21. Psalme." The second is more explicit on the identity of those enemies: "If thou wouldest have Christ to come conquere and beate downe the Sirians, Idumeans, Ammonites, Papistes, Antichristians, Nullifidians, Neutralles, and ungratious Pelagians, use the 68. Psalme." But the timeliest for an age in which the reforming minister often found himself in charge of a flock firmly attached to the long-established order is thus sympathetically prefaced: "If thou be thrust into a college, or into a parish, town or country, whose inhabitours are wicked, crafty, and malicious pickequarrels, wouldest be delivered from them, use the .120. psalme." [50]

But these directions to appropriate psalms are not followed immediately, as one would expect, by the Psalms. Instead, we find the canticles traditionally included in the Psalter, and these canticles are all provided with music for singing.[51] Then come a series of devotional-

instructional pieces of a character already familiar to us in the traditional expanded Psalter, such as a verse version of the Athanasian
Creed, "The Lamentation of a Sinner (O Lord turne not away thy
face)," "The humble sute of a sinner (O Lord of whom I do depend,
behold my careful hart)," a rhymed version of the Lord's Prayer, and
the Ten Commandments, also rhymed, and like all the foregoing
provided with music.[52]

Then at last come the Psalms, printed in verses, either with the accompanying music or a note as to which psalm tune they are to be
sung to.[53] In general this part of the book proceeds without any further
comment except for the traditional brief introduction before each
psalm. Upon the completion of the Psalms, however, the devotional
character of the volume is reënforced by the addition of exhortations
"unto the prayse of God" to be sung before morning and evening
prayer, and by a slightly expanded verse paraphrase of the Ten Commandments. The character of this latter composition may be suggested
by the first stanza:

> Attend my people, and geve eare,
> of ferly things I wil thee tel:
> se that my wordes in mynde thou beare,
> And to my preceptes listen wel.[54]

This paraphrase, like the Psalms, is provided with music, and so is
the accompanying rhymed prayer for grace to keep the Commandments. This is followed by a similar verse expansion of the Lord's
Prayer, and the Twelve Articles of the Christian Faith, both provided
with music.[55]

These quite traditional Psalter and Primer elements are supplemented by a series of versified prayers, also set to music. These include,
among others, a prayer to the Holy Ghost to be sung before the
sermon, which begins like the *Veni Creator* but takes a very different
course of more immediate application, a prayer for peace by E. G., a
couple of lamentations of sinners, a thanksgiving for use after the
Lord's Supper, and a versified prayer for preservation, addressed to
the Trinity by Robert Wisedome.[56]

But even this much of the song character of the book is dropped in
the next series of prayers, for they are all in prose: a form to be used
in private houses every morning and evening (a prayer made up of
various clearly traditional elements), a substantial series of prayers for

before and after meals, and prayers for various occasions, including "A Confession for all estates and times," "A Prayer to be said before a man begin his worke," and "A Prayer for the whole estate of Christes Church." [57] Here the devotional character of the book triumphs. A man possessing only *The Whole Booke of Psalmes* would find himself very well equipped with the minimum essentials of daily devotion, and that on what are on the whole, within the limits of the selections, traditional lines. Yet there is no doubt that in general orientation and flavor the book belongs firmly to the new order.

But that was not the only use of the Psalms. As we have seen above, the selection and rearrangement of the Psalms had been an ancient enterprise of Christian devotion. It was but a step from that to the quite plastic handling of the Psalms as a great quarry from which aspirations and phrases and sentences might be taken and reassembled into new wholes of confession or supplication or praise or whatever the type of prayer which the present author had in hand. That was how the maker of perhaps the most famous of these so-called psalters made his, the classic psalter ascribed to Saint Jerome, one of the most popular constituents of the medieval books of devotion. An early sixteenth-century *hore,* which we shall have occasion presently to study in some detail, averred that Saint Jerome made his selection with the help of an angel, and then went on to commend this immeasurably briefer composition to those who were for illness, travel, fighting, business, or any other good reason unable to say the whole Psalter.[58]

Another example of a rearrangement of the psalm material closely analagous to that attributed to Saint Jerome is the *Psalter of Saint Augustine* which he is said to have composed for the use of his mother,[59] and which continued to find a place in popular post-Reformation devotional books. Still another is the *Canticum Ambrosii et Augustini,* which was a staple of the traditional Primer.[60] This is a song of praise which Saint Ambrose assisted by Saint Augustine is supposed to have recited on his death bed. Again, this is a selection and rearrangement of the psalm material which found a conspicuous and enduring place in the Primer and after that in the sixteenth-century prayer books. A more modest example of the same process is to be seen in the famous *Versus sancti Bernardi,* which according to the helpful editor of the primer already referred to, Saint Bernard owed not to an angel but to the Devil himself.[61] Like the other special psalm selections it found a prominent and enduring place not only in the Psalter but, as we shall see presently, in the Primer as well.

The continuation of this process of adaptation and rearrangement is to be seen in a number of devotional books of the sixteenth century. Of these, unquestionably one of the most popular was that collection of psalms and prayers which was first printed by Thomas Berthelet, the King's printer, in 1544. This work occurs under two different titles at least. In the first edition it is called simply, "Psalmes or Prayers taken out of holie scripture." But a later edition of the same work, published in 1568 by H. Wykes, is titled, "The Kynges Psalmes," perhaps to match the copy of *The Queenes Praiers* uniformly bound up with it. This book consists first of all, and mainly, of fifteen psalms (one wonders if the number of the gradual psalms had anything to do with the choice of the number). These prayers are composed in verse fashion of materials found in the Psalter and in the Primer, shaped up into prayers, the purpose of which is specified in the accompanying title. The first of these so-called "psalms," a very long one, is "for the obteining remission of sinnes," [62] the second (sig. C7) and the third (sig. D5v) for the same objective, but the fourth slightly varies the heavily penitential effect: "a complaint of a penitent sinner which is sore troubled and overcome with sinnes" (sig. E4). The fifth abandons the penitential theme with a prayer for "the obteinyng of godly wise-dome" (sig. F6), the sixth is a prayer "A christian man praieth, that he maie be herd of god" (sig. G4v). The eighth, the ninth, and the tenth concern those enemies that in that age seemed so much to beset the godly (sigs. H5v–I7v). The twelfth is a prudent, "If god differre to helpe longe time" (sig. K5v); and in the thirteenth the successfully resistant devotee "giveth thankes to god, that his enemies have not gotten the overhande of him" (sig. L2). But there are some prayers of a less beleaguered nature, the seventh for "an order and direccion of good living" (sig. H2), the eleventh of "confidence and truste in god" (sig. I8), the fourteenth of praise of the goodness of God (sig. L7), and the fifteenth of thanksgiving for God's benefits (sig. M2v). In other words, this is a pretty comprehensive, even if pretty general, spiritual guide for the embattled Christian. Such a psalter would minister admirably to that somewhat militant psychology the cultivation of which has been noted above.

As for the prayers themselves, as so often happens even with the

Psalter of Saint Jerome, they have a way of glancing on and off the text of the Bible that is endlessly teasing. It would seem as if sometimes a definite scriptural phrase, notably the beginning of some popular psalm, had given the springboard from which the writer had taken off for his own composition. Again, a phrase not to be found in the Psalter yet echoes confusingly both the thought and expression of Scripture. Sometimes the echoes extend to other traditional prayers already well known in both Psalter and Primer. Probably not a little of this effect is due to the author's familiarity with the liturgical materials of his professional activity. But whatever the cause, the impression that results is at once of something very familiar and yet elusively different, with, on the whole, the sense of familiarity predominating. Here, as with so much of the materials of sixteenth-century devotion, the text is so full of echoes that one is in spite of past experience lured forth on a will-o'-the-wisp chase of origins that much of the time will yield little but a thicket of echoes and a mosaic of cognates and parallels. It is the fruit of a tradition so pervasive as to constitute almost a language rather than a source.

The sixth of these "Psalmes or Prayers Taken out of Holie Scripture" will suffice to suggest this curious relation to the scriptural originals. The opening is at once recognized as familiar, the beginning of one of the most popular of all the Psalms, the famous Psalm 101 of the Latin Psalter, *Domine exaudi orationem meam: et clamor meus ad te veniat* (Psalm 102 of the Protestant Psalter). But if we set the first four or five verses of this composition beside, say the version of the first Great Bible, headed, "A prayer of the afflyct, when he hath an hevy hart, and powreth out hys complaynte before the Lorde," [63] we shall see how soon it departs from its probably scriptural inspiration. Psalm 102 opens as follows:

Heare my prayer, O Lorde, and lett my cryenge come in unto the.
Hyde not thy face fro me in the tyme of my trouble: enclyne thyne eares unto me when I call, O heare me, and that ryght soone. For my dayes are consumed awaye lyke smoke, and my bones are brent up, as it were a fyre brande. My hert is smytten downe and wythered lyke grasse, so that I forget to eat my bred. [64]

In *Psalmes or Prayers,* "the syxte psalme, A christian man praieth, that he maie be herd of god," begins in this way:

O Lorde heare my prayers: and leat my crye come to the.
Tourne not awaye thy face from me in the day of my tribulacion.

What daye so ever I shall call upon the: here me (O lord god.)
For thou art great and workest wonders: thou only art god.
Also thy workes be great: thy thoughtes be very profound and depe.[65]

It is obvious from such a comparison that much of the imaginative poignancy of the original has been sacrificed in the interest of greater explicitness and coherence of development of the ideas involved.

Even where the psalm professes by number and description to be one of the Psalms of David, like "The .xxi. psalme of David, the complaint of Christ on the crosse," which comes after the fifteen psalms described above, the handling is very free. Again a comparison of a few lines will suffice to make the method clear. In the Great Bible David's psalm opened as follows:

My God, my God; (loke upon me) why hast thou forsaken me: and art so farre fro my health, and from the wordes of my complaynte? O my God, I crye in the daye tyme, but thou hearest not: and in the night season also I take no rest. And thou contynuest holy, O thou worshyppe of Israel. Oure fathers hoped in thee: they trusted in the, and thou dyddest deliver them.[66]

This becomes in *Psalmes or Prayers,*

My God, My God, why hast thou forsaken me? it semeth that I shal not obtein deliveraunce, though I seke for it with loude cryes.

My God, I will crye all the day long, but thou wilt not answere: and all the night long, without takyng any rest.

The meane time thou most holiest, semest to sit still, not caryng for the thinges that I suffre: whiche so often haste healped me heretofore, and hast geven to thy people Israell sufficient argument and matier to praise the with songes, wherwith they have geven thankes to the for thy benefites.[67]

Clearly the new psalm follows the main lines of the scriptural composition, but the editor of *Psalmes or Prayers* could not apparently resist a certain number of adaptations and expansions.

To a certain extent he might, of course, plead the example of the Vulgate version of the Psalter, in the making of which Saint Jerome had marked words or phrases not found in the Hebrew or the Septuagint which had been introduced to amplify or explain the meaning of the original.[68] But the extent to which the sixteenth-century editor carries the process of alteration would seem rather to indicate a desire to drive home the meaning of the psalm and enforce its lesson in homelier terms.

Sometimes the reënforcement of the psalm theme is carried out through a supplementary prayer. A typical example is to be seen in the earlier version of the popular Day prayer books, that of 1569, in which the editor prints, *Domine exaudi,* in an English version, "Heare my prayer (O Lord) and let my cry come in unto thee," with this heading:

> It seemeth that this prayer was appoynted to the faithfull to pray in the captivitie of Babilon. A consolation for the buildyng of the churche, whereof followeth the prayse of God to be published unto all posterities. The conversion of the Gentiles, and the stabilitie of the church.[69]

Then follows "A prayer taken out of the .CII. Psalme," which is in fact a confession of unworthiness of divine attention and a less formal and more immediate prayer for mercy and for hearing in need. In this the editor gives the more general petition immediate topical relevance by particularizing the danger which threatens the church as the persecution of Antichrist.[70]

But an even freer use of psalm material is to be found in a work that, as we have seen above, was often reprinted with the *Psalmes or Prayers taken out of Holie Scripture.* It is that collection of prayers known as *The Queenes Praiers,* first published in 1545 by Thomas Berthelet as *Queen Catharines Prayers* (for Catharine Parr), and reprinted at London by H. Wykes in 1568, as *The Queenes Praiers or Meditations.* While this is a fairly miscellaneous collection, the psalm type of prayer plays a conspicuous part in it, as may be seen in the "devoute praier," which precedes the Litany in the Wykes edition:

> Lorde, harken to my wordes, consider the thought of mine harte. Beholde, how loude I crie unto thee? Let my juste praier enter into thyne eares, whiche unfainedly cometh fro mine hart. Heare me Lorde: for I am poore, and destitute of mannes helpe.[71]

And there is the authentic psalm spirit, however attenuated and diffused, in the petition which immediately follows the Litany:

> But thou good lorde, that haste the Lordship over all, and power of the Sea, to asswage the rage, and surges of the same, arise, and helpe me, destroye the power of myne enemies, whiche alwaies make battaile against me, shewe forthe the greatnes of thy goodnesse, and let the power of thy right hande be glorified in me. For there is to me none other hope nor refuge, but in thee onely my Lorde, my God: to thee bee honor and glory everlasting.[72]

One other type of use of the Psalms for devotional purposes should be noted, and that is a sort of combination of meditation and prayer based on the Psalms. It was a thoroughly traditional type, well illustrated by *The Seven Penytencyall Psalms of David* by Bishop Fisher. This proved very popular, being published by Wynkyn de Worde in 1508 and 1509, by Pynson in 1510, and again by Wynkyn de Worde between 1525 and 1529.[73] Another example of this sort of psalm-meditation is to be found in a couple of compositions of what might be called the transitional period, the work of Jerome of Ferrara, better known to history as Savonarola. There is something dry, yet intellectually fervent about Jerome of Ferrara's "exposicyon after the maner of a contemplacyon" on Psalm 51 and his meditation on Psalm 30. Yet they clearly satisfied the editor of the Paris Primer of 1538, for instance, in his effort to initiate his readers into the art of meditation as a devotional tool.[74] In spite of the reputation of Savonarola among the reformers, these meditations of his are quite in the tradition of scriptural meditation of the rather old-fashioned type.

This traditional type appears in thoroughly Protestant guise in a translation by an unidentified I. S. of Beza's *Christian Meditations upon Eight Psalmes of the Prophet David* which was published in London in 1582. The combination of pedagogical and devotional provision which was so frequent a feature of sixteenth-century devotional literature is apparent in the translator's praise of the work on the ground that "besides the common helpe it brings to all, for more cleare understanding and expounding those eight psalmes: it is singularly medicinable to wounded and caste down consciences, who after their laborsome combat with sinne, and profitable humiliation therethrough, may againe by these sweete Meditations arise with joy, finding happie issue of their troubles."[75] Such use of the Psalms as a springboard for the devotional ingenuity of those scripturally-learned is not only a most characteristic but also a most persistent element in the development of the devotional literature of the sixteenth century.

IV

THE PRIMER

IMPORTANT as the Psalter is for the over-all history of devotional literature, it was in the developments of the first half of the sixteenth century eclipsed by its offshoot, the Primer. The story of the Primer is in itself an interesting one, among other things a very instructive example of the way in which devotional books, both liturgical and nonliturgical, expand and proliferate.

It begins with the early adaptation of the traditional synagogue use of the Psalms for common prayer to the purposes of Christian worship, especially for the canonical hours. The oldest of the hours are undoubtedly the night hours, vigils said originally in the middle of the night, and lauds recited at dawn. The day hours were recited at the divisions of the Graeco-Roman day, prime at six in the morning, terce at nine, sext at noon, none at three in the afternoon, and vespers at six. Later, prayers were provided to be said in the evening before going to bed, the office of compline. All of these offices go back for their basic plan to the most ancient pattern of Christian worship, consisting of the recitation of psalms, the reading of selected passages from the Old and the New Testament, a homily or sermon, some improvised prayers, and the singing of hymns. Though the individual offices vary in the constituent elements, the basic plan is the same: an invocation to God, a hymn appropriate to the occasion, preceding or following the psalms, psalms and antiphons, one or more lessons or a little chapter (shorter lesson) in place of a lesson, psalms with responsories, and finally a prayer by the officiating priest. The resulting offices varied not only with the hour of the day but with the day in the week and the season of the year—Advent, Christmastide, Septuagesima, etc.[1]

The full development of the cursus of the hours is really the work of monastic devotion, spreading out from the contemplative centers and finally embracing the whole church. It is a long story, extending for the western church from the fourth to the twelfth centuries. It is a story of monastic experiment and monastic preservation, the results of which were imitated and appropriated in turn by the more zealous of the secular clergy, and then finally imposed upon the secular clergy as a whole in the form of a daily office to be said privately by each individual priest as it was said in choir by the monastic orders.[2] The end product of that story is to be seen in compendious form in the breviary, to the daily use of which every secular priest in the Catholic church is still bound.

This was a quite natural evolution in view of the fact that the monk was, as we have seen, a specialist in the spiritual and devotional life, instructed and disciplined in the traditions of his order, with the necessary equipment, mental and spiritual, and the leisure requisite for the development of the life of prayer, while the parish priest was a busy man of the active world, usually without either the training or the opportunity for the specialized devotional undertakings of the monk. It was only natural, therefore, that he should for himself, and his bishop for him, turn to the laboratory of the monastery for the techniques of the more fully realized devotional life.

What he received therefrom was the fruit of the long and matured experience of a great number of men, stimulated, it is true, by the influence of learned and original and magnetic leaders like Benedict of Aniane, in the eighth century,[3] but in the final result of their labors achieving something like a corporate spiritual unity. By the end of the twelfth century the parish priest and the other members of the clergy with considerable social commitments had at their disposal in the compact and systematized form of the breviary a full scheme of devotion which enabled them, however isolated, to take part in and join their prayers to the corporate prayer of the church, each man reading his book by himself.

The basis of this compendium of devotion was, as we have seen, the Psalter, but it was supplemented by selections from a considerable portion of the Old Testament and most of the New, and further enriched through lessons and hymns from the masterpieces of the great leaders of Christian thought and feeling for over a thousand years. To name only a few of the major contributors to the making of this breviary, it gave the humblest village priest access to the experience and the genius for expression of men like Athanasius, Basil, Gregory Nazianzen, Gregory of Nyssa, John Damascene, above all John Chrysostom, among the Greek fathers, and, among the Latin, Augustine of Hippo, Gregory the Great, Ambrose, Jerome, Leo the Great. Although Augustine of Hippo led all the rest in the number of his contributions, the selections were not confined to the fathers of the church. The Venerable Bede made nearly sixty contributions, and in the high Middle Ages Bernard of Clairvaux almost fifty.[4] Although the breviary was by no means complete nor is, indeed, for that matter now, since it grows with every new feast or saint added to the calendar, still it may be said to have reached its maturity by the end of the twelfth century.

It was at once a rich storehouse of devotional materials, and an arsenal of tested and approved techniques of the spiritual life. As such, it was bound to challenge the emulation of a laity that was now growing in intellectual and spiritual culture. It was only natural that the earnest and aspiring layman should desire to enter into the devotional life of his church as fully as possible. For there is evidence from very early days of the attraction which monastic devotional practice held for the devout layman as for the secular priest. After all, the obligation to use every means available for the salvation of his soul and for the achievement of perfection in his degree rested upon the layman as well as the priest and the monk.

But the breviary, however tempting to lay ambition to emulate the clergy, was too exacting in its demands on time and learning for the majority of men. Just to find its directions and manipulate its techniques of order and arrangement, even with the guides available, was a formidable undertaking for the untrained reader. And the daily recital of the office imposed a very considerable burden upon the time of even a trained priest, familiar with its contents. What was needed for the layman, therefore, was a shorter, fixed service which he could follow without difficulty in church, or find for himself and recite at home. That demand was answered in some of the accretions which had with the passing of the centuries been gathering in the monasteries around the basic offices of the day.

These were, in general, of two types. The first were straight additions to the Divine Office, like the private recitation of the fifteen gradual psalms before matins, probably introduced by Benedict of Aniane in the eighth century and by the tenth universal among monks.[5] The second were the new offices, composed in imitation of the already established Divine Office, like those of the Blessed Virgin and the Holy Cross.[6] There are references as early as the middle of the eighth century to what must have been several different forms of an office in honor of the Blessed Virgin. But it does not appear to have been in common use until the tenth century. In the eleventh century it was generally recited by the secular clergy, and in the twelfth and thirteenth centuries it became a part of their daily office. By the fourteenth it was in almost universal use throughout the church, and its recitation was regarded as obligatory until 1568 when the Pope removed the obligation.[7]

The Office of the Blessed Virgin was based on the seven Hours of the Divine Office, but it modified that pattern by the frequent use of the Ave Maria, and by the choice of canticles, hymns, little chapters, versicles and antiphons that either paid tribute to the Virgin or could be considered appropriate to her. There were, of course, variations in this office as in any cursus, but they were slighter than in the established Divine Office, since only the antiphons of the psalms and canticles, and the little chapters varied with the seasons.

It was, therefore, relatively easy to frame out of it a fixed office. Indeed, when the primers came to be printed, the process of standardization went even farther. For they very commonly took one season only, that from Purification to Advent,[8] and while the local form used in other dioceses, especially that of York, was still to be found, most of the *horae* and primers for the English market printed the office in the form established for the diocese of Salisbury, the famous Use of Sarum.

With other elements to be noticed presently, elements in themselves invariable, it was possible, therefore, to make up a prayer book of fixed contents, or as it came to be called, probably from the Latin word *primarium,* in reference to the first of the day hours, a primer.[9] There was a good deal of latitude in the inclusion or the omission of certain of these elements, but practically all the primers that have survived contain the following: the Hours of the Blessed Virgin Mary, the Seven Penitential Psalms, the Fifteen Gradual Psalms, the Litany, the Office for the Dead, and the Commendations, or prayers following the Office for the Dead.[10] That was the practically universal core. So one can say that as early as the first quarter of the fourteenth century there was a single prayer book for the medieval layman, the *Horae Beatissimae Virginis Mariae,* or as it was known in England, the Primer. A similar development took place on the Continent, resulting in France in the famous *Livres d'heures,* and in Germany in the *Hortulus animae.* The enormous popularity of the genre is attested by the numbers of manuscript copies of these books which still survive from the thirteenth through the fifteenth century, including some of the finest extant examples of the scribe's and miniaturist's arts for that period.

As for the numbers of primers circulated in manuscript, it is impossible to make any guess. From the volume of references in medieval literature we can be confident that a good many were in circulation. They must have worn out in the course of time. And of those that did not, many were taken care of by the statute of 1549:

That all books called Antiphoners, Missals, Grailes, Processionals, Manuals, Legends, Pies, Portuasses, Primers in Latin or English . . . other than such as are or shall be set forth by the King's majesty, shall be by authority of this present Act clearly and utterly abolished, extinguished, and forbidden for ever to be used or kept.[11]

There is evidence that pious layfolk were in the habit of taking the Primer to the parish church with them and reciting the Office of the Blessed Virgin together during Mass.[12] But probably the most common use of the Primer was to read it alone at home, for, as we shall see presently, the book in the course of time was very much expanded with suggestions for the enrichment of private devotion.

However he used the Little Office of the Blessed Virgin, the book afforded the layman help in the fulfillment of a considerable number of his religious duties and enabled him to take advantage of a goodly number of his religious opportunities. To be more specific, it gave him a chance to express his devotion and perform his service to the Virgin, and in the accompanying psalms the universal sinner found help in expressing his penitence and begging for the always needed mercy. The litany enabled him to invoke not only the Blessed Trinity and the Virgin but all the enduringly popular saints of the calendar, for everyday aid, and the Office for the Dead made it possible for him to discharge his Christian duty of praying for the release and rest of the departed. On these grounds alone it would be easy to understand the enormous popularity of the Primer.

But it did much more than that for the devotional equipment of the layman, as may clearly be seen in what must be a notably fine example of the book at the height of its development, just before the forces of a new age challenged its centuries-enriched splendor. It is a sumptuous vellum edition of the *Hore Beatissime Virginis Marie ad legitimum Sarisburiensis Ecclesie ritum,* which François Regnault, one of the leading French printers of devotional books for England in the sixteenth century, published at Paris in 1527. The book is very handsomely illustrated with engravings, some of them nearly full page, others merely substantial expansions of the old initial picture. The subjects of these decorations are suitable to the prayers which they adorn, often representations of the saints to whom they are addressed. The pages are still further embellished by a rich marginal border, that, to judge from the frequency with which something like it is to be found in other fifteenth- and sixteenth-century primers, must have been a well-established feature of the Primer tradition. Sometimes this border is of a conventional scroll type embellished with symbolic and emblematic figures. But more often it is made up of a series of scenes, repeated again and again through the volume. Frequently this series is made up of scenes from Scripture, representing chiefly, but by no means exclusively, episodes in the life of Christ. Sometimes it has a more secular theme like a very rich and apparently well-established representation of a Roman triumph.[13] And several times it is the Dance of Death.[14]

Two elements make this treatment of the latter classic theme especially interesting, the detailed variety of costume in the dress of the various representatives of society involved, and the vivacity and versatility of the attitudes and even expressions of the figure of Death. It is hard to believe that the artist was not touching his grave theme with ironic humor in some of these pictures that present a very dapper, or mischievous, or teasing Death. Some of the enduring forms of social pretension are lightly underscored, too, in other figures in these scenes. Altogether this series makes up a good proportion of the total of the borders of the book. The final effect of the decorations is not only rich and diverting in its abundance of design but, also, highly suggestive in its reminders of biblical episode and moral precept. The use of such a book must have been at once pleasant and stimulating.

And, as we shall see from a summary scrutiny of its contents, it must have been highly educational for the layman who understood enough liturgical Latin to make use of its offerings. He would be in possession of the calendar with its constant reminder of the main events in the life of our Lord and its commemoration of great and influential figures in the Christian history. In this delightful edition the more solemn admonitions of the calendar were relieved by conventional but pleasant little quatrains bringing out the parallels between the passing months and the passing seasons of human life. A table of the movable feasts of the year and directions for finding them would be of obvious help. And so would a lunar chart (*situs lune*) with a picture on the obverse page of the zodiacal man with the twelve signs attached by scrolls to the proper anatomical places, and the seven planets distributed about him, with an explanation of their anatomical references. A summary of the properties of the twelve signs follows on the next page, and an account of the four complexions of man rounds out this little section of general information necessary to the orientation of the average man of the late Middle Ages. The summary of the life of Christ through selections from the Four Evangelists that follows is a classic feature of these primers, and so is the Passion according to Saint John.[15]

It would not be safe to regard the ensuing group of occasional prayers as in any sense unusual, but the offering is remarkable for the abundance with which it provides for the devotional needs of the average layman. A prayer to the Trinity opens with appropriate inclusiveness a collection of prayers for many occasions: the morning's thanksgiving for safe-keeping during the night past, the day's first leaving of the house, before a cross, when the priest turns "after the lavatorye," to be said when one sets out on a message or a journey, on entering the church, when taking holy water, and when kneeling down and beginning to pray. There are prayers for protection against carnal pleasure and temptation of the flesh, for true penitence, and prayers to be said at the canonical hours, a prayer ascribed to Saint Augustine to be said in the night and one of Saint Anselm for general spiritual help, a couple of prayers for a penitent sinner to say, prayers to be said when receiving the *pax,* when receiving the Sacrament, and after receiving the Sacrament.[16] Then come a couple of more general prayers, to get grace against sins and against evil thoughts.[17] These are followed by a series of prayers for various persons: for the king, for a friend living, for wayfaring men, for friends "in sykenes or in necessite," "for thy fader and moder deed," "for thy frend that is deed," "for the lyvnge and deed," for our "benefactours qwyk and deed" (this last a prayer often found in primers, asking Christ to put his passion and death between judgment and the sinner in the hour of his death),[18] and finally a prayer to be said to Blessed Mary after the Communion.[19]

As the foregoing list suggests, while some principle of classification, temporal or associational or functional, can now and then be discerned in the arrangement, no principle of organization holds the field for long. It would certainly be dangerous, for instance, to suggest that there was any rhyme or reason for putting the prayer for the king after the prayer against evil thoughts.[20]

One of the most interesting things about these prayers concerns the, for these years, always important language problem. The prayers themselves are in Latin throughout, but the group is prefaced by an injunction in English: "These prayers folowyng ought to be sayde or ye departe out of your chambre at your uprysynge." [21] The very presence of this note suggests some suspicion on the part of the editor of his readers' Latinity. And this impression is confirmed when one finds that most, though not all of these prayers, have English headings giving the purpose or objective of the prayer. And farther on in the book we shall find that many of the famous prayers of the Primer and the breviary are provided with elaborate explanatory notes in English, though the prayers themselves remain in Latin.

This would seem to be standard practice for this date, for there is a very fine *Hore Intemerate Virginis Marie secundum usum Romanum* from the press of Thielman Kerver in Paris of the year 1500 which furnished French headings for its daily and occasional prayers in Latin.[22] In fact, this book went farther than its English counterpart, for it furnished entirely French versions of certain popular prayers, and a very detailed form for the examination of conscience in French, too.[23] In both books there would seem to have been conservatism on the language issue, with some disposition to recognize the need of supplementary instructional aid in the mother tongue.

But whatever the attitude of the editor of the 1527 Regnault volume on the language question, there can be no doubt of the seriousness of his pedagogical intention. For it held even when he reached the Hours of the Blessed Virgin Mary, the core of the book, from which it took its title. There would not seem to be much that even so pedagogically-minded an editor could do with so fixed a liturgical feature, but here again the educational purpose of the book triumphs. For the constituent psalms are headed with explanations that relate the scriptural text to the liturgical purpose, very much in the manner of the traditional Psalter. For instance, the ninety-fourth psalm, *Venite exultemus,* is headed "Psalmus .xciii. in quo monet deum hilariter et devote laudare," and the eighth, *Domine dominus noster,* "Psalmus .viii. de exaltatione christi: et ecclesie dilatatione." [24]

In keeping with the general opulence of this book, the basic Hours of the Blessed Virgin are enriched with the Hours of the Cross at matins,[25] for example, and with the Hours of the Compassion of the Blessed Mary for all hours of the day,[26] an example of the tendency of liturgies to expand by accretion, and a not uncommon feature of the Book of Hours. The completion of the Hours of the Virgin is followed by a very extensive collection of prayers, addressed mainly but not exclusively to her.[27] Many of these prayers have since pretty much disappeared from popular Catholic devotion, but there are a number that still hold their place as classics. The prayer with which the collection opens, for instance, the *Salve Regina misericordiae* [28] is still recognized as one of the great and continuing Marian prayers. Perhaps the most remarkable of the prayers in this section of the book is the famous poem often ascribed to Jacopone da Todi, the *Stabat Mater dolorosa.*[29] Here it is printed in a solid block of type like any other prose prayer, with certain papal indulgences attached. And it is followed by a prayer to Christ for the intercession of his mother now and in the hour of our death.[30]

Again, the editor of the 1527 volume relies a good deal for instruction and exhortation of the reader upon brief notes prefaced to each prayer. Some of these are little more than Latin tags identifying the theme, like the phrase in the title of the *De profundis,* calling attention to its well-known penitential function: "Psalmus .cxxix. in quo monet ad penitentiam." [31] The English explanations are usually more ambitious than this. Some are historical notes on the provenience of the prayer in question. "A devoute prayer of the .vii. spirituall joyes of oure blessyd lady shewed unto saint Thomas of Cantorberi" [32] speaks for itself. Other prefatory notes detail the favors to be won by the pious who use these prayers. Some of these introductions, like the note prefaced to the *Gaude virgo mater Christi,*[33] are careful to specify the orthodox conditions of penitence and confession of sins for receiving so many days' pardon for saying a particular prayer. But others are not so cautious. For example, the introduction to the *Obsecro te domina sancta Maria* combines promises both of the Virgin's favor and of indulgence, which can only be regarded as rash.[34] The note before the *Ave Maria ancilla sancte trinitatis* combines both the promise and the account of origin of the prayer, when it assures the reader that "whoo that sayth devoutely thys shorte prayer dayly, shall not departe owte of thys worlde wythoute penaunce and mynystracyon of the holy sacrament: the whyche was shewed by an angelle unto saint Bernarde." [35]

But not all of the prayers even in this section are confined to the Virgin. "A generall and devoute prayer for the gode state of our moder the chyrche milytante here in erthe" is addressed to God and invokes the intercession of saints, angels, patriarchs, and so on, in addition to that of the Virgin.[36] And the collection closes with a couple of prayers to the popular Three Kings of Cologne.[37] Then follow in Latin the famous *Fifteen Oes* of Saint Bridget of Sweden, prayers of salutation, petition, and praise addressed to Jesus, and named from the interjection which opens each of the fifteen prayers.[38] Again, these are prefaced with very considerable promises for the delivery of souls out of Purgatory, and the helping of one's kindred to persevere in a good life. Still they serve only as a prelude to an even more extensive collection of prayers, this time mainly to Christ.[39] Many of these are ascribed to very famous names in the history of the church, among others, to Saint Gregory, to Pope Leo (who is said to have sent the epistle beginning "Crux christi sit mecum," to the emperor Charlemagne), to Augustine, to Bede, and to Saint Ambrose. Many of these prayers are simply brief invocations to various saints; others like Saint Gregory's prayer to the Trinity are more in the nature of substantial meditations. Some are remarkably enduring prayers, not only the staple of the Primer but later to be found often in sixteenth-century prayerbooks, like the *O bone Iesu,* commonly ascribed to Saint Bernardine of Siena.[40]

A number of the prayers in this section of the book are taken directly from Scripture, the prayer of the Old Testament character or characters being applied to contemporary personal needs or occasions. This appropriation and adaptation of Old Testament devotional materials to contemporary personal needs is, as we have seen, an old custom of

Christian private devotion. What is interesting here in view of later sixteenth-century devotional developments is the ease with which the present editor assimilates these materials to the over-all purpose of his book, applying them to a great variety of needs and occasions in the personal life of the sixteenth or, indeed, of any century. There is, for instance, "The prayer of Loth, Jacob and Moyses for them that have takem [*sic*] ony newe grete thynge upon them that they wolde have brought to good ende," from Exodus 34.[41] Equally apposite is David's prayer of thanksgiving from 2 Kings 7 with the prudent addition of a plea that the gifts of God to his people be continued.[42] And so is the distinctly inclusive prayer "for them that be in disease or have their frendes diseased or imprisoned: or falle in some grete synne: to praye god to delyver them out: as the good duke Neemie he prayed for them that were in the captivite of babylone the which were delyvered." [43]

In this section of the book the editor is obviously anxious to make as full provision as possible for the day-to-day needs of the average man in a by no means easy world. So he ransacks the piety of all ages, Christian and Jewish, and of all schools of devotion, to meet the joys and the griefs and the anxieties of his readers. There are prayers for all sorts of occasions and purposes, especially against temptations,[44] and there is an extensive group for the dying to be said in the last agony by the sufferer or by others for him.[45] There are prayers for "ony that falleth in disclander," for them that intend to be married or are newly married, of thanksgiving for those in sickness or adversity with an eye to their making satisfaction for their sins, and for those maliciously accused.[46]

And, of course, there are a number of prayers to help the layman perform his religious duties. Some are prayers to be said when assisting at Mass. For instance, there are half a dozen prayers for the Elevation, one for the "Sacring," another, really a small collection, to the Sacrament of the Altar, and another short series for "after the elevacyon of oure lorde." The section ends with a group of three Communion prayers.[47] Altogether it affords a varied and substantial supply of petitions for the daily life of the devout Christian.

The next section, devoted to the Seven Psalms and the Fifteen Psalms, is labeled appropriately and inclusively, "penitentiales." [48] It is another of the staple features of the Primer. Again, each psalm is prefaced by a preliminary explanation of its contents as is traditional in the Primer,

For instance, the third of the Seven Psalms, the thirty-seventh, *Domine ne in furore* is headed: "Oratio ad dei mitigandam iram: cum illa propter peccata in ipsum commissa timetur." [49] The *Letania sanctorum* is likewise another regular feature of the Primer, here given, of course, in undiminished fullness of homage to the riches of the calendar.[50] Again, the treatment of the prayers at the end of the litany is on the lavish scale characteristic of the volume. It includes the *Versus sancti Bernardi* with an explanation of their origin more, it is to be feared, in the spirit of the *Golden Legend* than of Saint Bernard. It is not difficult to see why not only the Protestant reformers but the Catholic were to eliminate it. Yet it has a certain faith in the interrelations of the powers of the universe and a certain confidence in the realism, if not the truthfulness, of the devil that make the story worth repeating:

Whan saint Bernard was in hys prayers the dyvell sayd unto hym. I knowe that there be certeyne verses in the sawter who that say them dayly shall not perysshe and he shall have knowledge of the daye that he shall dye, but the fende wolde not shewe them to saint bernard than sayd saint bernard. I shall say dayly the hole sawter. The fende considerynge that saint bernard shall do so moche profyte to laboure so he shewed hym thys verses.[51]

The *Vigilie mortuorum,* consisting of the *Placebo* and the *Dirige,* is another common fixture of the typical primer, one that, as we shall see presently, was to cause some of the sixteenth-century English editors of the book a good deal of trouble. Again, the psalms are prefaced with introductory summaries of their contents, like the note before the twenty-fourth psalm, "Oratio fidelium opem a deo poscentium cum ab inimicis iritantur: et ad divinam benignitatem confugientium." [52] And the same is true of the *Commendationes animarum,*[53] still another of the fixed features of the Primer. And, again, the prayers usually found at the end of the office are augmented this time by prayers to be said entering and leaving the churchyard.[54]

Two other common features of the Primer of the time are to be found in the Psalms of the Passion of Christ,[55] and the Psalter of Saint Jerome (the famous cento which we have already met in the history of the Psalter) with concluding prayers to and concerning Saint Jerome.[56] And then comes a cursus which, while not, as we shall see presently, a universal feature of the Primer, is often found in the fuller versions, the *Hore de nomine Iesu* (*hore dulcissimi nominis Iesu*).[57] The *Vespere* and *Completorium* of this particular book are of especial interest to students of English literature, because they are ascribed to "devoto Richardo de hampole."

Of somewhat the same optional character as the *Hore de nomine Iesu* is the supplement to the regular Office of the Blessed Virgin, made up of psalms and prayers to be said on special days and in special seasons.[58] The prayers which follow the conclusion of this supplement to the Little Office, include an appropriate prayer to be recited before the Divine Office, and the famous prayer to be said before a representation of the body of Christ, *Ad imaginem corporis Christi.*[59]

The encyclopedia-of-devotion character already suggested for the volume is borne out by the addition of the "forme of confessyon" entirely in English with its careful canvassing of the sinner's record with regard to the Seven Deadly Sins, and the Ten Commandments, not, it should be added, the statement of Moses but a more positive and practically interpretive statement of the injunctions of the Ten Commandments. This is reënforced by a very homely and practical summary of offences against the Ten Commandments, the Five Wits, the Seven Works of Bodily Mercy, the Seven Works of Ghostly Mercy, the Seven Gifts of the Holy Ghost, the Seven Sacraments, and the Eight Beatitudes.[60] Finally, another summary of the Ten Commandments in direct and everyday terms [61] completes this practical moral survey, on the whole a fairly comprehensive summary of the possibilities of human frailty for that or any other time.

This would seem to cover the field pretty completely, but there is still more to come, for at the very end the more purely devotional character of the book is restored in an English version of the *Fifteen Oes* of Saint Bridget, the famous series of petitions to Jesus which we have already met in Latin and of which we shall see more presently.[62] The practical note of the volume is reënforced by the concluding prayers: "A prayer agayne evyll thoughtes," and "A devoute prayer for the illuminacyon of mannes mynde." [63]

In this volume we have, then, a singularly full and rich version of the standard Primer. Not every version would, of course, contain all the supplementary material, but it may be doubted if there is a single item in this book that would not be paralleled in others of the time. Most of the contents of the book are to be found, for instance, in a much less pretentious volume published by Christopher of Endhoven at Antwerp in 1525. Indeed, much of the supplementary information even—the explanatory headings for the psalms and the notes of origin and indulgences and promises—is to be found in almost verbatim form in this primer. This resemblance is the more impressive because with the exception of an English version of the *Fifteen Oes* tucked away in the middle of the Latin text,[64] the book of 1525 is entirely in Latin.

The beautiful *Hore* we have been studying, then, is simply the classic Primer at its richest and fullest, edited with unusual solicitude for the reader who was in general conversant with liturgical and devotional Latin but who would appreciate a little English help when it came to finding in a hurry the prayers he needed. That this type of arsenal of private devotion was appreciated is apparent when we turn to the records of the publications of the early printers for the English market. No item in their output seems to have been more popular than the Primer, if we can judge from the number of copies that have survived the vicissitudes of the time.

V

THE PRIMER IN ENGLISH

LIKE its parent the Psalter, the Primer was caught up in the long and complicated controversy over the translation of religious books into the vernacular. The very fact that the Primer had come into being for the use of the laity made such an involvement inevitable. But in view of the relations of the Primer to monastic observance it is not surprising that it should long have clung to the language of its origin, especially when that language was still the language of most serious intellectual as well as devotional effort. In the beginning of the history of the Primer, at any rate, there were probably few people who either would want such a book or be able to make use of it who could not read Latin. Indeed, it may well have seemed to the makers of such books that they would be of doubtful utility to readers who did not possess that minimum of intellectual equipment. Furthermore, under the conditions of book-making before the invention of printing, even a much more modest book than the one we have outlined would be so expensive as to be entirely beyond the means of any individual except one possessed of considerable wealth, or willing like Chaucer's Clerk of Oxenford, to sacrifice every comfort for books.

But the growing importance and self-assurance of the educated middle classes who were at home only in English created a demand for a primer in the vernacular, and by the end of the fourteenth century there is evidence of a very considerable effort to satisfy that demand even within the limitations imposed by manuscript production. When Henry Littlehales undertook the publication of an English primer of about 1400, he sought out for collation all the surviving manuscript primers he could find for the period in English and Scottish libraries. He found thirteen entirely in English and one in Latin and English.[1] That figure is not insignificant when it is remembered that such manuscripts would in the very nature of things receive hard usage, to say nothing of the hazards of all ancient religious books in the sixteenth century. Little-hales assigned five of the thirteen entirely English manuscripts to the end of the fourteenth century, mainly on the strength of calendar items. Of the other nine, seven were assigned, chiefly on Maskell's authority, to the first third of the fifteenth century. Only one was put after 1460.[2]

As for the contents of these medieval English primers, there is no question that they were more fixed and more restricted than those of the Latin manuscripts, and, it should be added, than those of the later printed English primers.[3] Indeed, two of the English manuscripts contain nothing more than the bare minimum: the Hours of the Blessed Virgin Mary, the Seven Psalms, the Fifteen Psalms, the Litany, the Office for the Dead, and the Commendations.[4] And two add to that core but little, in one case the calendar,[5] and, in the other, an exposition of the paternoster.[6] Even when it was included, the calendar would seem to have been a much more modest affair than it was in the Latin versions or the printed English books. For example, the calendar in the late fourteenth, early fifteenth-century primer which Littlehales printed contained but three commemorations for April, and for November, the fullest month, no more than eleven.[7] In every respect the most elaborate of these medieval English primers fell far short of the sixteenth-century printed versions.

In view of what the editor reports as to the plainness of these manuscripts, and of the modest purchase price of two shillings for a primer recorded in the Paston letters, probably for 1474,[8] economy may well have been the motive. But the lack of leisure of the middle-class public for whom these books were probably made might well be another factor. The wax chandler's servant who mentioned a primer in his will of 1434 [9] probably did not have time for the elaborate additions of private devotion found in some of the Latin books of the age.

But even such a limited prayer book as that which Littlehales printed would make available to the literate and earnest Christian who read only English the aid of a considerable number of the Psalms for expressing his praise of God, his sorrow for his sins, and his petitions for support in the various emergencies of life; it would help him to express his devotion to the Blessed Virgin, and in the litany to call upon the most commonly invoked of the saints, and it would help him to pray for the dead. If he happened to be near a cathedral or a conventual church, he might use his book to follow the popular Little Office of the

Blessed Virgin, or he might take it to his parish church with a friend to recite it with him. It is easy to understand the popular appeal of such a book, and the resulting demand for it, quite apart from any other considerations such as those that presently made such translations so complicated and controversial a business.

There is no question that the demand for these books had increased by the end of the fifteenth century and the beginning of the sixteenth, as one would expect from the growing prosperity and ambition of the middle classes. And the cheapening and the increasing availability of books which the invention of printing made possible certainly served to increase the public that would be interested in the vernacular primer.

Some effort was made, as we have seen, to satisfy this interest in the Latin primers; it took the form, as in the Regnault *Hore* of 1527, of the insertion in the Latin text of one or both of two English elements, either notes of explanation, usually of occasion or of indulgence, before Latin prayers, or the provision of English prayers among the Latin, perhaps to enable the Latin-reading owner of the book to share it with some less learned member of his household. Examples of both devices are to be seen long before the Regnault *Hore* of 1527 in a *Horae* of Sarum Use which Johannes Jehannot printed for N. Lecomte in Paris in 1498.

For at the end of this Latin book was added a typical group of what may be called occasional prayers,[10] practically all of them to be found in the larger group of prayers at the beginning of the Regnault *Hore* of 1527.[11] The remarkable thing about this group in the earlier book is that they are not only the same prayers but that they are for the most part arranged in the same order and with the same identifying headings as the prayers of Regnault's *Hore* of 1527. Some of these headings are English, in general the same, word for word, as those of the 1527 book, fresh proof of the established and traditional character of this material.

But even more interesting from the point of view of concessions to the demand for the vernacular is the inclusion in the very heart of the book in a group of what might be called occasional prayers, between Compline and the Seven Penitential Psalms, of a few prayers in English.[12] Two of these are prayers to Jesus, "O Glorious jesu O mekest Jesu," and "O the most swetest spouse of mi sowle." There is also a well-known prayer to the Trinity, and a prayer beginning, "O Lord god almyghty alle seeing althynges."

This insertion of English prayers in the Latin text seems to have been a well-established custom by the end of the fifteenth century, for the same prayers in the same version and in the same position are found in the *Hore* of Sarum use which Thielman Kerver printed at Paris for Johannes Ricardus Mercator in 1497.[13] And they are found again likewise in the same version and in the same position in the *Hore* which Philippe Pigouchet printed at Paris in 1502 for Simon Vostre.[14]

But the editor of the *Hore* which Christopher of Endhoven printed for Francis Byrckman at Antwerp in 1525 went farther than that. For he printed the usual preliminary pedagogical material of the Primer, the Our Father, Hail Mary, Creed, and Ten Commandments, in English.[15] But the offices and the prayers were printed in Latin with the English notes described above. The one further provision for the non-Latinate was the printing of the *Fifteen Oes* entirely in English at the beginning of the collection of prayers between the Litany and the Vigils of the Dead.[16]

A still more advanced stage of this vernacular development is represented by *Thys Prymer off Salysburye Use* which Yolande Bonhomme, the widow of Thielman Kerver, printed for Johan Growte in 1533. For though, with one exception to be noticed presently, this book still printed the actual Little Office, etc., in Latin alone, it included "The maner to lyve well," in Robert Copland's translation,[17] "An invocacyon gloryous named the psalter of Jesus," [18] a considerable group of occasional prayers,[19] the *Fifteen Oes*,[20] "Certayne questions what is synne with the order of confession," [21] and "The XII artycles of the fayth" and the Ten Commandments, all in English.[22] Such a book would clearly be of a good deal of use to the man who knew no Latin or had only a very imperfect grip on the meaning of the Latin which he read or heard read.

But even that would hardly suffice to meet the requirements of the now expanding middle-class reading public. There is evidence that here, as so often, the opportunities of such a situation were seized upon more readily by the critics of the existing order than by its defenders. The role of the "English books" in the spread of revolutionary religious ideas will be remembered by any reader of Foxe. The Primer plays its part in that story, too. An English *Hortulus animae* (a parallel layman's devotional book, very popular in Germany) is mentioned in a list of books of 1529, and in 1530 is found in a list of prohibited books.[23] In the next year both the *Hortulus animae* and the Primer in English were proclaimed at Paul's Cross, and Richard Bayfield was charged with importing the Primer in English. In 1532 Sir Thomas More reported that he had heard of an English primer by George Joye.[24] And in 1534-35 came what were, so far as we can at present tell, the first English primers to be printed, the Godfray primer and the first of the Byddell-Marshall primers. These were unquestionably revolutionary primers both in form and intention, as is hardly surprising in view of the stage which the controversy over the English books had reached at that time.

But in view of the long history of English elements in the Primer, to say nothing of the complete English primers, it would have been surprising if someone had not attempted the publication of a straight translation of the traditional Primer as it stood.

That, with certain qualifications which we shall examine shortly, is what happened in a group of primers coming out of Rouen and Paris in these same years. Apparently the first of these, and certainly the first of these to survive, is a book of 1536, printed at Rouen without any indication of the printer's name. The copy which I have been using in microfilm, that at Cambridge University, is defective at the beginning to the extent of the first eight signatures, about sixteen pages. That means that the title page, the Almanac, the Calendar, and about two pages of preliminary materials are missing. As it survives, the book at present begins with the Life of Christ after Saint John.[25] A leaf is also missing from the Litany, and three leaves from the prayers after Compline,[26] including part of the first of the *Fifteen Oes*. But we can be fairly sure of the missing materials. Hoskins records a reforming preface to the copy available to him,[27] a preface clearly, from his summary, the same preface as that to the 1538 edition which we shall presently discuss, a preface which puts the basic position of the book on such crucial issues as honor to the Virgin and saints beyond doubt. And, as we shall see presently, we can be sure of the general character of the missing Calendar and section of the Litany from the 1538 editions of the book, for in that edition both are still highly traditional in spite of the more outspokenly reforming character which the book has assumed by that time.[28]

At any rate, the bulk of the Rouen primer of 1536 remains even in this mutilated copy, and it is quite clear that, except for a very few changes which we shall examine shortly, it is the traditional Primer, which we have been studying, but with the Latin text in the margin and the English translation in the center of the page. Beginning with the Life of Christ according to the Four Evangelists—as we have seen, a very ancient type of scriptural harmony—it prints in the traditional order and form both Latin and English versions of the Passion according to Saint John the Evangelist, the paternoster, the Ave Maria, the Twelve Articles of the Faith, the Ten Commandments, both in scriptural prose and in "metre," in other words, all the traditional introductory materials of the Primer.[29] After an "Invocacyon unto the Holy Trinitye, to be sayde in the mornynge, whan thou shalt ryse up," the complete Little Office of Our Lady is printed, with the Matins of the Cross and the Hours of the Compassion of Our Lady.[30] Then follow the *Fifteen Oes*,[31] the Seven Penitential Psalms,[32] the Litany and Suffrages,[33] with a number of brief prayers following, the *Dirige* and Commendations,[34] the Psalms of the Passion,[35] and the Psalter of Saint Jerome.[36] The book ends with a final brief selection of prayers usually found in the Primer, a couple of Communion prayers, the *O bone Iesu* of Saint Bernard, "A prayer unto the ymage of the body of Christe" (*Conditor celi et terre*), and four scriptural prayers, two for wisdom from the Book of Wisdom, and two prayers of Solomon's, one for wisdom to govern "ryghtly," and one for a "competency of lyvyng." [37] This primer is constructed, in short, on the basic pattern of the Regnault *Hore* of 1527, and all its contents are thoroughly orthodox and traditional in every way.

But quite apart from language, there is a very striking difference in the over-all effects of the Regnault *Hore* of 1527 and this Rouen primer. The latter book seems barer, more businesslike than its opulent Paris predecessor. Part of this is due to the more modest format of the latter book. Though finely illustrated, it is not so richly embellished and decorated at every point as the Regnault 1527 book. But that difference, though striking enough, is not so important as the difference in the handling of the contents.

As we have seen, the Primer in its tendency to grow by accretion had enriched its liturgical core with a good many prayers of various types. Most, if not all, of these prayers were dogmatically orthodox and psychologically sound. The difficulty was in the promises that sometimes as a consequence of half legendary source-reporting, sometimes as a result of the enthusiasm of the promoters of a new form of devotion, sometimes as a response to the hunger of the worshiper for assurance of spiritual safety for himself and his family and friends, had been offered without due regard to prudence or even common sense. These promises were to be attacked, and with justice, by the reformers of various stripes of opinion, on the ground that they were conducive to superstition and idolatry. The sixteenth century was not very precise in its discriminations between idolatry and magic. Sometimes the promise offered certainly smacked of the magical formula, although there was nothing in the prayer itself of that character. The need for some reform was apparent, and this primer of 1536 represents one approach to the problem.

By and large the promises of supernatural help have been eliminated. The source notes have been eliminated, too, or condensed. The most colorful and the most uncertain details of the circumstances under which the prayer was first composed have vanished in the process. The result is a loss for the lover of the picturesque legend and a distinct gain for good sense. But there is more than common-sense reform at work here. The promises of indulgences have been eliminated, too, and that is an important hint as to the editor's position.

And there are still others. The multiplication of devotions to saints had been one of the features of later medieval devotion, one that was to be severely challenged by the pioneers of some of the new movements of the time. The editor of this Rouen primer of 1536 made no concessions on the principle of the honoring of the saints and the invocation of their help in the struggles of the universal Christian community. But he was quite obviously aware of the enormous multiplication of devotions to which the changing fashions of piety had given rise, and the danger of clogging litanies and commemorations with the sheer numbers of saints to be remembered. A comparison of the lists of saints remembered or invoked at various points in the Regnault *Hore* of 1527 and this primer of 1536 reveals some very interesting condensations or omissions. For instance, in the later book [38] some seven saints are dropped from the earlier list of commemorations at the end of Matins.[39] Saint Panthaleone, martyr, and Saint Sitha, virgin, are not at first sight important one way or another. The omission of Saint Thomas the Archbishop of Canterbury is more significant. But the omission of the special commemoration of Saint Paul the Apostle when that of Saint Peter and Paul is kept is hard to explain on any basis but that of the desire for economy.

The desire for economy is certainly to be seen in the omission of most of the occasional prayers and the large collection of Marian prayers that are so striking a feature of the Regnault 1527 book.[40] But there is probably nothing more than economy to it, because the 1527 collection was unusually rich in both categories. Certainly, no effort was made to attenuate the Marian character of the Little Office as was so often to be done in the Protestant reformers' primers.

Nor is any more significance to be attributed to some of the other omissions of material found in the unmistakably fuller *Hore* of 1527. For instance, a couple of prayers for the dead [41] are eliminated in the incidental prayers between the *Dirige* and the Commendations,[42] but prayers for the dead are kept elsewhere, and the Vigils and the Commendations themselves are reproduced in full. There is no reason to suspect the editor of any heterodoxy on this point. But he is clearly anxious to eliminate some of the duplication perhaps inevitable in any collection of materials from so many different sources.

There are a few cases of alteration in the text of a prayer that raise interesting questions in view of the controversies of the time. Perhaps the most striking example is the change in the final petition of the classical prayer, *Conditor celi et terre,* "Oh maker of heaven and earth." That is one of the most popular of the Primer prayers; it was used, for instance, in the *Hore* of 1527, as a preparation for confession with the heading, "Oratio ad imaginem corporis christi." [43] This prayer the editor of the 1536 primer prints in identically the same Latin form in the margin of his page, and in the middle of the page he translates it faithfully until he reaches the last petition: "ut perducas me ad bonum finem: ad veram penitentiam, puram confessionem, et dignam satisfactionem omnium peccatorum meorum. Amen." This he briefly sums up in the general petition, "that thou bryng me to the blysse, that never shall ceasse." [44] Such a change at the end of a prayer that is fundamentally a confession of sin on the basic Seven Deadly Sins pattern and a prayer for mercy raises the question as to which it was that the editor objected to, the notion of satisfaction for sin, or the notion of the sacrament of confession. But in the main there is no question of the unknown editor's desire to conserve the traditional book, as will become clearer when the later history of his work is considered.

That history is an obscure one, but enough can be deduced from a comparison of succeeding editions to make clear certain very curious and important facts. For it is not difficult to trace this book even though the printer's name is missing, because the version used for the Psalms that, as we have seen, are the core of the Primer, is different from any known elsewhere.[45]

Two years after the publication of this Rouen primer of 1536, another edition was published in the same city that may be viewed as either a more explicit disclosure of the intentions of the earlier publication or a fuller development of its implications. This time, though no printer's name is given on the title page or in the colophon of the Primer itself, Nicholas le Roux is named as the printer in the colophon of the uniformly printed edition of *An Exposycyon after the Maner of a Contemplacyon upon the LI Psalme,* etc., bound up with it. The preface to this work, as we have already seen, makes clear the position of the editor on what obviously seems to him the most important of current controversies, that over the honoring of the Blessed Virgin and the saints:

The due honour to god (as me semyth) is. That we shulde neyther worshypp, feare, ne sarve nothyng but hym only: which opinion I wold nat that men shuld interprete so straitly as though myne intent were to with drawe from sayntes and temporal rulers theyr due worshyp and obedience . . . . For evyn as it is a poynte of christian prudence and circumspeccyon nat to receyve any thynge for certayne and undoubted, whiche is nat expressyd in manyfest scripture, so contrary wyse is it a poynte of presumptuous perversite and arrogance proudly to rejecte that thing whiche the religious contemplacion of good and godly men have eyther taughte, to the solace and conforthe of them that beleve, or lefte to the instruction of the unlerned multitude . . . . Yct am I nat ignorant that some people have ben greatly deludyd of longe tyme about the veneracyon of sayntes and suche lyke thynges, partly by ignoraunce, and partely thorowe impure persuasyons of false preachours. For the reformacyon wherof almyghty god of his eterne providence hath put in the mynds of his electe princes, and true pastors of his flocke to purge the fylthynes of false doctrine out of the hertes of them that have ben seducyd by blynde guydes.[46]

It took the author of that preface quite a while to get to that last point, but when he did there is no mistaking the fact that he took some of the classic Marian prayers as the main illustrations of the abuses which he condemned.

Yet in spite of that preface, the edition of 1538 begins traditionally enough. The Calendar is the full calendar such as one finds in the

Regnault *Hore* of 1527, an important point for the basic orientation of any book of this period, since the calendar was one of the earliest and most persistent targets of the Protestant reformers. True, there is some evidence of what might be called weeding-out. For example, the commemoration of Ignatius, Pope and Martyr, for January eleventh has been dropped, and so has that of Thomas Aquinas for January twenty-eighth, while the feast of "Agnetis secundo" is left for the latter date. For the fourth of May, the "Festum corone spinee domini" is omitted, and so are the commemorations of Boniface Martyr for the fourteenth and Hubert the Bishop for the thirtieth of that month.[47] One might form some conjecture as to possible explanations, but in view of the extensiveness of what is kept, the motive is probably the same one already noticed in 1536, the desire to reduce the number of commemorations. Curiously enough, that of Saint Thomas Martyr is kept for December twenty-ninth.[48] But throughout the Calendar the words "bishop of Rome" are substituted for "pope," as for instance, on March twelfth, where the *Hore* of 1527 lists "Gregorii pape et confes.," this edition lists "Gregory byshop of Rome." [49] This was to be the practice of the Protestant primers to comply with the statute of 1534 which forbade the use of the title of "Pope" for the Bishop of Rome.

The Litany is another place where the editor of 1538 seems to have seen a chance to cut the list of commemorations,[50] but here he seems to have proceeded on a different basis. Certain saints are left out entirely: Saints Cletus, Sixtus, Damian, Prime, Felician, and Dionysius with his comrades, a list of omissions which falls with a disproportionate heaviness on early popes that can hardly be accidental.[51] There are a good many more omissions, however, conspicuous among which is that of a long list of feminine saints, some famous ones about whom little is known, like Perpetua, Felicitas, and Praxedis, but others, like Scholastica and Wenefreda, who have very considerable legends.[52] This would appear to suggest some lack of enthusiasm for female saints. And there is reason in the omission of the invocation of "Omnes sancti monachi et eremite," and of "sancte vidue et continentes," [53] to wonder what the editor's attitude toward the monasteries was. But he has kept the usual litany prayer that all the degrees of the church in holy religion be preserved: "Ut donum apostolicum et omnes gradus ecclesie in tua sancta religione conservare digneris." [54] But, again, the editor's obvious desire to cut down on the contents of his book should not be forgotten.

In spite of this desire for economy, however, the editor of the 1538 Rouen primer took up a good deal of space for a device which the *Hore* of 1527, like a good many of the traditional books, had used freely and which the editor of the 1536 primer had eschewed, namely, the expository introduction to various elements of the Primer. Those introductions or notes, it will be remembered, had been used mainly to suggest the purpose for which a prayer might be used or to give some account of its provenience and potency to interest the reader in its use. The editor of the 1538 Rouen book revives this old device. Sometimes he uses it very much as it had often been used before, to identify in a fairly stereotyped fashion the material he is about to print, as when he prefaces matins and lauds [55] with brief notes explaining the meaning of those offices.

But sometimes he uses this device for a very different purpose. For instance, he prefaces what he calls "The .xv. prayers of saynt brygyde" with the following note:

These .xv. prayers followyng, called commonly the .xv. oos, are set forthe in dyvers latin prymers, with goodly paynted prefaces, promysyng to the sayers therof many thynges bothe folyshe and false, as the dely[v]erance of .xv. soules out of Purgatory, with other lyke vanyties: yet are the prayers selfe ryght good and vertuous, if they be sayd without any suche superstitious trust or blynde confidence. And therfore are they called the prayers of S. Brygyde because that holy virgin used dayly to say them (as many write) before thymage of the Crosse in saint Paules Churche at rome.[56]

Now such a note is capable of more than one interpretation. It might be an attempt to defend traditional prayers under attack against people who would drop them because of their associations, quite the plain sense of the passage, in fact. But it might, also, be a device for furthering the attack on the Golden Legend elements of the Primer in quarters where attachment to the traditional book was strong.

There is something of the same ambiguity (in view of the controversies of the time) in a rather lengthy preface to the *Dirige:*

The makynge of this service (that we call Dirige) some do ascribe to saynt Isidore, and some to saynt Gregorie: but whether of them it was, forceth not moche, for certayn it is, that all is conteined therin, (the colletes excepte) may as well be applyed for the lyvyng, as for the deade, yet (as Platina wryteth) Pelagius, byshop of Rome dyd fyrste ordeyne the commemoration, or prayenge for the deade. Whiche thynge, (after the mynde of Isidore) was received as a tradition of the apostles, howe be it S. Ambrose affirmeth, that it was derived of an olde custome had amonge the Hebrewes, which used longe lamentation for the deade after theyr departyng, as they dyd for Jacob the space of .xl. dayes, and for Moyses .xxx. But we that are under the newe lawe, are taught of god by the mouthe of Saynt Paule his apostle, not to mourne or be sorye for them that be departed, in the faythe of Christe, but to rejoyse as in them that rest in the sleepe of peace, for so is it dayly remembred in the Masse, untyll they shall be called unto the laste judgement. Never the lesse I thynke it very charitable, and to procede of a good and godly mynde, in that we use any worldly obsequies aboute the deade, or do pray for them for Saynt Augustine in his Euchiridion saythe: It is not to be denyed, but that the soules departed are greatly releved by prayer. Whiche usage is very commendable, for asmoche as it hath continueth [sic] in the christen churche, evyn from the very infancie therof.[57]

Again, the plain sense would seem to be that he agreed with an objection often advanced in those years against the traditional office but still found value in the office. Certainly, the Protestant reformers who were attacking all praying for the dead as basically useless and misguided would hardly be satisfied with such a defense. At the same time, the apparent defense does contain an admission of a position that, as we shall see presently, was used in the reforming books to attack the basic meaning of the *Dirige*.

And this sense of a cautious moving out of old positions in the direction of new is confirmed by one or two changes in the content of the prayers themselves. Of these the most striking again concerns this much-debated matter of praying for the dead. In the customary series of prayers for the dead that, as usual, follow the *Dirige* and the Commendations, the 1536 primer includes one quite traditional one which it titles, "A prayer to god for them that be departed, havynge none to praye for them."[58] The 1538 editor keeps all the series but this one. This he drops and he puts in its place a prayer often found elsewhere in the traditional Primer, "The prayer of the prophete Jonas delyvered out of the whales belly."[59]

One other change of significance for contemporary emphasis or value rather than doctrine is the insertion in the litany right after the prayer for the souls departed, of a prayer for the king. That is striking enough in itself. But the prayer is interesting because of its implications not only of the expected loyalty but of a general sympathy with the king's position, hardly to be misunderstood by anybody interested in the carrying on of the traditional Primer by this year of 1538:

Lorde of god hostes, kynge most myghtye and stronge, by whom kynges do reigne, and in whose handes are the hertes of all kynges: graunte unto thy wel beloved servaunt. H. our kynge continuall helthe of body and soule, that his herte alwayes enclynynge to holsome and godly counselles: and the enemyes of the common welthe beinge vanquished we may longe enjoye under hym perpetuall peace, and brotherly concorde.[60]

What all this amounts to is not easy to judge precisely. The editor is certainly committed to the traditional Primer; he is not disposed to undertake any startling innovations in its basic plan, or, on the whole, to change its contents. But he is very much aware of the points at issue, and though he is clearly not disposed to go to the extremes to which some of the people who raise these points have gone, he has not dug himself in against the first attack the way in which most defenders of the tradition would. He is psychologically poised between two worlds, and one wonders if on one or two points he may not have already gone farther than he is yet ready to admit, notably on the issue of paying honor to the Virgin and the saints.

But whatever his precise position, there is no question of the thoroughgoing seriousness of his pedagogical intention. That becomes quite apparent in two additions which he makes to the book of 1536. Both are printed with separate title pages and separate signatures, but both are printed in every respect uniformly with the Primer and obviously designed to be bound up with it as parts of one book. The first of these two supplements is the "exposycyon after the maner of a contemplacyon" of Hierom of Ferrara, on Psalm 51, and the unfinished meditation of the same author on Psalm 30.[61] These two treatises are translated from *Fratris Hieronymi Ferrariensis expositiones in psalmos,* published at Venice in 1505.[62] Jerome of Ferrara is, of course, Savonarola, the famous reforming friar whose difficulties with ecclesiastical authority made him an object of sympathetic interest to the Protestant reformers. In spite of the reputation of Savonarola for his difficulties with church authority, his doctrinal orthodoxy was not challenged. The addition of these meditations to the traditional Primer does constitute a novelty. But the type of meditations on the Psalms is, as we have seen, quite in the medieval tradition, and there is nothing in these meditations out of keeping with the general position of the Rouen primer of 1536. So far as the general purposes of the book as a whole are concerned, these meditations would not only help to deepen the reader's understanding of the Psalms, but they would give him example and practice in the use of the important religious tool of meditation.

In the same fashion, a third volume is uniformly printed with the foregoing and bound up with them, to complete this compact encyclopedia of devotion, and that contains "the Pystles and Gospels of every Sonday, and holy Daye in the Yere." This, again, is an innovation, this being (with the possible exception of another book of the same year to which we shall turn presently) the first time apparently that such a collection appeared with the Primer. In itself such a collection is not, of course, a novelty, for there is evidence that in the late fourteenth and early fifteenth centuries some of the English-reading laity used to take manuscript copies of the Epistles and Gospels to church to follow the Epistles and Gospels of the Mass in the vernacular.[63] But it is a new addition to the Primer. And the particular form it takes is significant, for the translation used is that of Tyndale.[64] Again, this section of the expanded Primer puts the non-Latinate reader in direct possession of a very considerable portion of his inheritance, namely, those portions of the Old and New Testaments most often used in Christian devotion. For these are the sections that bring out most explicitly the central episodes in the life of Christ, the foundation of the ecclesiastical year.

In other words, there is nothing in the character of these additions in themselves incompatible with the traditional Primer character of the original Rouen primer of 1536. But the spirit and atmosphere of the 1538 edition of the Rouen primer as a whole still remains very different from that of the earlier book. This becomes even clearer when one turns to another primer of the year 1538, a book which has not, so far as I am aware, been hitherto associated with the Rouen books but which clearly belongs with them. This is a finely printed and illustrated book of about the same general degree of ornamentation as the two Rouen books; it was published at Paris in 1538 with no indication of publisher or editor. It is indeed much closer to the 1536 primer of Rouen than the 1538 primer. The most striking physical evidence of this relationship is that the same plates are frequently used to illustrate and decorate the beginnings of the various hours, etc. These plates usually represent a scene or action central to the meaning of the service, such as that before the Seven Psalms of a very seductive Bathsheba standing naked in her bath tub with a mirror in her hand for the temptation of King David, or a terrifying animated corpse with serpents gnawing at his torn flesh and exposed vitals and Death behind him, before the *Dirige*. Identical plates are also used close to the beginning of the two books before the Passion according to Saint John, before lauds, before the sixth and the ninth Hours of Our Lady, before the Evensong of Our Lady, and before Compline.[65] These plates are the same in so many cases as to raise the possibility of some relation between the two shops in which these books were printed.

The clue to that relationship is to be found in the *Prymer in Englysshe after the Use of Salysbury* which Nicholas le Roux printed at Rouen for François Regnault in 1538. Nicholas le Roux was, as we have seen, the printer of the Rouen primer of 1538, and François Regnault we have already encountered as the Paris printer of the very complete Latin *Hore* of 1527, and, it should be added, for more than forty years a leading French printer of devotional books for England.[66] This primer is, as its title indicates, completely in English, but it is the English text of the Rouen Latin-English primers with the reforming introductory notes of the 1538 edition.[67] These facts suggest the possibility, if nothing more, that the unidentified printer of the Paris primer of 1538 is François Regnault.[68]

But quite apart from that possibility, there is no question that the Paris primer of 1538 is another edition of the Rouen primer of 1536, and although it is expanded at certain points, it is closer to the primer of 1536 than the 1538 Rouen primer. It does not, for instance, have any of the substitutions or ambiguous explanations of the 1538 primer. Indeed, it lacks even the reforming preface.[69]

The Paris primer of 1538 has the same calendar and the same litany [70] as the Rouen primer of that year, and in view of the relations between the two Rouen editions there is no reason to believe that the primer of 1536 would have any less conservative a calendar or litany.[71] The Paris book contains the same elements as the Rouen primer of 1536 plus certain other elements that in their total effect reënforce the general impression of the book of 1536. Indeed, the inclusion of these elements simply carries a little farther the original intention of the decision to print the Primer in Latin and English, namely, to put the layman in as full possession as possible of the resources of his religious tradition. The first of these added elements is a guide to the spiritual life of which we shall see more when we come to study that genre, "The preface and maner to lyve well" of "mayster Johan quentin . . . doctour in dyvynyte at Paris," translated out of French by Robert Copland, printer of London.[72] The French original was already a classic of the Roman Use *hore* designed for French readers, and in Copland's translation it came to enjoy a wide popularity among English readers as well. We shall examine it in detail when we come to study the field of the guides to the devout life in another chapter.

Like the Rouen primer of 1538 this of Paris adds to the Primer the uniformly printed volumes of the Savonarola meditations and the Epistles and Gospels for the Sundays and holy days of the year. And in both cases, the same English text is used. These additions to the primer of 1536 not only in no way change its basic character and emphasis and technique, but rather, I think, carry to its logical completion the basic purpose of the Rouen book of 1536, namely, to put the non-Latinate layman in possession of the resources of his tradition in a compact and accessible form, and so to give him practical help in the development of his spiritual life. It may well, therefore, be taken as the representative of the whole group and will so be taken in this study.

The general position of this whole group of primers in the history of the Primer is an interesting one with some very obscure and even puzzling features. As we have seen, there is no question that the general choice of materials was thoroughly in the Catholic tradition. Indeed, it has been suggested that the makers of the Rouen primer of 1536 may have been Catholic, and the fact that this version of the Primer is the basis of the Marian primer of 1555 has been cited in support of that possibility.[73] That is certainly impressive evidence that this version is so Catholic as not to be unacceptable to Catholic authority in 1555, but it is far from conclusive as will be seen when we examine the character of that by no means entirely traditional book. More important, I think, is Mr. Butterworth's suggestion that some part at least, if not the whole, of the Rouen version of the Primer may have been in existence before 1536. He cites the fact that the Rouen version of Psalm 51 was used in a meditation on Psalm 51 (Savonarola's) in the Marshall primers and in the John Gowhe primer of 1536,[74] certainly proof that the Rouen version of that psalm at least was in existence before 1536. This raises two possibilities, of course, that of an earlier primer or simply an earlier psalter. But it would take more than one psalm to argue the existence of either.

There is other evidence, however, for some of the non-psalm elements. An interesting example is to be found in a primer which William Rastell printed at London on the thirtieth of April, 1532. At first sight this book seems to be simply another example of the type of primer we have already met—the Latin Primer with English headings, the form of confession, and some special prayers in English. But there is more to it than this. The hours are given for the most part in Latin only, but every so often there is a translation. These translations seem (the copy I have seen in microfilm is mutilated) to be confined to the Hours of the Cross and the Hours of the Compassion of Our Lady. Their character may be judged from "The englysshe of Hora prima domina videns":

> When owre lady in the mornynge behelde
> Her only sonne, skorgyd and fowle arayde
> Bobbed, knokt, and hys face wyth spyt deffylde
> God wot in hert she was full sore dysmayde
> But yet alas, hyth makyth myne hert affrayde
> To thynke how she felle in grevous wepynge
> And how dulfully her handys she gan wrynge.[75]

Beginning with the Matins of the Cross and the Matins of the Compassion of Our Lady, these English versions run through the hours of both offices, adding up in the sum total to a continuous story of the Passion of Christ, with especial emphasis on his mother's grief. Now this same series of verses is to be found in the same place in the Rouen primer of 1536.[76] And it is to be found in the *Primer* of Yolande Bonhomme, widow of Thielman Kerver, of 1533,[77] which we have already had occasion to notice, a fact which suggests a common, well-known source for this element at least.[78]

But there is other evidence for the prior existence of some at least of the materials of the Rouen-Paris primers. For instance, the English primer which Thomas Godfray published in London in 1534-35 used the version of the Prayer of the Prophet Jonas which the Rouen primer of 1538 had substituted for one of the usual prayers following the *Dirige* and Commendations.[79] And the first Byddell-Marshall primer of probably early 1535 used not only the Jonas prayer [80] but the old

Primer prayer, "O Lorde Jesu Christe the sonne of the lyvynge God, put they passion, crosse, and thy death betwene the judgment and our soules," this latter in the version of the Rouen primer of 1536.[81] And the June 1535 edition of the Byddell-Marshall primers prints the famous *O bone Jesu* of Saint Bernardine of Siena in what is, except for one or two insignificant changes in wording, the version of the Rouen primer of 1536.[82] There is no question that a good many of the materials of the Rouen primers were in existence before 1536.

It would be a large undertaking to check through all the English passages in the surviving Latin primers, but it would yield some very important evidence not only on this point but on the whole involved matter of the relations of various groups of primers. The present writer on the basis of a rough examination of a limited number of such books would be surprised if such an examination would yield anything like a complete translation of either the Primer or the Psalter, but would also be very much surprised if it did not prove the existence of widely accepted and much used common versions of many of the elements of the Primer, especially the groups of special and occasional prayers.

But however obscure the origins of these Rouen-Paris primers, there is no question of the important part which they played in the development of later versions of the Primer. They found their way into the hands of the printers in England. Hoskins lists a primer printed by Robert Redman in London in 1537 that sounds very much like the Rouen 1538 version.[83] And Robert Toye republished the Paris book of 1538 in London in 1542 under the very comprehensive title of "The Prymer in Englishe, and Latyn wyth the Epystles and Gospelles: of every Sonday, and holye daye in the yere, and also the exposycion upon *Miserere mei deus,* with many other prayers." There are, of course, a number of small changes, such as one finds in succeeding editions of the same book throughout this period, but they are none of them of any special importance or significance. Of all these perhaps the most revealing for the psychology of the time is a prayer which combines a petition to the Deity with an exhortation to the reader, a device to be found increasingly in the devotion of this period. In the light of this dual function it is appropriately styled, "A prayer for the reader, expressynge after what sorte scrypture shuld be red." The author of this prayer is clearly enthusiastic over the new dispensation, for he compares the work of Henry in promoting the circulation of the

Title page of the sumptuous vellum edition of the *Hore* published in Paris
by François Regnault in 1527

(*See page 58*)

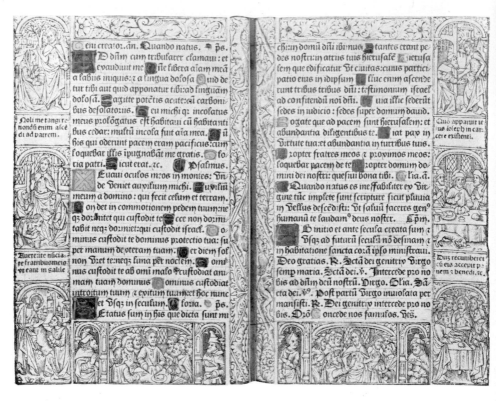

The *Hore presentes ad usum Sarum* published in Paris in 1502, opened
to sig. e6v-7

Scriptures in English to the work of King Joshua in the Old Testament. But before the prayer ends he has sounded a very significant note of warning in the following petition:

Graunte us moost favorable father whych art wonte to gyve good gyftes to thy chyldren, thys thy gracyous gyft, graunted by the, and receaved by oure soveraygne ruler under the, thanckfully to receave, and ryghtely to use, to the glory of thy holy name and safegarde of our sinfull soules[.] Graunte us O Lord here all to lerne perfect and faythful obedyence unto the, and to our governoures ordayned by the. Graunte us mooste mercyfull God to rede it wyth al reverence to studye it wyth al dylygence, and in our lyvinge to put it in ure.[84]

The man who wrote that prayer was clearly in sympathy with the over-all course of the changes which had taken place in recent years, but he was quite aware that there were other issues involved in the Christian life beyond those which had engaged so much of public thought and attention in those years.

Influential as these succeeding editions of the Rouen-Paris primer doubtless were, the most important contribution which they made to the development of sixteenth-century devotional literature was un-questionably the part which they played in the formation of the official prayer books of the middle of the century, the English and English-Latin primers of Henry VIII in 1545, and the Marian primer of 1555, for this primer is the foundation of both.

But before the Paris primer of 1538 could become the official primer of 1545, it would have to undergo a number of changes beyond any-thing which its original makers could have contemplated. For I think it is quite clear that the men responsible for that Paris book were men who valued the rich tradition of the Primer and had no thought of giving it up. They were committed, too, in the main to the general body of ideas and patterns of thought and feeling embodied in that tradition. And they unquestionably believed that they were strengthen-ing it by thus making available the riches of that tradition to the ex-panded vernacular-reading public made possible by the development of the new techniques of publication. So far, the book of 1538 would seem simply the traditional Primer reformed and directed to the needs of the day.

But there are those antimonastic, and antipapal, and possibly anti-confessional touches to the revision. It is, of course, not impossible that they were made in a spirit of compromise or accommodation to avoid raising issues that would impede the circulation of the book among the English readers for whom it was designed. But in the year 1538 that was not likely. The controversial line-up had become too clear. What is more likely is that the editor of this book was still hoping to maintain a position which had been held, and was indeed still held, by a good many Englishmen of the time. It was not necessarily Erastian, but it was at least willing to acquiesce in, if not indeed support, the minimizing of the Pope's position; it was certainly lacking in enthusiasm for the monastic glorification of celibacy. It had taken the offensive on the acknowledged prevalence of superstition, and it was ready to push the vernacular not to the point of rejecting the Latin, but to the point of providing the layman with a complete translation. But with the possible exception of confession it had no intention of breaking with tradition in doctrine or practice. As expressed in this book, it had every appearance of confidence and conviction. But, historically, it proved unable to maintain itself. This book would become the foundation of the Henrician primers of 1545, but in the process it would be transformed by forces for which the Rouen editor of 1538 shows some signs of sympathy but of which the editors of the other two books seem scarcely aware. To understand those forces we must turn to the books of men who were much less interested in preserving the tradition than in changing it to fit their convictions.

VI

THE PRIMER
AS AN INSTRUMENT OF
RELIGIOUS CHANGE

EANWHILE much more radical experiments with the Primer were under way in London. It will be remembered how Sir Thomas More in his well-known "Preface to the christen reader" before *The Confutacion of Tyndales Aunswere* of 1532 had mentioned a report that George Joye had translated the Primer, leaving out the litany in order to keep people from praying to the saints.[1] If that primer could be found, it would take away from the Byddell-Marshall primers of 1535 the primacy usually accorded them among printed English primers. But it has not been surely identified, and no surviving English primer can be dated that early.

There are two primers surviving from this period, however, that do fit this element in Sir Thomas More's description. Neither is dated, but one can be clearly identified with the earlier effort at an English primer described in the well-known Byddell-Marshall primer of 1535. Since we shall be discussing that version in some detail in a few minutes, we shall postpone the consideration of this earlier book until we can discuss its relation to the whole series of Byddell-Marshall primers. The other primer is more puzzling. In the copy which I have used, the title page is missing, but the table of contents gives the title of the book as "A primer in Englysshe with dyvers prayers and godly meditations," and the colophon identifies the place of printing as London and gives the name of the printer as Thomas Godfray but gives no date. There is, however, a very striking indication of date in the Calendar, for a number of saints there commemorated still carry the description "Pope," as, for instance, on March 12 "Gregorii pape," and "Felicis pape" for May 30, etc.[2] That would seem to indicate that this calendar was made before Henry VIII, after his break with the Pope in 1534, directed that the name and word "pope" be expunged from all calendars, prayer books, service books, etc. and that "bishop of Rome" be substituted. It is hard to see how such a calendar could be published much later than the end of 1534 or the very beginning of 1535 by a leading London printer, especially in view of the materials that follow that calendar. For they are such as to indicate that their editor and compiler would welcome the official proscription.

At first sight they bear out the traditional appearance of the calendar, "A christenmans lernyng devysed in thre partes," generally orthodox in character, followed by instructions on the Ten Commandments, the Creed, the paternoster with a quite full exposition of its meaning, and an "exhortation for them that receyveth the blessed sacrament of the auter."[3] The catechetical dialogue for children[4] that follows these familiar elements is not traditional; in fact, from 1526 on it appears more than once in lists of prohibited books.[5] Less novel is the general confession for sinners, the type of thing again to be found in primers of every orientation.[6] The hours themselves begin properly enough with "Matyns," but there are some suggestive changes. For instance, a brief hymn of praise[7] is substituted for the familiar *Quem Terra pontus ethera,* "The governore of the triple engyn whome the earthe, the sea, and the hevynes dothe honour."[8] There are cuts in the praises to Mary, and substitutions of New Testament passages concentrating attention on Christ for the traditional Marian lessons.[9]

The progress of the hours is interrupted after lauds by the insertion of the Passion of Christ in ten parts. This differs from the usual Passion according to Saint John, for it is a lengthy running account made up of selections from the various Evangelists, as the author explains in a still uncontroversial preface.[10] It is a device, often used at this time, for getting in a good deal of fairly straight Scripture. The next striking innovation in the progress of the hours is the insertion of a short series of Old Testament prayers, including the prayer of the Prophet Jonas so often found in the traditional primers.[11] The little essay on the theme of "Prayer peaseth goddes wrath" begins disarmingly enough with the citing of Scripture on the need of prayer to appease God's wrath, but presently this seemingly orthodox prayer has turned into a plea for the Englishing of the Psalms:

Consyderynge therfore prayer to be of such efficacy and vertue, and that christ him selfe commaunded us to praye also in these peryllouse dayes, me thynketh it necessarye that the laye people shulde have the prayers moost convenyent for this tyme, which prayers are the Psalmes and that in Englysshe, that their faith mighte the more encrease, and their devotion.[12]

The normal Primer appearance is resumed with the Seven Psalms,[13] but after them one looks in vain for the Fifteen Gradual Psalms, the litany, and the *Dirige*. The Commendations are printed right after the Seven Psalms, and then the Psalms of the Passion.[14] It is, indeed, a radical departure from the traditional Primer pattern.

But this primer is interesting on another score, and that concerns the text of the materials used. Some of the prayers follow virtually the same text as that of the Rouen primers, for instance, the prayer of the Prophet Jonas found after the *Dirige* and Commendations in the Rouen primer of 1538.[15] But the text of the Psalms is quite different. That is the version of the English psalter of 1530. The note before Commendations [16] copies even the argument to Psalm 109 which we have already had occasion to comment on: "This psalme declareth in howe great price and reverence the sayntes or holye men have the lawes of god," etc.[17] This may mean simply that in the years between 1530 and early 1535 (the outside limit for the publication of this book on the basis of the calendar) some unknown primer-maker took the psalter of 1530 and made it the basis of his work. But it will be remembered that it has been suggested that George Joye was the author of that version. If that were true, then this primer might well be the missing English primer of George Joye to which Sir Thomas More referred.

But this Godfray primer has very close relations to the other of these early radical primers without litany or *Dirige*. Again, it is a work with place and publisher but without date. This time, however, we have some external evidence to help us with the problem of dating. It is *A Prymer in Englyshe, with Certeyn Prayers and Godly Meditations,* which, according to the colophon, John Byddell published for William Marshall. Now we know from the explanatory note which the editor of the Byddell-Marshall primer of June 16, 1535, prefixed to the Litany in that volume that he had already tried a primer without

a litany in it and, as he then explained contemptuously, "diverse persones of small judgement and knowledge in holy scripture," had been
offended.[18] While this undated work has much in common with the
book of June, 1535, so much that there is no doubt that it is the work
of the same editor or compiler, it represents not only a more radical
but a more frankly reforming volume than the later one, the sort of
book from which in those years even a fairly bold man would have to
retreat. For it not only omits the litany and the *Dirige,* but it tries some
pretty radical experiments with the calendar, that make this from the
very beginning look like a very different book, say, from the Godfray
primer. For January for instance, there are but two dates marked,
January first, "The Circumcision of our Lorde," with the scriptural
reference to Luke 2, and a quotation from Genesis 17 on Circumcision, and January sixth for the appearance of the star with the
reference to Matthew 2. By August his repugnance to the calendar
must have relaxed a little, for he begins with "Peters presonment
called Lammas day," for the first, with the scriptural reference to
Apostles 12, and the note, doubtless significant for readers of his way
of thinking at that time, "Peter was prysoned for prechynge goddes
worde." He then goes on to include the Transfiguration with the reference to Matthew 17 for the sixth, Saint Lawrence the tenth, the
Assumption of Our Lady the fifteenth, Saint Bartholomew the twenty-
fourth, Augustine Bishop and Doctor the twenty-eighth, and the
"headyng of John Baptist" the twenty-ninth, this last alone with a
textual reference, to Matthew 24, and a lengthy explanation of the
circumstances, doubtless very interesting to the author and his friends,
who must have felt that they knew what it was like to preach reform
to deaf authority.[19] It is not difficult to imagine the criticisms which
such a calendar would evoke at that time.

While this is a quite different work from the Godfray primer,
it does contain some of the same distinctive material found in the
former book, for example, the Passion in ten parts, the dialogue
catechism, and "Prayer peaseth Goddes wrathe." [20] Like the Godfray
primer it uses prayers already found in the Rouen primer of 1536,
fresh proof again that some at least of the materials found in that
book were current before 1536, for example, "O Lorde Jesu Christe
the sonne of the lyvynge God, put thy passion, crosse, and thy death
betwene the judgment and our soules," etc.,[21] from the Matins of the

Cross. And like the Godfray primer it uses the psalter of 1530 for the psalms.[22] Again, the possibility of Joye's authorship is interesting, for if he wrote the Godfray primer, it is probable that he wrote this, too, and the whole series of the Byddell-Marshall primers which we shall look at presently.[23]

But this is a much larger work than the Godfray book, and a much more elaborately pedagogical work. For it includes some very forthright instructions on faith, "The worke of Faythe," and good works.[24] What the editor had to say of faith was again more radical than could be maintained, for it was to vanish from the edition of 1535. It is not difficult to understand why when one reads the following very forthright sentences:

The power of fayth is to justefye us, that is, to despoyle us frome all oure vices and laye them on Christs backe whiche hathe pacefyed the fathers wrathe towards us: and to endue us with an others ryhtwysnes, that is christs, so that I and all my synnes are Christes, and Christ with all his vertues are myne, for he was borne for us and geven unto us. Esaye.ii. Roma.viii. To obteyne this ryhtwisnes god the father requireth nothing of us but that we believe in hym and make hym no lyar.[25]

Whoever wrote this book, and whenever he wrote it, he had certainly learned his lesson by June of 1535. As the preface to the Litany quoted above made clear, the omission of the litany had been the feature of his earlier book most objected to. The fact that he kept the litany in this book is proof enough that he felt this complaint was to be reckoned with, but in the same preface to the Litany already referred to he apparently feels obliged to explain that he had not made the earlier omission out of "any perverse mynde or opinion" that the Virgin or saints might not in any way be prayed to.[26] In other words he had learned by experience the necessity of going cautiously on matters of devotional usage.

However, his mood is still clearly prophetic. The frontispiece strikes the keynote dramatically, for it presents a very substantial female figure, allegorically and totally naked, labeled "truthe, the doughter of tyme," in process of being dragged out of a bankside or cave by a winged old gentleman who hardly needs his label of "Tyme reveleth all thynges," for identification. The whole lively action proceeds under the puffs of a dragon-winged and serpent-locked cherub, labeled, "Hipocrisy." Beneath is the significant text, Matthew 10:

> Nothyng is covered, that shall not be discovered.
> And nothynge is hydde, that shall not be reveled.

This exciting keynote of bold revelation is immediately justified in the first sentence of "An admonition to the reder," on a theme which, as we have seen in the Rouen primer of 1536, had already engaged the sympathetic attention of men who were on the whole conservative in their attitude toward orthodox doctrine, that of the superstitious promises which had been attached to the prayers of the Primer. This was a theme on which the present editor could clearly count on wide sympathy for reform. So he plunged into it with a confidence that matched the promises of the frontispiece:

Amonge other innumerable pestilent and infeccious bokes and lernynges, with the whiche the christen people have ben pituously sedused and deceyved, broughte up in diverse kyndes of diffidence and false hope, I may judge chiefly those to be pernicious, on whom they have ben wonte commonly hytherto in every place superstitiously to pray, and have lerned in the same with moche folyshe curiosite, and as great scrupulosite to make rehersal of theyr synnes by herte, and that for this cause. For these bokes over and besides that that they habounded in every place with infinite errours, and peryllous prayers, sclaunderous both to god, and to all his holy sayntes, were also garnyshed with glorious titles, and with redde letters, promysing moche grace, and many yeres, dayes, and lentes of pardon, whiche they coulde never in dede perfourme, to the great decepte of the people, and the utter destruction of theyr soules.[27]

The editor then proceeded to illustrate his thesis with a series of horrific examples, in the discussion of some of which there is the usual confusion between magic and idolatry.

In other words, the attack opened on lines with which well-informed readers of the time were already familiar. The earlier lack of an effective general censorship of popular books of devotion, beyond a certain few points of obvious heresy, had doubtless led to very real abuses in these widely disseminated instruments of popular piety. It was apparently not so much the content of the prayers, although this was presently to be attacked, as it was the promises which were attached to many of the prayers, that drew the first attack of the reformers, and there is no question that they were, as we have seen, in many cases dangerously rash, quite without warrant in official theory or prescription, but doubtless very appealing to the credulous and the optimistic.

In this attack on superstition, then, the author of this book had taken up his stand on firm ground.

But when any movement of reform is once under way, it is very seldom that it stops short of goals far beyond the first intention. So it proved here. The ground of superstition was swiftly and almost imperceptibly broadened to include matters of a very different order. For instance, patriotism and iconoclasm were alike invoked in an extension of the indictment of the Primer to other allied books of the time.

The same judgement and reformation that is mente of the bokes before named, is also to be had of the bokes of passions, and sayntes lyves, called Legende auries, of Festivalles, of Manipulos curatorum, of Eccius, of Cocleus, and of Hocstratus bokes, with suche lyke dreggs, and draffe, wherin the popes false usurped power, and his moste wycked lawes ben mayntayned, and defended, to the great and daungerous infeccion of our moste gracious soveraigne lorde the kynges liege people, and the unlaufull withdrawyng of their hertes from his graces majestie, by suche myschevous bokes.[28]

There was no mistaking the author's intention here. But it should be noted at the same time that he was very anxious to avoid if he could the odium of the innovator, especially the charge of rushing to extremes:

For asmoche than, as this shorte simple admonition procedeth neither of blynde zele, or affection, neyther of wyll or purpose to offende or displease any man, moche lesse than to displease any saint in heven, and in no wyse than our blessed lady, but evin of very pure love to the honour of god, and helthe of mennes soules.[29]

This very eloquent and tendentious preface then ends with a final petition against the idolatry of the offending books, as if protection from idolatry were the most pressing need of the English worshiper of the time as it was the favorite point of attack of some of the reforming parties.

Indeed, whoever wrote this "Admonition to the reder," there is no doubt that he was a master of that technique of stressing the importance of the changes he wished made and the relatively trifling aberration, if not complete innocence, of the books advocating such changes which the Bishops had been objecting to, that was one of the reformers' most effective weapons in the propaganda of the transitional period. It was just after his arraignment of some of the superstitious and dangerous promises of the primers and what he considered the blasphemous emphasis of some of the petitions that he concluded:

Wherfore I most humbly beseche almyghty god, that I may ones se men as diligent and busy, to ensearche, call in, and condempne these, and suche, bothe abhominable heresies, and therto ryght open and manifest treasons, in the Decrees, Decretals, and other lawes of byshops of Rome, with other boks, at this tyme over many to be rehersed, as heretofore they have ben to call in, condempne, and ensearche, suche bokes privileged, as wherin I thynke that no greate harme, yea no harme at all can be founde (specially worthy of condempnation) yf they were indifferently, and charitably oversene and judged.[30]

As for the contents of the book itself, the author evidently felt he now had to move cautiously, but move he did. In the calendar that as usual preceded the prayers, the old calendar is kept even to the feast of "s. Thomas Martyr" (Saint Thomas of Canterbury) on the twenty-ninth of December.[31] But there was a tendency throughout to omit certain vigils, like that of Laurence Martyr on August ninth.[32] The most significant change in the calendar is still the changing of the title "pope" to "bishop" or "bishop of Rome," as in the case of "s. Gregory byshop" for March 12.[33]

The same spirit of cautious but discriminatingly persistent modification of traditional materials is to be seen in the handling of the basic materials of the book. The primacy given to the Ten Commandments and their exposition, the Creed, the Lord's Prayer, and the Salutation of Our Lady is in the main Primer tradition, but the full exposition of the meaning and significance of these staples of Christian devotion is more in the tradition of the special books of guidance for householders and for others who have to instruct the simple and the young than in the Primer tradition.[34] And two very substantial compositions, "A generall confession for every synner," and "An instruction howe, and in what maner we oughte to pray to almyghty god," intervene between the Creed and the Lord's Prayer and "The salutation of our lady." [35] By and large these expositions are fairly traditional but the handling of the Ave Maria betrays noticeable anxiety that the angelic salutation should not be stretched beyond a mere giving of honor or praise of a guarded sort.

This disposition to attenuate the emphasis on Mary is to be discerned especially in the changes which were made in the Little Office of the Blessed Virgin, which still remained the backbone of this book as of the traditional Primer. The key to them is to be found in the substitution of the scriptural promise, "Come unto me all ye that labour and are laden: and I shall refreshe you," [36] for the Ave Maria, customarily employed for the invitatory between the opening petitions and the first psalm of matins,[37] and between the verses of the ensuing psalms.

In the same spirit a praise of Christ and the Trinity was substituted for the usual hymn, *Quem terra pontus ethera,*[38] which pays more honor to the part of the mother of Christ in the process of the redemption than the editor of this book thought it proper to recognize. Of the same nature was the substitution of a brief "anteme" of acknowledgment of sin and hope for mercy, again in traditional terms, for the usual "anthem" of praise to Mary [39] at the end of the next three psalms:

The anteme:

Ro.iii.   All we are synners, and have nede of the glory of god.

The versicle

Ephe.i.   In what thynge standeth the glory of god?

In the free forgyvenes of synns of his clere mercy only.

In the same way, scriptural substitutions, one from the New Testament and two from the Old, are made for the three lessons in praise of the Virgin usually found after the paternoster and the Ave Maria at this point in the traditional office.[40] The prayers which follow were left untouched, probably because they are for the most part selections from the Psalms; but wherever, as in the anthem that in lauds follows the Benedictus or "songe of zachary," the theme is praise of the Virgin, we shall find that in this book either a hymn of general praise to God has been substituted for the Marian prayer, or as here,[41] a collect or brief exhortation to faith in God. This type of change runs throughout the hours. One notable exception, the retention of the Magnificat in the "Evensonge," [42] probably a tribute to its scriptural origin, but reënforces the point of view responsible for these changes.

To proceed with the other fixtures of the Primer, the Seven Penitential Psalms apparently gave no difficulty beyond their title, for they are printed here under the simple title of "the seven psalmes." [43] But the litany, as we have already seen, was another matter. The editor

clearly would have liked to dispense with it as he had in an earlier
version, but he had felt compelled to yield to the pressure of his critics.
But though he did print the litany, and that in a still clearly traditional
form,[44] for the most part Luther's litany of 1529,[45] he consoled himself
by descanting at length on the superstitious manner in which these
petitions had been abused and by insisting on the sole mediatorship
of Christ. And he revenged his surrender to compulsion by explaining
that it was to satisfy the above-mentioned weak brethren "and som-
what to beare theyr infirmities" that he included it this time, hoping
they would not abuse it. For a final thrust he raised the question of
whether some of those whose names are included in the litany are
really saints, however they may have been canonized by the bishops of
Rome.[46] So what starts out as an explanation ends up as a fairly inclusive, albeit moderately calm, reassertion of the editor's objections
to the litany.

After the accompanying prayers and collects of the litany, he then
proceeded to "An exposition after the maner of a contemplation upon
the .li. psalme, called Miserere mei deus," the work, although he does
not name the author, of Jerome of Ferrara, or Savonarola,[47] it will be
remembered, one of the elements printed with the Paris and Rouen
primers of 1538.

The story of the Passion of Christ is another common feature of the
Primer. In the version of 1527, it was told through selections from the
Four Evangelists, followed by the Passion according to Saint John.[48]
But the Paris primer of 1538 had used another ancient device of com-
bining excerpts from the Four Evangelists, in a very brief summary
of the life of Christ from the cosmic beginning of Saint John to the
burial of Christ as narrated by that writer, with excerpts from the other
Evangelists in between.[49] What this primer of 1535 does is to make a
continuous and extended narrative, giving credit in the margin to the
respective writers from whom the specific episode is derived.[50] In
general this narrative is faithful, but occasionally there is an interpolation to underscore a point or to draw an edifying lesson or inference.
For instance, after the speech of the "petie captayne" and his fellow
guards who at the death of Christ said, "This man was the very son of
god," the editor goes on, giving credit to Luke in the margin: "And
all the comen poore symple people, that thyther came to se, consyderyng
these unwonte and wonderful thynges that thus happened in tyme

of his deathe, knocked them selves upon theyr brestes, with greate feare, and reverence." [51] This appeal to the poor and the simple is quite typical of the reforming literature of the time. But in general the handling of this material is fairly traditional, possibly because there was very little opportunity to raise contemporary issues in an account which begins at the end of the much controverted Last Supper.

The same cannot be said of the meditation which follows, "A devoute, frutefull, and godly remembraunce of the passion of our saviour Jesu Christ." Here the author has some very shrewd things to say about the superstitious use of the Mass for good luck. The criticism itself is orthodox enough, but the terms in which he drives it home very definitely suggest the Protestant reformers' commemorative view of the Mass rather than the traditional sacrificial view: "They consydre not that the masse was institute of Christe to make us more holy, thrugh the devoute remembraunce of his passion, with a pure faythe, and not to preserve us from adversities, whiche god sendeth us for the correction of our evyll lyves." [52]

There is much the same interweaving of the traditional and the new in what he has to say of the abuse of the consideration of Christ's Passion, particularly on the emotional side. The actual discussion of the effect which the contemplation of the Passion ought to have on a devout mind is presented in quite traditional terms with extended borrowings from Saint Bernard's third sermon on the birth of Our Lord for the "sorowe and tremblyng" which the good Christian should feel in the contemplation of Christ's Passion.[53]

But the terms in which the editor expresses his censure of foolish preachers who abuse the theme of Christ's Passion are again such as to suggest a basic attack on the traditional handling of the emotional and imaginative elements involved:

These do petuously sorowe and mourne for Christ, and complayne that he was innocent, and gyltles put to death, evyn lyke as the women of Jerusalem, whom Christe hym selfe dyd reprehende, advertisynge them that they shulde lament them selves, and theyr chyldren. Neyther is it any mervel, for the preachers them selves are sicke of the same disease, whiche for the most parte whan they entreate this mater, leape out of the frutefull and holsome storie, into these their comen places, How Jesus toke his leave of his disciples. And with what dolorous sighes his mother Mary petied hym, and suche other thyngs. On these they bable at length and discante theyr pleasures, rather to the weryenge, than edifienge of the audience.[54]

This complaint should not be emphasized unduly, but it is safe to say that we have here evidence of the beginning of a very important divergence in emphasis on the elements to be developed in the contemplation of Christ's life, a divergence to be widened by the spread of the Ignatian type of meditation on the one hand, with its strong appeal to the imagination and the feelings, and, on the other, the rigorously doctrinal consideration and exhortation of the Puritan devotional writers.

The ebb and flow of controversial spirit in the book is illustrated by the fact that the "Remembraunce of Christis passion" is followed by some quite innocuous material, "A frutefull and a very christen instruction for chyldren" which in addition to the paternoster, the Ave Maria, and the Creed provides fairly brief, nonliturgical morning prayers, several forms of grace, and evening prayers of the same character, obviously for the simple as well as for children. "A dialogue betwene the father and the sonne, askyng certayne questions. and the father answerynge," provides a rudimentary species of catechism, giving simple instruction on faith, the Trinity, the Commandments, and sin, clearly indicating in the limited choice of topics the author's reforming point of view, but in general avoiding the raising of controversial issues in the handling of them.[55]

But the author speaks out again when it comes to another of the classic fixtures of the Primer, the *Dirige*. Apparently, as in the case of the litany, the author did not deem it prudent to omit the *Dirige,* one of the universal elements of the Primer, but he prefaced the printing of the traditional prayers for the dead with a very urgent warning to the reader, the theme of which was that there was no reason why these prayers should be said for the dead any more than for the living:

Amongest all other works of darkenes, and deepe ignoraunce, wherin we have blyndly wandred, folowynge a sorte of blynde guydes, many dayes and yeres, I accompte not this one of the leaste, that we have ronge, and songe, mumbled, murmured, and pituously pewled forthe a certayne sorte of psalmes, herafter ensuyng, with responses, versicles, and lessons to the same, for the soules of our christen bretherne and sistern, that ben departed out of this worlde, whiche psalmes and lessons (I beseche god I dye) and if they make any more for any suche use and purpose, that is to say, that they ought or may be used any rather for them that be departed, than for them that be in lyfe and in good bodely helthe, than may Te deum, or Gloria in excelsis.[56]

A certain reserve with regard to nonscriptural elements which we have already observed, is to be seen in the handling of the prayers usually inserted in the middle of the *Dirige,* in the Paris edition of 1527, for instance, to the number of six.[57] Of these the present editor keeps but one, a brief traditional prayer for mercy, *Deus qui proprium est,* "God, to whom it is appropried to be mercyfull ever."[58]

As for the incidental prayers used between the psalms, the editor, compared with some of his contemporaries, is exceedingly sparing. But he has kept some of the favorite nonbiblical prayers that had long been the staple of the Primer. One of the most interesting of these is the famous *O bone Iesu,* ascribed to Saint Bernardine of Siena. Except for one or two insignificant changes in wording in the English version of the 1536 Rouen primer, this is given with great faithfulness.[59] And the theme of this prayer is the petition of an acknowledged sinner for the mercy of his Redeemer. This disposition to retain the old devotional classics when they stress the heavy score of the sinner and his dependence on Christ for forgiveness will be, as we shall see presently, one of the main characteristics of the new collections of prayers. But there is in this prayer, as in so many of the devotional compositions of its period, an emphasis on the sweetness and mercy and lovableness of the Redeemer that is not found so often among the new makers of prayers as the more functional stress on the significance of the Redemption. This, however, the editor does not disturb.

But he is not always so forbearing. These incidental prayers offer too good an opportunity to use the long established and the familiar for the insinuation of new emphases and new applications. Probably the most ingenious and effective examples are to be seen in some of the incidental developments of prayers that begin in a fashion familiar enough to the readers of such literature and then take a sudden turn into a new path. A good instance is the prayer that follows "A dialogue betwenc the father and the sonne." This "prayer for the molifyinge and supplyenge of our harde hertes, the lyghtnynge of our blynde hertes, and the true convertynge of our impenitent hertes," sounds like a well-established, to say nothing of abundantly justified, approach to the perennial problems of the Christian life. And the beginning of the prayer, reminding God, to whom it is addressed, of Christ's old promise to hear petitions, and asking for mercy, especially for the most wretched of his children,

the author of the present petition, is certainly in the main highway of
the familiar. But as the prayer progresses, a new direction of topical
relevance becomes clear:

The kynges herte is in thy handes (oh lorde) that where thou wylte, thou
mayst incline it, for so saythe thy scripture. Incline his herte to this purpose
(oh father) that it wyll please him to commaunde his prelates of his realme,
no longer to kepe from his people, his lovynge subjectes, the lyghte of thy
worde, the lyghte of holy scripture, the lyghte of the testament of thy dere
sonne, our saviour Jesu Christe, the lyghte wherin he that walketh erreth
not, neither stumbleth at any stone. Put in his mynde lorde to commaunde,
that lyke as through thy secrete inspiration, other nacyons alredye have: so
his people also by his commaundement may have in to their tongue truely
translated thy holy scripture, wher in they may lerne and perfectly knowe
thy godly wyll and pleasure, obediently submitte themselves unto the same,
folowe it, and expresse it in theyr lyvynge.[60]

The same adroit taking of opportunity by the forelock is to be seen
in the instruction on "Good Workes," which follows "Thoffice of all
estates." This begins with unmistakable relevance to the current situation in the very first sentence of the instruction: "Amonge good workes,
the chiefe are, to be obedient in al things unto kyngs, princes, judges,
and suche other officers, as farre as they commaunde civile thynges that
is tosay, suche thyngs as are indifferent, and not contrary unto the
commaundementes of god." [61] Then after enjoining obedience to father
and mother and respect for family obligations, he takes up the problem
of our relations to our neighbors. Here, particularly significant are the
terms in which the traditional appeal for care of the clergy among the
works of charity is expressed: "Amonge these ought we to have respecte
unto the preachers and ministers of the worde, that they may be had in
honour, and well provided for." [62]

This book must have had better luck than the editor's first in finding
public favor, for he issued another edition with astonishingly few
changes soon after, probably in 1537. Of these the most interesting is
undoubtedly the change in the Calendar which enables us to put it after
the foregoing in the Byddell-Marshall series. It is the dropping of the
commemoration of "Saynt nabor and felyx" for the twelfth of July and
the substitution of "Erasmus of Roterdame desessed. 1536." [63]

The most substantial change in the work, however, is the addition
of "A goodly exposition upon the .xxx. psalme In te domine speravi,"
of Jerome of Ferrara, this time with the author's name,[64] usually printed

as in the Paris-Rouen primers of 1538 with his exposition of Psalm 51. That composition still holds its place after the Litany as in the earlier edition of this primer. The most interesting thing about the printing of the meditation on Psalm 30 in this edition is the page which precedes it, a page of comment on false prophets, with a tribute to Henry VIII as a pioneer in the work of harkening to God's word, a thanksgiving for the same, and a prayer that what has been begun may be continued.[65] In its high degree of generality in the terms of the remarks and of warmth in the feelings suggested, this tribute is an admirable example of the editor's tact.

These Byddell-Marshall primers are not by any means the only reforming primers of the time. There was, indeed, a good deal of experimenting going on in these unsettled years. In 1536, for instance, John Gowhe brought out an English-Latin primer based like the Byddell-Marshall series on the English Psalter from the text of Feline of 1530, but, also, making use of the psalter which George Joye published in Antwerp in 1534.[66] The most interesting feature of this book is the addition after the Compline of Jesus of "devoute meditations and prayers with contemplacions called the paradyse of the soule." [67] The *Paradisus animae* is one of the classic Catholic collections of both the general and the occasional types of prayers so often found in the Latin primers.

One of the most interesting features of this version is the collection of prayers for every day in the week,[68] a devotional element that, as we shall see presently, became increasingly popular in succeeding primers. The generally eclectic character of this primer is reënforced by the addition of a series of texts from Scripture on basic points of doctrine, especially the much controverted theme of faith, called "The nosegay or posee of lyght to lede and comfort al synner that walke in darknesse gadred out of the new testament." [69] Such a primer well illustrates the range and variety of experimentation that was going on within the limits of traditional devotional forms during this period.

Such experiments are interesting and important, not only because of the light they throw on the changing points of view of the time but because of the testimony which they afford as to the prestige and influence of the Primer. It was clearly one of the readiest ways to influence the religious thought and feeling of the average literate English layman. The reformers seem to have seen this clearly and to have acted on that insight with a good deal of tact and resolution. The fact that many of the changes which they made fell in line with the criticisms of loyal supporters of the old order made their changes more acceptable. Such a book as the 1535 Byddell-Marshall primer must have commended itself to a good many already Erastian Catholics as something preserving most of the familiar features of the old Primer with omissions and warnings that might well escape a good many of the less alert, for the Primer was always a flexible instrument of devotion with a good deal of room for selection. That such books did much to familiarize the average layman with a new point of view and a changed set of values cannot be doubted.

VII

THE PRIMER
AS AN INSTRUMENT OF
RELIGIOUS SETTLEMENT

W E MAY be quite sure that the demonstration which the success of these reforming primers gave of the usefulness of the
Primer as an instrument for influencing public opinion in desired
directions was not lost on statesmen so acute and so experienced in that
area as Henry VIII and Thomas Cromwell. The progress of the
changes which the former had set in motion had already by the end
of the fourth decade raised hopes in reforming circles that Henry
clearly had no notion of satisfying, and the menace of the resulting
tensions to the settled religious and civic order always dear to the
heart of Henry was becoming only too apparent. In this field of private
devotion as in every other aspect of religious activity, the problem of
something like an official settlement was growing more acute.

The first actual step in that direction was taken when Cromwell
commanded John Hilsey, the Bishop of Rochester, to prepare an edition
of the Primer. John Wayland published the resulting book in 1539, only
two years after the third of the Byddell-Marshall series which we have
been studying. The dedication to Thomas, Lord Cromwell, was signed
by Bishop Hilsey himself.

As might well be expected of a book appearing under such circumstances, the general position taken up therein is that which the Henrician religious policy had reached at that date. It is clearly designed
to consolidate the King's supremacy in religious matters, as against
Rome, but equally designed to preserve as much as possible of the
traditional observances of religion in the teeth of more extreme Protes-

tant demands for change. This book is, therefore, quite explicitly Erastian and antipapal, as is evident, for instance, in the "Office of all estates" with its emphasis on the necessity of the submission of the people of all classes to their prince, and its general warning that the Bishop of Rome and his adherents are the destroyers of all estates.[1] At the same time "An instruccion of the maner in hearing of the Masse" defends with equal vigor the doctrine of the Real Presence against the heretical opinions of the "Sacramentaries."[2]

In the handling of the traditional fixtures of the Primer both the process of alteration in the Protestant direction and the development of the possibilities of the traditional layman's prayer book as an instrument for the inculcation of approved opinions in the public mind have been carried to a point considerably beyond that of the Byddell-Marshall primers. This is apparent at once at the very beginning of the book in the treatment of the calendar. Here the process of reform has been carried beyond anything envisaged by the earlier editor. Moreover, Bishop Hilsey is at some pains to let the reader know what his principles of calendar reform are in a statement well worth quoting because of the light it throws on a very important element in the psychology of the time. He begins his "prologe to the Kalender" with a confidence that is bound to disarm any reader who prides himself on keeping up to date:

The straungenes of thys Kalender (gentel reader) shal not move the to marvail very much the cause ones knowen, for the newe fasshion here of hath a double commodite. The one is brefnes, for where the other kalender had a great nomber of sayntes wythout profyte to the unlearned thys hath but only such festes which are kept holydaye and the epistle and gospel that are red in the church on such holydayes set forth in the kalender. The seconde is, that where the nomber of saintes were set, there have we appoynted wekely certayne places of the scripture whych the church doth use to reade at Matens, that the reader may knowe what scripture the church do use thorow out the yeare, and to study and use the same.[3]

This is quite typical of the editor's over-all approach to his problem. He shares the desire of the editor of the Byddell-Marshall primers to eliminate what he considers superfluities and corruptions, but he has his own pedagogical ambition to organize the materials of the Primer in such a fashion as to realize to the utmost their potentialities for popular education. "The prologe to the whole worke" makes this abundantly clear.[4] It is the popular character of the Primer as the book commonly in the hands of the people and especially the first book for the instruction of youth that he emphasizes in his approach to the reader. He is not content just to restore to Christ the prayers and praises which he feels have been dangerously arrogated to his mother, but he proceeds to rearrange the traditional materials into a complete scheme of direction for the Christian life.

This is organized in three parts. As the editor himself explains,

in the fyrst parte thou art taught thynges of fayth, where in thou hast the simbole or crede of Athanase, the .xii. artycles or crede, a lesson of eche of the foure Evangelistes puttynge the in remembraunce of the fayth that thou art bounde to have to the gospels and worde of god. In the seconde parte thou hast thynges concernynge prayer. Fyrst the beades, the pater noster, and the salutacion, a prayer to be sayd in the mornynge, grace afore dyner, grace after dyner, grace before supper, grace after supper, a prayer whan thou goest to bedde, a prologe to the Matens wyth the houres, then the matens and houres, a prologe to Evensonge, Evensonge, a prologe to Com- plene, Complene, salve rex misericordie, O bone Iesu, conditor celi, the .xv. Oos, with theyr prologe, the seven Psalmes wyth the prologe, the letany wyth the prologe, a treatyse of the sacrament of the aulter wyth thre prayers, the Dirige wyth hys prologe. In the thyrde parte thou hast thynges concernyng workes, as the commaundementes set forth at large wyth a declaracion of the kyndes of workes, these have I set out, both in englysh and laten for the more parte to thende that the devoute (for hys choyse) may reade whether he wyll.[5]

What this suggests, at first sight, is a simple rearrangement of the traditional Primer in the interest of its more functional use for the spiritual orientation of the layman's life. But, of course, there is a good deal more to it than that. What that is becomes apparent in the use to which the editor puts the prefatory notes, which, as we have seen, were a feature of the traditional Primer. At first, these seem to be merely historical or expository notes designed to deepen under- standing and appreciation of the traditional prayers. But when these notes are examined, they are soon seen to be very skillfully designed to inculcate the desired attitudes on points of doctrine or usage that were being especially controverted at the time.

A very good example of one type of note is the preface to Matins, for it reveals the kind of challenge which the defenders of traditional ob- servance were meeting on all sides at this time and the kind of defense to which an apologist for a transitional position such as that of this writer was likely to resort:

The fyrst limitacion or appointment of houres was not by mans invencion or devyse, but (as I reade) was of God. In the seconde boke of Moses I fynde that almyghtye God commaunded that twyse in the daye they shulde do sacrifyce, etc.

He goes on to point out that the division of the day's worship into seven parts was due to David, and then traces the evolution of the service of the hours through Daniel and Saint Jerome, with reminders of the example of Peter and John to reënforce the scriptural and apostolic warrant.[6]

In the same manner on the controversial issue of the *Dirige* he appeals to Hebrew lamentation for the dead and the scriptural accounts of last rites for various Old Testament worthies. He canvasses the various suggestions current at the time for the author of the office, Saints Isidore, Gregory, and Pelagius, without making any choice among them. He quotes Saint Paul as to the care Christians should take in avoiding any appearance of despair for their dead, and he reminds his readers that the psalms of which the *Dirige* is composed are no more appropriate to the dead than to the living, a conclusion, it will be remembered, that had already been reached by the editors of the Byddell-Marshall primers and the Rouen primer of 1538. But on the moot question of whether in the beginning these psalms were to be said for the souls of the departed, he concludes characteristically:

I wyll make no doctryne of it, but this I know wel that the reder of these may have a great lernynge and knowlege of the miseries and shortenesse of the lyfe of man, and maye learne hereby to dye well, and to have a hope and trust of the last resurreccion. And for this only cause have I also set furth in this primer a dirige of the which the thre fyrst lessons are of the myseries of mans lyfe, the myddel of the funerall of the deade corps, and the last thre are of the last resurreccion.[7]

In other words, the editor of this book is moving in the same direction as the editor of the Byddell-Marshall primers, but his instinct is even more clearly to conserve all that he can and use it to his purpose. Here in the case of the *Dirige* he follows the choice and order of psalms of the Paris primer of 1538 rather than that of the Byddell-Marshall primers, but with one exception in a different version, that of the Coverdale Bible of 1535.[8] This would seem to be due to the policy explained in the prologue to the whole work:

But where there shal seme to the reader in the psalmes ony difference betwene the Laten and Englysh, let the same remember that the englysh is accordaunt to the Hebraicall psalter translated by saynt Jerome, and the laten is the usuall psalter, whych in some places are not correspondent in all thynges, and thus have I joyned them, that such as delyteth in the englysh, myght have the playner sentence, and that the other that redeth the laten shuld not thynke that we shulde brynge in ony straunge psalmony.[9]

This is an example of a certain critical reserve in the handling of the Latin version of the book that we shall later see reflected in Elizabethan practice.

This same desire to keep material long found valuable is apparent in his retention of the *Fifteen Oes,* in a version that is substantially that of the Paris primer of 1538.[10] He prefaces them, however, with a guarding note repudiating the promises associated with the prayers as, for instance, in the Regnault *Hore* of 1527,[11] that reprints much but not all of the warning preface of the 1538 reforming Rouen primer verbatim.[12] One may easily discern a tendency in this book to rescue elements from the traditional primer that had in general been rejected by the editor of the Byddell-Marshall primers, even to the retention of the same phrasing. Another striking example is to be seen in the various "memories" of lauds—"of the holy ghost," "of our Lady," "of all sayntes," "of the passyon of Christ," "of the compassion of our Lady"—in which the fuller lauds of the traditional version like that of the Paris primer of 1538 [13] have been raided for special prayers, borrowed not only in substance but verbatim.

This same verbal resemblance is apparent elsewhere in the book, for instance, in the Seven Psalms, in which the version of this book of 1539 is practically identical with that of the Paris primer of 1538, and quite different from that of the Byddell-Marshall primers.[14] But the most striking example of this resemblance is to be found in the prayers at the end of the Litany. These latter are totally different from the Byddell-Marshall prayers; indeed, all but one of them may be found with very slight and unimportant verbal changes at the end of the Paris primer of 1538.[15] It would be easy to conclude from this that the Hilsey primer of 1539 was really closer to the Paris primer of 1538 than to the Byddell-Marshall primers, but it should not be forgotten that Bishop Hilsey is explicit, quite as explicit as the editor of the Byddell-Marshall primers, in his commitment to the extirpation of what they held to be idolatry, especially the arrogation to the Virgin and the saints of homage due only to God himself. Hilsey's eagerness to cut down the number of saints in the mind of the devout is especially evident in the Litany. Here there is a marked reduction even over that already made by the Byddell-Marshall editor. For where forty-nine were included in the Litany of his primer of 1535, only twenty-nine are named in Bishop Hilsey's book.[16]

In brief, this primer of 1539 is a Protestant book to the extent that the official English position was Protestant at this time, and it is committed to the defense of that position quite wholeheartedly. But throughout it is clearly motivated by a desire to preserve as much as possible of the devotional materials of the traditional Primer. That is a very important undertaking in view of the character of the various Elizabethan prayer books which we shall consider shortly.

In a curious fashion both the process of salvage and the process of modification were accelerated in the years that followed. This becomes especially clear in a book that may be taken as the epitome of the whole process of adaptation of the Primer to the progress of the Reformation in England. It is the book which the royal printer, Richard Grafton, published at London on the twenty-ninth day of May, 1545, with every circumstance of official approval. The title page is eloquent of the intention of this publication: "The Primer, set foorth by the Kynges majestie and his Clergie, to be taught, lerned, and read: and none other to be used throughout all his dominions." This is the first of the official primers.

It is the progress of change that is first apparent when one opens the book to the Calendar. For that most fundamental of all fixtures is practically unrecognizable. Most of the old feasts have vanished entirely. Perhaps the lowest rate of survival is that of the month of March. Of the twenty-nine saints commemorated by name in the Byddell-Marshall primer of around 1537 only Saint Gregory survives with a fast on March twenty-fourth. The Annunciation of Our Lady on the twenty-fifth, and the Resurrection of Jesus Christ on the twenty-sixth complete the commemorations. March has suffered most, but the other months have not fared much better. The divisions of the Roman calendar and the movements of the sun through the signs of the zodiac fill in some of the blank spaces, but only a skeleton of the old liturgical calendar remains.[17]

Of the fixtures of the Primer the following remain among the usual preliminary materials: the Lord's Prayer, "The salutation of the Angel to the blessed virgin Mari," the creed, the Ten Commandments, and a series of graces and short prayers ending with, "God save the churche, our kyng and realme, and God have mercy upon all christen solles. Amen." [18] The Little Hours from matins to compline follow, and then in due order the Seven Psalms, the Litany and Suffrages, the *Dirige,* the Commendations, the Psalms of the Passion, the Passion according to Saint John, the Prayers of the Passion,[19] and then a final array of prayers which will be noticed shortly.

All this looks much more traditional than one would have expected from the Calendar. But there have been within this familiar framework a good many changes, the significance of which is in some cases obvious, in others harder to determine. To begin with, there have been some extensive omissions, surprisingly enough, of selections from the Psalms. Some of these omissions are relatively easy to account for, others not. The group of psalms known as the *Dirige* had long been a recognized problem. It will be remembered that the editor of the 1535 Byddell-Marshall prayer book examined above had prefaced these psalms with a series of explanations designed to substantiate his claim that since there was nothing peculiar to the Office of the Dead in these very popular prayers, they might just as well serve as prayers for the living.[20] But in general he had kept the psalms and prayers of the old primer. The editor of 1545, however, found a much more radical solution for the problem.

He kept the title and the opening psalm, but he cut the office as a whole down to little more than a third of its usual extent.[21] And in the selection of the psalms to be included, he displayed a preference for psalms of thanksgiving and praise over psalms of penance and petition for mercy. This preference was quite unusual in the reformers of his time, who as a rule ran heavily to the graver themes of the religious life. The result is probably the most triumphant and cheerful *Dirige* on record. One searches in vain through these abbreviated pages for the gloomy splendor of the *De profundis,* one of the most impressive and popular of the prayers of the old Vigils of the Dead. It is, on the whole, however, not a matter of substitution but of judicious selection, underscored by the prefatory notices before each psalm. For instance, Psalm 38, *Ego dixi,* "I sayd, in the middest of my dayes I shall go to the gates of hell," is headed: "Thankes for recovery of health." [22]

As one would expect, the prayers for the dead that follow this office

came in for their share of revision. They are still prayers for mercy
for the souls of the departed, but a good many changes have been
made, ranging from slight turns and twists that subtly but unmistakably shift the emphasis and direction to the complete substitution
of a petition. The resulting difference in emphasis and direction may
be seen once and for all in what is the most complete and explicit of
these changes. It is found in that very well-known prayer for the
dead which opens this collection of prayers in the 1538 Paris primer as in
the 1527 Regnault *Hore*.[23] The Paris 1538 English translation ran as
follows: "God, to whom it is appropried to be mercyfull ever, and to
spare, be mercyful to the soules of thy servauntes of eche kynde, that
they beynge losyd from the bondes of deathe, may deserve to ascende
unto lyfe. By Chryst our lorde." But the primer of 1545 series opens
with the following, a prayer which in a sense performs the same
function but with a very different emphasis and over-all effect:

O God, whiche by the mouth of sainct Paule thyne apostle hast taught
us, not to waile for them that slepe in Christ: graunt we beseche the that in
the commyng of thy sonne our Lorde Jesu Christ, both we and all other
feithful people beyng departed maye be gratiously brought unto the joyes
overlasting, whiche shalt come to judge the quicke, and dead, and the worlde
by fyer. Amen.[24]

The questions raised by the *Dirige* do not seem to have troubled the
editor when he came to the Commendations. These psalms are printed
in full down to the end where one psalm, Psalm 138, *Domine probasti
me,* is omitted. But the first of the psalms, Psalm 118, *Beati immaculati,*
has a fairly elaborate preface:

This Psalme is the .A.B.C. of godly love, the paradise of lerning, the
shop of the holy Gost, the schole of truth. In which appereth how the saintes
of God esteme his holy lawes, howe fervently they be geven unto them, howe
it greveth them that they shulde be despised, howe fervently they desire to
learne them, to walke in them, and to fulfyl them: finally, howe the trans-
gressours and adversaries of them shalbe punished and destroyed.[25]

In view of the tone of this and the changes discussed above, it is not
surprising that the concluding prayers for the dead of the traditional
primers are simply omitted.[26]

Something of the same treatment is given to the Psalms of the
Passion, another of the almost universal fixtures of the primers of the
time. The number of psalms is cut in half from ten to five; after

the first psalm the old order is abandoned, but in this case what results is not a selection of the old psalms, but a substitution of new ones. To judge from the prefatory notices before each psalm, the only apparent motive would seem to be the desire to carry the reader's thoughts from the contemplation of Christ's Passion in itself to the consideration of the fortunes of Christ and his church and his disciples in an age of persecution. As for the usual brief prayers at the end of the Psalms of the Passion in which the intercession of the Blessed Virgin Mary and Saint John the Evangelist played a conspicuous part, the author of 1545 simply failed to provide any prayers at this point.[27]

The inclusion of the Passion of Christ as told by Saint John is in the Primer tradition, but it is more usual, as we have seen, to put it, not as here after the Psalms of the Passion but at the beginning of the Primer.[28] The "Praiers of the Passion of our saviour Chryst," which now follow, are very different from the usual Passion prayers of the classic Primer.[29] They bear every mark of being designed to draw the pious reader's mind from the emotional and imaginative contemplation of the Passion of Christ to which the editor of the Byddell-Marshall primers had earlier objected,[30] and direct it to a more systematic consideration of the lessons to be drawn therefrom, with especial stress on satisfaction and redemption.

Something of the same disposition to change emphasis is to be seen in what is done with some of the traditional choices of hymns. It will be remembered, for instance, that the hymn in praise of the Virgin, *Quem terra pontus ethera*[31] of the usual Little Office of the Blessed Virgin, had become in the 1537 Byddell-Marshall primer a hymn of praise to God for giving us Christ as our saviour.[32] In view of the way the wind was blowing at that time there was nothing surprising in that substitution. No such doctrinal significance is to be seen, however, when the 1545 primer drops that hymn in turn and substitutes the famous dayspring hymn, *Iam lucis orto,* "Now the cherfull day doth spryng."[33] It would seem more reasonable to suppose that the purpose of the shift was to emphasize the matutinal character of the whole exercise in such explicit terms that the not too liturgically minded could not miss that significance.

The same thing is true of the anthems and of the lessons. The three lessons of Matins, all three in praise of the Virgin, had already been changed in the Byddell-Marshall book of 1535 to three lessons on

the moral undertakings of Christ's followers.[34] Now they are changed
again to three readings, one from Isaiah 11, the other two from Luke 1
on the promise of the Redeemer and the Annunciation.[35] This change
was probably made in the interest of greater emphasis on the redemption, but as against the earlier change it certainly resulted in a clear
gain in coherence and simplicity. Probably something of the same
desire for simplicity motivated the general condensation of the offices
by the omission of scriptural materials which could hardly be challenged on any other grounds. It is hard to know how else to account
for the omission, for example, of Psalm 93, *Dominus regnavit,* and
Psalm 100, *Iubilate,* and Psalm 63, *Deus deus meus,* in the office of
matins,[36] all three of which had been kept in the Byddell-Marshall
primer of 1535,[37] or the omission of about half of the office for the third
hour.[38]

But it is in the handling of the litany that the greatest change is
apparent. The old Litany of the Saints is represented only by the
opening prayers to the Three Persons of the Trinity and by three
condensed petitions to the Blessed Virgin Mary, to "All holy Angels
and Archangels, and al holy orders of blessed spirites," and to "All
holy Patriarkes, and Prophetes, Apostles and Martyrs, Confessours, and
virgyns, and al the blessed company of heaven." [39]

The petitions that follow these opening prayers cover most of the
collective and individual needs of the membership of the church.
Many of them are regroupings and expansions of the petitions which
followed the invocation of the saints in the old litany. Some, however,
are new creations to meet the exigencies of the times. One of these is
especially interesting because of the now quite frank endeavor to promote hostility to Rome as a Christian duty: "From all sedition and
privy conspiracy, from the tyranny of the bishop of Rome, and all his
detestable enormyties, from al false doctryne and heresy, from al
hardness of harte and contempt of thy worde and commaundement:
Good lorde deliver us." [40]

As for the six prayers which follow the completion of the litany,[41]
three are traditional, with occasional expansions in the interest of
reiteration and emphasis of the original doctrine; two, prayers for mercy
and protection, are obvious substitutes for prayers for the dead, which
had taken for granted the intercession of the Blessed Virgin Mary and

the saints, and the last is a prayer from Saint Chrysostom, which emphasizes the public character of the exercise of prayer just completed. This is one of several cases where the primer of 1545 is closer to the old Primer [42] than the Byddell-Marshall primer of 1535. That had provided only half the number of prayers, two of them clearly compositions to meet immediate and contemporary needs, and the third a prayer for forgiveness, with emphasis on the latter end of the petitioners.[43] There is, however, one slight but striking modification that runs throughout this group of prayers. Where the Paris primer of 1538, for instance, had ended each prayer with "By Chryste our lorde," the primer of 1545 used syntactical variants of the phrase "through our mediatour and advocate Jesu Christ," [44] thus underscoring Christ's mediatorship as the sole mediatorship to be invoked.

In all of these changes and adaptations the book of 1545 is a basically Protestant book. But there are certain other points at which it emphatically looks back to the tradition from which it had come. To begin with, although the handling of the materials of the hours carries forward the tradition of the experiments of the Byddell-Marshall and Hilsey primers, it is clear that for the form of the prayers the editor is not depending upon the versions of 1535 and 1539 but is going back to the Rouen-Paris primer or some book like it. He has obviously gone afresh to the Latin, and in the reforming spirit of his time made a good many changes of his own, but it still is clear that he has before him as he works either the English version of the Rouen-Paris primer or one a good deal like it. For the verbal resemblances are too sustained to be accidental, even for renderings of the same materials. The only reasonable explanation is that the editor of 1545 had some English-Latin version like that of the Paris primer of 1538 before him as he worked, and that where he was not moved to a fresh translation, he took up what was at hand.

This textual relation is well illustrated by a comparison of what is the first of the Seven Psalms in the Paris primer of 1538, and the fifth in the primer of 1545, Psalm 101, *Domine exaudi*. The version of the Paris book of 1538 begins as follows:

Lorde heare my prayoure: and let my clamoure come unto the.
Tourne nat thy face frome me: when so ever I am troubled bowe thyne eare unto me.

In what so ever daye that I am troubled: here me hastely.

For my dayes have vanysshed as smoke: and my bones waxed drye as a fyre bronde.

I am strycken and my harte wythered lyke hey: for I forgatte to eate my breade.

With the noyse of my mournynge my bone hath cloven to the flesshe.[45]

In the official primer of 1545 the same psalm runs thus:

Lord heare my prayer, and let my cry come unto the.

Turne not thy face from me, whensoever I am troubled, bowe thyne eare unto me.

In what day soever I cal upon the heare me spedely.

For my daies are vanyshed as smok and my bones are waxed as dry as a fyre brand.

I am stricken, and myne harte is wythered like haye, so that I have forgot to eate my bread.

Wyth the noyse of my mournyng my bone cleveth to my fleshee.[46]

But striking as is this illustration of the immediate indebtedness of the editor of 1545 to the earlier form of the Primer tradition, there is still more impressive evidence in what is for the student of the devotional literature of the time perhaps the most interesting part of the volume, a considerable collection of prayers for various occasions, much in the style of the traditional accretions to the Primer with which we are already familiar.[47] In view of the condensations and omissions already noted, the amount of space given to these prayers is impressive. A good many of them are, as might be expected, selections from the Psalms, chosen with an eye to particular needs and particular occasions. For instance, the sixtieth psalm, "How hast thou O lorde, humbled and pluckte me doune?" is presented as "A prayer for patience in trouble," and the sixty-eighth, "Aryse Lord, let thyne enemyes be scatered, thy haters put too flyght," as "A prayer for concorde of Christes Churche." Some of these prescriptions are obviously prompted by the needs of the moment. For instance, a selection from Acts 4, beginning "Lord, thou art God, whiche hast made heaven and thearth," is labeled, "A prayer to speke the worde of God boldely," a petition that must often have seemed relevant in a time of such swift religious and political changes.[48] These immediately scriptural prayers form a very considerable portion of the total.

Closely related to these psalm prayers is another group which reflect some basic difficulty for the editorial policy of grounding everything on Scripture and at the same time bringing devotion to bear as directly and practically as possible on the spiritual needs of the individual in all the particular emergencies of the time. Usually in this group the prayer is a flexible but in general faithful translation of the original psalm on which it is based, but that original has undergone a certain amount of condensation and selection. On the whole, this makes for greater brevity and a sharper focus on the objective of the petition. A good example is to be seen in "A prayer agaynst the enemies of Chrystes trouth," which is a slight condensation of Psalm 139 (140), "Deliver me O lord, from the ungodly styffe necked personnes." The changes are relatively slight, but they all move in the direction of greater sharpness and coherence of statement.

Deliver me O lord, from the ungodly and styffe necked personnes, for thou seest how in their heartes thei imagin mischeve, and have greate pleasure to pycke quarelles, theyr tonges be more sharpe then any adders styng. And under ther lyppes lurketh poyson of adders, but O mercifull lorde, let me not fall into their handes, that thei handle me not after their owne lustes. Thou only art my GOD, thou must heare my piteous plainte, lorde that rulest all together, that art the strength and power of my defence, be thou as a salet on my hedd whensoever the ungodly shal assaulte me; neither suffer thou not the wicked thus to prosper in their matters. Suffer not their croked and malycious stomakes to increace, and spytefully revile the. Loke upon thy poore wretches cause, and rydd me out of these dayly grevaunces, then shall I with a right up heart and pleasaunt countenaunce extolle and magnifie thy holy name. Amen.[49]

There is, of course, some loss in the comminatory splendor of the original, but none in the force of the petition, and the total result is certainly more direct and compact in its movement.

Of the nonscriptural prayers a good many are clearly traditional, the stuff of contemporary primers and manuals of prayer, both Catholic and Protestant.

From "a praier in the mornyng" to the concluding prayers against the devil, and for the desire of the life to come, the organization, such as it is, and the themes of the prayers are traditional.[50] There are prayers for trust in God, "for the kepyng of a good name," "agaynst worldly carefulnes," prayers against pride, envy, and anger, prayers to be said in adversity and prosperity, and a general confession of sins to God, to name some of the outstanding.[51]

It is interesting, too, to find among these prayers some of the traditional Primer favorites that have a temper and a tone which one would hardly expect the reformers of the time to find congenial. Perhaps the most striking of these survivals is that prayer usually ascribed to Saint Bernardine of Siena, called *O bone Iesu,* which is described here simply as "A devoute praier unto Jesu Christ called, O bone Iesu." [52] Its spirit may be judged from the first petition: "O Bountefull Jesu, O swete Jesu, O Jesu the sonne of the pure virgin Mari, ful of mercy and truthe, O swete Jesu after thi greate mercy, have pitie upon me."

At first sight this would seem more like what one would expect to find in a French devotional prayer book of the next century than in a resolvedly Protestant English prayer book of this. The whole type of devotion which it represents, what one may call the contemplation of affection, would seem about as alien as anything could be to the more rigorously functional and theological prayer characteristic of this period. However, as we shall see shortly, it was to prove one of the hardiest devotional survivals of the time.

By and large, then, the great majority of these prayers are to be described as traditional in type and content if not always in precise form. But there is one notable exception, the longest and one of the most eloquent of them all, Erasmus' famous "praier for the peace of the churche." [53] In its main movement, and in its temper, this is also traditional, but at one or two crucial points it takes a turn that is strikingly relevant to some of the most controverted issues of the day. The beginning is large and timeless:

Lorde Jesus Christ which of thyne almightynes madest all creatures bothe visible and invisible, whiche of thy godly wisedome governest and settest al thinges in moost goodly ordre, whiche of thine unspeakable goodnes kepest, defendest, and furtherest al thinges, which of thy depe mercy restorest the decayed, renewest the fallen, raysest the deade.

This is a classic salutation. The description of the crisis in which the author of the prayer appeals for help is couched in similarly classic terms, but here the crisis envisaged in the biblical passage on which this is based is presented not as a prophecy but as an immediate actuality: "Thou seest (O good shepeherde) what sundry sortes of wolves have broken into thy shepecotes, of whom every one cryeth: Here is Christ, here is Christ so that if it were possible the very perfect persons shulde be brought into errour." [54] The author then proceeds to acknowl-

Title page of Richard Day's *Booke of Christian Prayers,* edition of 1608, known as Queen Elizabeth's Prayer Book

(*See page 191*)

The 1581 edition of *A Booke of Christian Prayers,* opened to sig. B3v-4

edge that this confusion is the proper and due reward of the sins of the faithful, surely a universally safe admission.

But the innermost heart of the time, the secret of its hopes and its fears alike, is to be caught in the noble celebration of the work of the creator of the world that follows. For all its large metaphysical movement it yet goes to the center of the crisis of the time:

Thou alone bringest thinges that be never so out of order, into order agayn: which art the only authour and mayntainer of peace. Thou framedst that old confusion which we call *Chaos,* wherin without order, without fashion confusely lay the discordant seedes of thinges, and with a wonderfull order the thinges that of nature fought together thou didest alie and knit in a perpetual band. But how muche greater confusion is this wher is no charitie, no fidelitie, no bondes of love, no reverence, nether of lawes nor yet of rulers, no agrement of opinions but as it were in a misordred quire, everi man singeth a contrari note.[55]

It is to restore order to this confusion that the author prays:

Stei this confusion, set in order this horrible Chaos (O Lorde Jesu) let thy spirit stretch out it selfe upon these waters of evyll wavering opinions. And because thi spirit, whiche accordyng to thi prophetes saiyng containeth al things, hath also the science of speakyng, make, that lyke as unto al them which be of thi house, is all one light, one baptisme, one God, one hope, one spirit: so thei may have also one voyce, one note and song, professyng one catholike truthe.[56]

But the shrewdest touch of all is to be seen in the picture of an ordered society for which the author prays as the remedy of all this disorder:

Geve unto princes and rulers the grace to stand in awe of the, that thei so maye guyde the common weale as thei should shortly render accomptes unto the that art kyng of kynges. Geve wisdome to be alwaies assistent unto them, that whatsoever is best to be done, thei may espye it in their myndes, and pursue the same in their doinges. Geve to thy bishops the gift of prophesy, that thei may declare and intepret [*sic*] holye scripture, not of their owne brain, but of thine inspiring. Geve them the threfold charite which thou once demaundest of Peter what time thou diddest betake unto hym the charge of thy sheepe. Geve to thi priestes the love of sobernes, and of chastitie. Geve to thy people a good wil to folow thy commaundementes and a redines to obey suche persons, as thou hast appointed over theim. So shall it come to passe, if through thi gift thi princes shal commaund that thou requirest, if thy pastures and herdmen shall teache the same, and thy people obey them both, that the old dignitie and tranquillitie of the church shall returne againe with a goodly order unto the glory of thi name.[57]

In this last section of the prayer there are one or two phrases that are especially interesting because they represent a change in the text of Erasmus that makes the total effect rather different from that of the original. For example, the original of "suche persons, as thou hast appointed over theim" is "per quos juxta tuum animum voluisti res humanas administrari," not quite so explicit on the social and political hierarchy. Again, "si principes tuo munere te digna imperunt, si pastores te digna doceant" is not nearly so Erastian as "if through thi gift thi princes shal commaund that thou requirest, if thy pastures and herdmen shall teache the same." [58]

It is the peaceful state ruled in all things by the prince, with a reformed clergy to teach the people the way they should go, that was the great dream of the Henrician statesman and of a considerable section at least, of the clergy of the time, that is so presented as the answer to the fears and anxieties of the age. This prayer is a fitting climax to the very adroit labor of public persuasion that had gone into the editing of this official primer of 1545.

VIII

THE LATER OFFICIAL PRIMERS

OMETHING of the old view of the Primer as a layman's prayer book for use in church as well as at home still survived in the primer of 1545. It found its most forthright expression in the directions prefixed to the litany for the saying of "this commune prayer of Procession":

And suche amonge the people as have bokes, and can reade, may reade them quietly and softly to them selfe: and suche as can not reade, let them quietly and attentively geve audience in time of the saide prayers, havyng their mindes erect to almyghty God, and devoutly praiyng in their hartes, the same petitions which do entre in at their eares, . . .[1]

For this purpose the Primer was, of course, superseded by the official Book of Common Prayer, first published in 1549.

But though the Book of Common Prayer settled for the average member of the Church of England the problem of the layman's service book, it obviously did not succeed in satisfying, indeed, made no pretense of satisfying to any considerable degree, the other purpose of the Primer, that of helping the layman with his own personal and private devotions. True, there were still a good many of the earlier reforming primers still in existence. But though they had been carried to the point we have already studied in the book of 1545, they must still have seemed perilously close to the ancient tradition in the eyes of the makers of the Book of Common Prayer of 1549 and still more that of 1552. It was imperative, therefore, from the point of view of those who were directing the religious developments of the reign of Edward that some provision more in accord with their conception of the spirit of the time be made in the field of private devotion.

The readiest way to solve this problem was to take the existing Primer, and revise it in the interest of the desired objectives. The result was the book which William Seres published in 1553, the year after the publication of the second Book of Common Prayer of Edward VI. The importance of the undertaking is recognized in the title of the book: "A Primmer or book of private prayer, needful to be used of all faithful christians. Which book is auctorised, and set forth by the King's majesty; to be taught, learned, read, and used of all his loving subjects." [2] This book certainly accomplished its purpose of bringing the provision of devotional material up to date, and in so doing it made full use of the opportunities afforded by the unique position and history of the Primer to consolidate the religious position that had been established in the second Book of Common Prayer.

The way in which this was accomplished becomes clear when this primer of 1553 is compared with the books that preceded it. The first and most striking difference to be noticed is that so many of the central fixtures of the traditional Primer have completely disappeared. Indeed, one may say that the core of the book is gone, for the familiar hours that had, in however modified a form, still remained a vital part of the various reforming primers through that of 1545 have disappeared, and so have the *Dirige* and the Commendations, and the psalms and prayers of the Passion. The second difference, and this may be taken as the defining characteristic of the whole group of primers which we shall later see stem from this book, is its close assimilation to the Book of Common Prayer of 1552. The calendar strikes the keynote in that the saints' days for which the Book of Common Prayer of 1552 provides an Epistle and Gospel are printed in red (with the exception of Saint Barnabas), while other saints' days are printed in black.[3] Then follows "A Catechism, that is to say, an instruction to be learned of every child before he be brought to be confirmed of the bishop," the same catechism which had previously been printed in the Book of Common Prayer of 1549.[4] And likewise, the 1549 framework of the order of private prayer for morning and evening is the framework of matins and evensong in the Book of Common Prayer of 1552.[5] The litany, practically the same as that of the Book of Common Prayer of 1552 except for some additional collects, is now placed in the "Morning Prayer for Sunday," as in the Book of Common Prayer.[6] Finally, "the Collects for Sundays, and Holy days throughout all the year," are the same as those of the Book of Common Prayer of 1552.[7]

The third change is not so immediately apparent or so easy to define, but when we have completed our study of the development of devotional literature for this century, it will be seen to be hardly less significant than the foregoing, and that is the general character of the large collection of "godly prayers for divers purposes" which now fills so large a portion of the book. Some of them are, of course, the prayers with which we are already familiar, particularly in the primer of 1545, but by far the majority of them are not. A good many of them bear familiar titles, or titles very close to those with which we are already acquainted, as "For a competent living," "For a patient and thankful heart in sickness," or a "Thanksgiving unto God for all his benefits," to name just a few which provide for conspicuously unchanging human needs, but the prayers themselves are new.[8] And, significantly in line with the devotional developments of the time, a good many of these new prayers are prayers for special classes and conditions of men of a type which we are presently going to find a very conspicuous feature of the new books of private prayer, as for instance, prayers for landlords, for merchants, for laborers, and for "men of occupations," etc.[9]

In other words, in this primer of 1553 the traditional Primer quite disappears in what is a layman's everyday combination of the Book of Common Prayer and the book of private prayer of the more practical, informal, nonliturgical type that was already in process of defining itself in these years.

But whatever its prospects of future influence, the official primer of 1553 at the time of its first appearance did not have much chance to make its way. For the accession of Mary in the year of its publication naturally brought almost immediate steps to counteract the influences which it represented. From the new sovereign's well-known disposition to restore the things that had been thrust aside by recent ordinance, one might anticipate the simple reprinting of the standard Primer, as is suggested by the title of the new book which came out by royal authority in the year 1555, "An Uniforme and Catholyke Prymer in Latin and Englishe," like the preceding official books "to be only used (al other sette a parte) of al the kyng and Quenes majesties lovinge subjectes throughe oute all their realmes and dominions." [10]

The determination to restore what had been lost is at once apparent when upon opening the book we find the old calendar in its full glory. But in view of that beginning it is surprising to encounter next an extensive collection of prayers for the mornings of the week, to which we shall presently have reason to return. The next item is more familiar. It is the Athanasian Creed as found in the classic Primer, followed as usual by the summary of Christ's life as told in selections from the Four Evangelists.[11] Thereafter all the central features of the classic Primer are restored, interestingly enough in the form of the Paris primer of 1538, both Latin and English. Many of the supplementary features of the ancient book are here, too, as is to be seen in the insertion between Compline and the Seven Penitential Psalms of that great favorite of the old English primers, the *Fifteen Oes,* still destined, as we shall see, to an interesting history in the later sixteenth-century prayer books.[12]

But in spite of the obvious desire to restore what had, as we have seen, been so altered and so substituted for in the volume of 1553, the restoration of traditional materials in this primer of Philip and Mary stopped short of completeness. One looks in vain for any sign of two types of prayers which had filled a good deal of space in the Regnault *Hore* of 1527 and had certainly not been entirely eliminated in the Paris primer of 1538, and these are the Marian prayers, and the special invocations, often fairly extensive, of particular saints. It was certainly not because of any hesitation about the Catholic character of the book, or any compromise of its basic commitments that these prayers were not put back even by token. For the thoroughly Marian character of the Little Hours was restored in the liturgical part of the book, and recognized in the heading in liturgical red before the opening of the first of the hours, "The matyns of our Lady." [13] But one looks in vain for the often beautiful and almost always colorful prayers that pay tribute to Our Lady and ask her aid on so many pages of the old primers. And the same is true of the prayers to the saints, except in so far as they fall within the limits of the liturgies included in the earlier sections of the book. Whether it was the haste of the work, or a feeling that it would be wiser to avoid any suspicion of over-emphasis in a region where conflict had so bitterly raged, it is not possible to say. But the fact remains that there is this striking evidence of regard to opposing points of view even in the restoration of the old primer in this book of Philip and Mary.

Indeed, the most remarkable thing about this primer of 1555 from the point of view of the development which we have been studying is the evidence of its indebtedness to preceding primers of a Protestant charac-

ter. Perhaps the most dramatic example is the prayer for the ruler
in the litany. It is the same prayer which was found in the litany of
Hilsey's primer of 1539.[14] It has been changed from the one-ruler form
of 1539 to the plural needed for Philip and Mary, but the heading, red
"For the kinge," with a little above it to the right in black, "And Quene,"
suggests a much rougher adaptation than would under the circumstances seem tactful.[15] There may be other possible explanations, such
as the unaccustomed situation with the woman ruler, but what the
change most looks like is an afterthought. At any rate the very presence
of such a prayer at this point in a quite traditional devotional series
following the litany proper suggests an interesting concession to the
spirit of the time.

The influence of the primer of 1553 is to be seen, too, especially in
what is one of the most immediately noticeable features of the book.
That is the extensive collection of special morning prayers for every
day in the week that has been inserted between the restored calendar
and the Athanasian Creed.[16] Such a provision of an order of prayer
for every morning and evening of the week was, it will be remembered,
one of the distinctive features of the primer of 1553. This scheme is now
followed at least to the extent of furnishing prayers for each morning
in the week. In the primer of 1553 the basic framework of these provisions was the matins and evensong for each day of the week to be
found in the Book of Common Prayer of 1552, where they were
frankly offered as a substitute for the traditional hours. But in this
book of 1555 they are supplementary to the traditional hours.

The influence of the recent reforming primers is, also, apparent in
the handling of even these classic materials, especially in the effort to
bring the traditional prayers more closely and more practically to bear
upon contemporary day-to-day needs and occasions. A good example
is the treatment of the classic prayer of thanksgiving to God for having
brought the grateful Christian safely through the night. The original
is one of the most popular of all the ancient primer prayers, "Piissime
deus et clementissime pater laudes et gratias ago tibi domine iesu christe
omnipotens eterne deus: qui me indignum famulum tuum in hac nocte
custodisti." [17] The 1555 editor takes this for his Friday morning prayer,
opening on quite traditional lines: "O Mercyfull Lorde God and
heavenly father, I render moste high laudes, prayse and thankes unto the
that thou hast preserved me bothe thys nighte and all the tyme and

dayes of my lyfe hetherto." [18] So far the prayer proceeds on quite traditional lines, but it soon diverges from the original, seemingly in the interest of a more exact specification of the ills which the reader prays to be delivered from during the coming day, ills, it need hardly be said, almost exclusively of a very general spiritual nature. Especially significant is the rendering of the final petitions. In the Latin of the Regnault *Hore* of 1527, for example, they run as follows:

. . . ut concedas michi diem venturam sic peragere in tuo sancto servitio cum humilitate, discretione, devotione et dilectione benigna: ut tibi servitutem meam debitam et placabilem in omnibus operibus meis valeam persolvere: et fac mecum tua gratia vivere semper et omnibus diebus vite mee tibi commendo corpus meum et animam meam.[19]

In contrast to this large statement of what might be called general and enduring principles of the moral and religious life, one may discern something of a response to the challenge of the present crisis in the version of 1555:

. . . and I beseeche thee hartely that thou wilt vouche safe to receyve me thys daye and the residewe of my whole lyfe from hensforth into thy tuicion, ruling and governyng me with thy holy spirite, that al maner of darknes of misbelefe, infidelitie, carnall lustes and affeccions maye be utterlye chased and driven out of my hearte, and that I maye be justified and saved bothe body and soule thorough a ryghte and a perfecte fayth, and so walke in the lyghte of thy moste Godly trueth, to thy glorye and prayse, and to the profite and furtheraunce of my neighbour, thorough Jesus Christe oure Lorde and saviour Amen.[20]

But striking as are the evidences of the influence of the primers of 1539 and 1553, they are much less important than that of the thoroughly and conclusively Protestant book of 1545. Indeed, one may go so far as to say that the editor or editors of the primer of 1555 kept as much as they could of the materials established in the 1545 volume, both the English primer discussed above and the English-Latin version which Richard Grafton published on the sixth of September of that year. The Prayers of the Passion are a good example. Though thoroughly traditional in spirit, they were not a universal feature of the Sarum primer. The Latin and English primer of 1545 had printed them after the characteristic primer feature of the Passion according to Saint John, at the end of the liturgical portion of the book.[21] The editor of 1555 kept them, printing them in the miscellaneous material at the beginning of the primer, before the Hours, even before the selections from the Four Gospels.[22]

But a still more impressive evidence of this relation is to be seen in that series of prayers labeled simply "Godly prayers," inserted between the "Psalmes of the passion" and the final "forme of confessyon," that closes this book of 1555.[23] These prayers are given only in English. Both in total effect and in position this collection of prayers is strongly reminiscent of the collection of prayers for all sorts of occasions and needs at the end of the English primer of 1545.[24] Although the title in the table of contents of the primer of 1555 is given as "Fyftie devoute Prayers contayning severally what so ever is mete to be prayed for, as by their tytles doeth appere," [25] there are more than sixty prayers in this collection, ranging in length from a single sentence of ejaculation [26] to more than three closely printed pages of carefully articulated prayer and meditation.[27] While some relation of theme may be discovered in the juxtaposition of certain prayers as when, for example, a prayer "in prosperitie," follows immediately upon a prayer "in adversitie," [28] in general these prayers are not arranged in any special order. They are simply massed for the reader to make his own selection and his own use. To this end, many of them are labeled as above so that the reader will be guided in his efforts to find specific satisfaction of a particular spiritual need, but a good many still bear only the noncommittal label, "A devoute prayer," or a bare ascription to the known or supposed author, such as "A prayer of Jeremie." [29]

In view of the traditional character of this primer it is not surprising that many of these prayers are the inheritance of generations of primers and other devotional collections. Conspicuous examples of this purely traditional prayer are the *Conditor coeli* and *O bone Iesu,*[30] to be found in almost every primer one comes across. Less universally popular but no less traditional are such prayers as "A prayer for kepynge of a good name," beginning: "That wise man which was privie of thy secreates O heavenlye father," or "A prayer agaynst worldly carefulness," beginning: "O Most dere and tender father, our defender and norisher, endue us with thy grace." [31]

Some of these prayers had for various reasons been dropped from the more Protestant of the transitional primers. Distinctively Catholic communion prayers were among the most conspicuous of these; so their restoration in a Catholic primer was to be expected.[32] Of different, though analagous, significance is the restoration of the famous prayer of the Seven Words, ascribed usually to the Venerable Bede,[33] which had been one of the perennial favorites of the Primer. It involves, however, issues of taste and tone in the handling of Christ's Passion which Catholic and Protestant opinion in this period tended to regard differently. Its restoration here is a reaffirmation of the general character of the book.

And so is the form of confession,[34] not to be found, of course, in the primer of 1545 or even in the Paris primer of 1538. In fact, it goes back to the Regnault *Hore* of 1527, for it is quite the same form as that given in English in that edition except for a few changes in wording. Typical of these is the substitution in the confession of sins committed in wrath, of "cruel wordes" for the "evyll wordes" of 1527.[35]

But the most remarkable thing about this collection of prayers, in view of the general purpose of the book, is to be found not in the differences between this and the corresponding collection of 1545 but in the elements that are either identical or similar. Th collection of prayers at the end of the 1545 volume numbers (exclusive of the prayers of the Passion which have been placed earlier in the 1555 primer) thirty-five prayers. About two-thirds of these have been retained in the book of 1555. Some of these, as suggested above, are prayers that are found in most of the primers, commonplaces of this type of literature. Others are prayers for the daily needs, morning and evening prayers, confessions of sin, and petitions for help, as in adversity or affliction, like "A prayer for patience in trouble, psal. lx."[36] Others are prayers for enduring spiritual needs, for trust in God, for help in "great trouble of conscience, psal. .cxxxiiii," "For the desyre of the lyfe to come," etc.[37] These might be considered staples of the life of devotion.

As regards the text, they seem in general to come from a common source. It is rash to generalize on the relations of particular prayers to a source one can only guess at. But some rather interesting tendencies emerge from a rough comparison of these prayers with each other and with the text of the Paris primer of 1538. In general, the editor of 1555 faithfully copies the English version of the primer of 1538, even where that translation differs from the Latin original beside it, and in one case at least, even where the editor of 1545 had corrected a slight omission of

no importance. In the old primer favorite, *O bone Iesu,* the first of the
two sentences, "Hoc nomen Iesus nomen dulce est. Hoc nomen Iesus
nomen salutate est," is to be found in the Latin of the Paris primer of
1538, but through some carelessness in editing, it has dropped out of
the English version on the same page.[38] In other respects the version
of 1545 is a faithful copy of the translation of 1538, but at this point the
editor of the English primer of 1545 had clearly checked over his
translation with the Latin or had access to a more accurate copy of the
basic English translation, for he restored the sentence.[39] On the other
hand, it disappears in the version of 1555,[40] suggesting that the editor
of that book relied here as in the bulk of the book on the English translation of the Paris primer of 1538, or the basic version behind it. Too
much stress should not be put on this point, for, as we have already
seen, there is a good deal to indicate that this book was prepared rather
hastily with considerable carelessness in copying and proofreading.

But in some cases the difference between the two versions of what is
basically the same prayer is not only considerable but significant of a
real difference in mood and feeling. A very good example is to be seen
in the prayer labeled rather generally in the 1545 edition, "A fruitfull
praier to be sayde at all tymes," [41] mainly a prayer for help to do the
will of God in all things, a translation of a somewhat adapted version
of an old prayer of Saint Thomas Aquinas, said to have been translated
in the main by Queen Mary herself when she was eleven years old.[42]
In both cases the prayer proceeds in general along the same lines with
such a degree of agreement as makes it clear that it is the same prayer
in the two different versions. But at the end, there is a difference in
the wording that, although not of importance for substance of doctrine,
is suggestive for tone and temper. The version of the primer of 1545 is
in this case the smoother and the more compact:

My lorde, graunt me wytte to knowe the, diligence to seke the, conversation
to please the, and finally, hope to enbrace the, for the precious blud sake of
that immaculate lambe our onely saviour Jesu Christ. To whom with the
father and the holy gost thre persons and one God, be al honour and glory
worlde without ende. Amen.[43]

But what looks in the beginning like the same petition soon takes a
very different turn in the version of 1555:

Graunt to me my swete lorde god, understandinge, that I maye knowe thee,
diligence that I may seke the, wisedome that I may finde thee, conversacion

that I may please thee, long perseveraunce, that trustily I may abide for the, and sure hope that fynally I maye clappe me to thee, graunte me here to be afflict with paines and tormentes in the way of this life, to have use of thy benefites by thy grace, and to have fruicion of thy joyes and rewardes in thy heavenly contrie by everlastinge glory. Amen.[44]

Certainly, that ascetic note at the end is something very foreign to the tone and temper of the earlier version. Here as so often the prayer of 1555 represents an older approach, that of 1545 the more contemporary, so far as the prevailing climate of the prayer books of the time is concerned. The version of 1555 is a little more diffuse, more homely, and ascetic. That of 1545 is less passionate, more compact, and most significant of all, more rigorously logical. The version of 1555 is more interested in the component elements of the experience hoped for, 1545 in the significance of it.

But perhaps the most interesting example of the curious and involved relationships between this restored Catholic primer of 1555 and the official Protestant primer of 1545 is to be found in the material drawn from contemporary devotional literature. The book of 1545 had drawn upon some of the Catholic devotional writers of the time. One of these men, Erasmus, was, not entirely without reason in view of the ambiguous character of a good deal of his history, often counted as an ally by Protestant writers of the time, and would seem so to have been counted by the editor of 1545, for he printed at length "A praier for the peace of the Churche," with its graphic description of the doctrinal confusions of the times and its clearly perceptible terror of threatening chaos.[45] Erasmus' position, however viewed finally, is certainly very different from that of either the extreme reformer or the conservative anxious to restore an old order that has been nearly destroyed. It is, therefore, the sort of prayer that one would be more apt to find in a book of 1545, a book written by conservative men who were committed to the new movement but fearful of its wrecking itself upon the rocks of sectarian discord and contention than in a Catholic book of the all too sadly experienced restoration of 1555. It is not surprising therefore that it did not find its way into the 1555 book, though a more controversial spirit might have supplied ample justification for its misgivings over the way the world was going.

The situation with Vives is quite different. He was a reformer, too, and a humanist, and although like Erasmus he came under suspicion in certain quarters, there is no reason to doubt his basic loyalty to the Catholic church. However, there was something in the topical immediacy of the sentiment of Vives' prayers that commended them to the Protestant writers without raising any question of the doctrine involved. The editor of the primer of 1545 was only one of a number of Protestant writers of the time who drew on Vives. For instance, his prayer against the devil was a direct borrowing, while his prayer "For the desyre of the lyfe to come" is a good example of a new prayer expressing the sentiments and often the turns of expression of a prayer of Vives on the same theme.[46] Both of these prayers were kept by the editor of 1555.[47] The fact that the prayers of a moderate Catholic reformer could be taken over by Protestant reformers, and still later from them by Catholic conservatives, anxious to recover ground lost, is fresh proof of the general fluidity of the devotional field at this time, at least, in England.

Some of this may, of course, have been merely a matter of prudence. The editor of 1555 had restored the ancient hours and the *Dirige* and the litany and the other essential parts of the traditional Primer in the old form and the old text without any hesitation. Since these were matters of liturgy, involving, incidentally, basic theological issues like those of honoring the Blessed Virgin and the saints, or of prayers for the dead, one can understand why the restoration of the old book should have seemed imperative. But the occasional prayers were a different matter. Obviously the editor of 1555 had checked them over. Some were simply omitted; others were either restored to their original form or pointed up and sharpened to greater effectiveness from the Catholic point of view. But the surprising thing is not that some prayers were omitted and some changed, but that so many were kept, and in substantially the same form.

The fact would seem to be that the editors of 1555 were not hypersensitive in their scrutiny of the prayers that had recently proved so popular. A very interesting example is to be seen in a prayer not found in the primer of 1545 but in one of the devotional works of Becon, published at least as early as 1551, *The Flower of Godly Prayers*. It was in this book that Becon printed that prayer to God as the diligent Watchman who forever takes care of his people,[48] which the primer of 1555 reprinted, with a few verbal changes so slight as to be of no real consequence, for the Saturday morning prayer. What makes the

acceptance of this prayer so noteworthy is the fact that it approaches
the theme of the day's work in a spirit usually regarded as more
characteristic of the Protestant of the time than of the Catholic; for
the pious man is made to pray finally,

that all myne enterprises may be agreable unto thy most blessed wil, which
is alwaye good and godly, doing that that may avaunce thy glory answere to
my vocacion, and profit to my neighbour whom I ought to love as my selfe:
that whansoever thou callest me from this vale of misery I may be founde the
child not of darknes but of light, and so for ever rayne with thee in glorye
which art the true and everlastyng lyght, to whom with thy derely beloved
sonne Jesus Christ our alone saviour and the holy gost that most swete com-
forter, be al honour and glory. Amen.[49]

Probably nothing could better illustrate the essential flexibility and
responsiveness of the Primer as an instrument of religious organization and religious expression than this fact. Even in a monument of
thoroughgoing restoration the influence of the time is to be seen, and
points of view expressly repudiated yet have their weight in the determination of the activities of their adversaries. But if any further proof
of this general character of the sixteenth century Primer is needed it is
to be found in the first Elizabethan primer, that of 1559. "The Primer
set forth at large, with many godly and devout prayers," so runs the
title of the book which the Assigns of John Wayland brought out in
London in that year, with the classic "forbidding all other to print this
or any other primer." [50] As might be anticipated, this book returned to
the primer before Mary, but it did not, as one might well expect, pick
up the pre-Marian primer at its latest development in the reformed
direction, the Edwardian primer of 1553. Rather it went back to the
type which we have already studied in its full maturity in the primer
of 1545. Although that primer had gone through certain developments
in a number of intervening editions in the reign of Edward, notably
the Grafton primers of 1551,[51] the basic type had persisted, and it is to
that that this first primer of Queen Elizabeth returned.

The recovery of the Protestant tradition was emphasized by the reprinting in the opening of the book of a preface ascribed to Henry
VIII and printed originally not in the 1545 edition of the English
primer but in the Latin and English primer of 1545. The main emphasis
of this preface is on the language question, advocating the use of the
vernacular that men may understand what they are praying, "so that

the depe contemplacion or ravishyng of the mynde folowe the pithinesse
of the woordes, and the guidyng of reason goe before . . . ." This
preface of 1545 was followed by Henry's injunction, "for the autorisyng
and establishyng the use of this Primer," the same as that printed in
the English primer of 1545.[52]

But the Primer had not by any means stood still. The calendar of
this primer of 1559 includes only those saints' days (with the exception
of Saint Bartholomew) for which the Book of Common Prayer of
1549 had provided an Epistle and Gospel.[53] The relation to the Book
of Common Prayer was emphasized by the fact that right after the
introductory material noted above, "An order for Morning prayer
daily through the year" was inserted such as was printed in the Book
of Common Prayer of 1552 and that of 1559.[54] This was followed
by a series of Communion prayers, and only then did the usual introductory material of the traditional Primer, such as Creed, Com-
mands, and Graces appear, all in the form of 1545.[55]

The basic materials of this primer are, we may say at once, those of
1545. But there are certain alterations that are significant of the change
that has taken place in the position of the Church of England since
that time. Of these the most significant are those which concern the
Marian character of the Primer. For instance, the form of matins is
that of 1545, but the Hail Mary has been left out,[56] and substitutes have
been found for anthems and lessons or chapters where there was an
emphasis on the Virgin in the original.[57] The Litany [58] likewise shows
the results of the same development reflected in the calendar. The
supplications to Mary, the angels, and patriarchs, the martyrs and
confessors, of 1545 have all been omitted.[59] It is in substance the litany
of Grafton's 1547 edition of the official primer.[60]

But the traditional character of the book then asserts itself. The
Dirige is the Dirige of 1545, with the same title and the same choice and
text of psalms. The Commendations of 1545 are reproduced even to
the prefatory note, and so are the Psalms of the Passion. Even the
interpretative descriptions inserted between the opening words of the
Latin psalm and the text of the psalm itself are the same. The same
version of the Prayers of the Passion is used, too. And perhaps most interesting of all, the rich collection of occasional prayers which is such
a striking feature of the primer of 1545 is reproduced here without
change.[61]

In other words, with the exception of the modifications in what may be called the public devotion sections of the book, Calendar and Order for Morning Prayer and Litany, the stage which the Primer had reached in 1545 was restored with one notable exception, and that was the specifically Marian materials. Above all, the occasional prayers were preserved without change.

We have no way of knowing how popular this book proved, nor how far it succeeded in accomplishing what must have been one of its purposes, the elimination of the various surviving Catholic primers. At least four editions of this type of primer, either alone or with the catechism, are known to have been printed in the reign of Elizabeth.[62] And though they lie outside the scope of this study, since they are in Latin, the fact that the *Orarium* of 1560, and the *Preces Privatae* of 1564 with its later editions of 1568 and 1573 belong to this general type of primer should be noted as evidence of the enduring interest in the traditional Primer.

But this was not the only type of primer to be printed during these years. There was another which enjoyed equal if, indeed, not greater popularity. And that is the series of primers which Hoskins traces back to the primer of 1553, discussed above, authorized by Edward VI and printed by William Seres.[63]

It is significant that, although when she first revived the Primer Queen Elizabeth took the older and more traditional form for her first book, in the next year the primer of 1553 was revived in a volume which William Seres published with the royal commendation on the title page: "A Primer or Book of private prayer, needful to be used of all faithful christians. Which book is to be used for all our loving subjects." This book restored the "Seven penitential psalms" and added several prayers for the woman with child.[64] But otherwise it followed the basic plan of the primer of 1553. And the same was true, so far as can be ascertained, of the five other editions of this type of primer known to have been published in the reign of Elizabeth. There will be various modifications here and there in the litany and collects, and there will be changes, usually in the form of additions, in the collection of miscellaneous and occasional prayers.[65] But the type remains constant. The persistence of this type even more than that of the 1559 primer, demonstrates the continuing concern about the needs of private devotion. For it carries forward the disposition already noted to rely less upon liturgical aids for private prayer and to provide more abundantly for the needs of special classes of men and special circumstances in the life of the time.

Such was the story of the sixteenth-century Primer, a story of tradition and innovation and repudiation and experimentation and compromise, with a constant tension between the different parties in a very confused and complicated and fluid situation. In the light of such a story it is not at all difficult to understand why the average sixteenth-century Englishman seems so often to have shown scant appreciation of the issues involved in the changes of the time and, even on occasion, indifference. In such a situation it was not at all easy for a man to know just where he was, unless he were more alert to the implications and the premises of successive changes and more eager to face difficult and obscure decisions than the average man is in any age.

IX

SCRIPTURE FOR PRIVATE
DEVOTION

IMPRESSIVE as is the story of the development of the Psalter
and the Primer, the use of scriptural material for the quarrying
of new forms of prayer was by no means confined to the Psalms. There
were too many other sections of the Old Testament and the New which
provided either patterned and directed prayers or the materials from
which such prayers might easily be framed. Such prayers from Scripture had already, as we have seen, found their place beside the prayers
based on the Psalms in both the expanded Psalter and the Primer.
They were destined to enjoy a no less prominent place in the various
types of books which came in varying degrees to take their place.

Indeed, some of the most popular prayers of the sixteenth century
were quite direct and acknowledged borrowings from Scripture. They
are to be found in almost all the devotional collections of the time, to
some extent, and they play a major role in a number of volumes. Of
these the most direct and probably the most influential is a book quite
explicitly titled: "Praiers of Holi Father, Patryarches, Prophetes, Judges,
Kynges, and renowmed men and women of eyther testamente," which
Richard Grafton printed, probably in 1540. This work ran through a
number of editions and proved a rich source of material for succeeding
editors of devotional collections. As the title suggests, the book is made
up of prayers taken directly from the Old and New Testaments. It is
hard to imagine anything more centrally representative of the scripturalism of the age than this collection. It opens, appropriately from the point
of view of time and theme alike, with the "praier of Moses to the Lorde,
for the synnes of the people," from Exodus 32: "Lord, why waxeth thy
wrath hote against thi people, which thou haste brought forthe of the

lande of Egipt with a greate power." [1] After that classic opening the
collection ranges widely and largely through Scripture in a fashion that
may be suggested by a sampling of the titles of some of the prayers:
"The praier that Baruch prescribed unto the captives in Babilon for
their synnes," from Baruch 23; "The praier of Joshua what tyme the
people fled in the battaill," from Joshua 7 : 10; "The prayer of quene
Hester for her selfe and all her countrye menne," Esther 13 : 11; "For
benefytes receyved at Goddes hande, the prayer of David," 2 Kings 7;
"The songe and thankesgyving of Mary the virgyne," from Luke 1.[2]

Sometimes, the old scriptural prayer is applied especially to some
contemporary occasion, even at the risk of a colorful anachronism. A
dramatic example is the description of the battle prayer of King Asa
from 2 Paralipomenon 14 in the following heading: "In warres againste
Turkes and invadours, the prayer of kyng Asa." [3] But in view of the
difficulties which the various reformers were experiencing in their en-
deavors to persuade civil authority to accept their prescriptions at the
time when this book first appeared, probably the most satisfying description was that of "The prayer of the preestes againste the tiraunt that
he might not prospere against the holines of God," from Maccabees 7.[4]
As we have seen from his handling of the Psalms, the editor of the
Praiers of Holi Fathers was much exercised about the ancient problem of
the tyrannical ruler.[5] This was, however, for all the attention to be given
to the ruler in the later prayer books of the century, one type of prayer
that was destined to disappear. The orthodox Elizabethan editor would
explain this, of course, on the ground that with the happy reign of Elizabeth there was no longer any need to think about tyrants and persecutors.
But when this book first appeared, there was much less general confidence in the status quo.

But whatever the occasion to which the scriptural prayer is directed,
one feels throughout the book the dramatic exhilaration of the Old
Testament, the sense of large and urgent matters of cosmic importance moving forward, an atmosphere thoroughly congenial to the
excitement and the almost apocalyptic tension of so much of the devotion of the sixteenth century. This does not mean that the more joyous
and triumphant verses of the Psalter altogether failed to find a place in
the volume. Psalm 103, "Prayse the Lorde, oh my soule and all that is
within me, prase his holy name," for instance, is headed: "A merie
thankesgevyng for all the benefites conferred unto us by Christ." [6]

But the major emphasis and drive of the book is not unfairly represented by the main headings of the table of contents which gather up the various prayers into seven main groups: "Praiers for the synnes of the people"; "Prayers in tyme of adversitie, and for a mannes owne synnes"; "Thankesgevinges and prayses unto God of the Fathers"; "Praiers for succoures and releifes of life, for wisedome, for humilitie, and for other naturall gyftes"; "Certain Psalmes picked forth miete for daily prayers unto God"; "Certain praiers shorte and of divers sortes"; "Psalmes of David agaynste tyrannes and persecutoures of Goddes woorde." [7] Again one is conscious of the main preoccupation of so much of sixteenth-century devotion, the devotion of an age conscious beyond most of its sins and its shortcomings, and yet confident with the confidence of Armageddon of the final rightness of its own position. In short, both in the source and the selection of the prayers and in the massing and organization of them, this seems at first sight to be a typical reformer's book of devotion.

And yet probably the most remarkable thing about this collection of prayers is that a very large number of them had been already picked out and given currency in the primers we have been studying. This may be illustrated in a very striking fashion by a comparison of the *Praiers of Holi Fathers* with the Regnault *Hore* of 1527. In this latter book there is a considerable section of "suffragia" composed of several types of prayers, but running largely to petitions to various saints, and prayers for a wide assortment of emergencies.[8] Among them, however, is a group of Old Testament prayers which have been applied to various spiritual and moral needs. A good example of the approach is to be seen in the description prefaced to one from Exodus 33: "The prayer of Loth, Jacob, and Moyses for them that have takem [*sic*] ony newe grete thynge upon them that they wolde have brought to good ende." Another is the prayer of Nehemias 1: "Thys prayer is for them that be in disease or have their frendes diseased or imprisoned: or falle in some grete synne: to praye god to delyver them out: as the good duke Neemie he prayed for them that were in the captivite of babylone the which were delyvered." [9]

There are some eighteen of these prayers, all in Latin, in this scriptural section, and of these fully half are to be found in translation in the *Praiers of Holi Fathers*. In view of this fact it can hardly be accidental that the first of the *Holi Fathers* series, as noticed above, is a selection from the first prayer in the series of the *Hore* of 1527.[10] The *Holi Fathers* prayer, titled the "praier of Moses to the Lorde, for the synnes of the people," begins about a third of the way through the 1527 prayer with the dramatic question: "Lord, why waxeth thy wrath hote against thi people . . . ?"[11] On the other hand, the prayer of the *Holi Fathers* takes more of the seventh chapter of the second book of Kings in "For benefytes receyved at Goddes hande, the prayer of David,"[12] than does the *Hore* of 1527 for "Thys prayer is to thanke god of his gyftes, askynge them to be continued in us and in all his people."[13]

Perhaps the most suggestive fact that emerges from this comparison is that a number of these prayers, those of Manasses, Judith, Susanna, Jonas and Nehemias, occur in both series in that quite unscriptural order,[14] although of course, in some cases, notably in the *Holi Fathers* volume, other prayers intervene. In general the introductory and explanatory headings of the *Holi Fathers* collection keep closed to the scriptural situation and make less effort to suggest the bearing of the prayer on the problems of contemporary life than do the introductory headings of the *Hore* of 1527. For the Jonas prayer, for instance, the editor of 1527 explains at some length:

This prayer is for them that stande in disease and distresse unlykely to be delyveret: and yet let them trust to be delyvered: and to come out of theyr peryl et Jebardi as jonas that was cast in to the depnes of the see, trusted yet in the grete goodnes of god to be saved, and to prayse hym therfore in his temple: and so it was. Jone .i.[15]

But the editor of the *Praiers of Holi Fathers* contents himself with "The prayer of Jonas when he was as yet in the fishes bely."[16]

As for the principles that govern the translation of these scriptural prayers, they may be illustrated by the versions of one or two of the most popular Primer prayers. One of these is that prayer of Manasses, which is found in the Regnault *Hore* of 1527 with the heading:

Thys is the prayer of the synfull kyng manasses that shed the blode of innocentes and of prophetes, and dide many other synnes as scripture wytnessed more than ony other that was afore hym or after folowynge reynynge. And yet after all thys he besought god of mercy entierly and dyde penaunce and hath mercy.[17]

Now this prayer is to be found in the Great Bible between "The story of Bel and of the Dragon," and "The first book of the Maccabees."[18] This version is printed in its entirety in the *Praiers of Holi*

Fathers [19] with an occasional word or phrase moved or changed in the direction of a more literal or more homely phrasing.

There is evidence of a tendency in *The Praiers of Holi Fathers* to cut down or condense some of the scriptural prayers of the Primer, by omitting the nonscriptural devotional additions characteristic of that book. For instance, that prayer "for them that be malyciously accused," *Deus eterne qui absconditorum cognitor es,* which the Regnault *Hore* of 1527 printed with the reference "Susanne .xiii.," [20] is cut down by about a third in the *Praiers of Holi Fathers* version where it is credited to "Daniell : 15." [21] The most significant of the omissions is that of the concluding petition for the spirit of resignation and acceptance of her death as the will of God. The result is that the prayer now stands simply as the scriptural lamentation of one falsely accused.

On the whole, the editor of the Regnault *Hore* of 1527 was primarily concerned with fitting these prayers to specific occasions while the editor of the *Praiers of Holi Fathers* would seem to have been more interested in presenting a selection of traditional prayers without too much modification of their scriptural character. But he is not too exacting as to the immediate scriptural source, for he does not hesitate to include [22] that selection and rearrangement of the Psalms attributed to Saints Ambrose and Augustine, which was printed in the primers as a portion of the Matins of Our Lady.[23] And what is still more interesting, he uses what is, except for some minor recastings of phrase of little significance, the same English version as that in the Paris primer of 1538.[24]

Closely related to the *Praiers of Holi Fathers,* but quite independent of it, is the collection of "Certayne other devout Prayers taken out of the Byble" which was added to the version of *The Psalter, or Boke of Psalmes,* "after the first copye of James Nycolson," [25] which John Whyte published somewhere about the middle of the century. The title in the text is even closer to the one we have been studying: "Here folowe certayne prayers of holy men and women, taken out of the Bible." [26] Many of these prayers are the same ones which were included in the *Praiers of Holi Fathers,* as they had been included in the expanded Psalter and the Primer from time immemorial. There are some striking parallels between the two collections. For instance, the *Praiers of*

Holi Fathers opens with the "praier of Moses to the Lorde, for the synnes of the people" from Exodus 32.[27] The first prayer in the later collection is a prayer "for the synnes of the church or congregacyon," entitled, "A prayer forthe people murmuring agaynst Moses," but now the text is taken from Numbers 10 : 11.[28] And the order in which the familiar prayers of Nehemias and Manasses and Queen Esther and the rest come along in the volume [29] is quite different from that of the *Praiers of Holi Fathers* and, of course, the Regnault *Hore* of 1527.

But it is when it comes to the prayers from the New Testament, that this work becomes really interesting. For it includes not only the "songe and thankesgevying of Mary the mother of Christ," and the "prophecy and thankesgevyng of zachary John Baptistes father," from Luke, but a number of Christ's prayers, as for example, "The prayer of Christ unto his father against the pharasaical enemyes of his worde," from Matthew 16, "The prayer of Christ upon the mount," from Matthew 26, and "the prayer of Christ on the crosse for them that crucyfyed hym," from Luke 23. And still more remarkably perhaps, it includes "the prayer of the Publicane," Luke 19, "the prayer of the Murtherer on the crosse," Luke 23, and the prayer of Stephen from Acts 7.[30] But the most picturesque part of the collection is a series of prayers toward the end, three of which are "the song of the fowre beastes," from Apocalypse 4," "the thankesgevyng of the angels," from Apocalypse 7, and "the prayer and thankesgevyng of the .xxiiii. Elders," from Apocalypse 12.[31] The total effect is a varied and rich one, inspired obviously by a desire to enable the devout reader to pray as directly as possible in the language of Scripture.

A much freer attitude toward scriptural material is to be seen in a book by an unknown author which proved so popular that eight editions still survive from the years 1563–1581, *The Treasure of Gladnesse*.[32] The title page of the 1568 edition of the work suggests that it was even then more than two hundred years old.[33] That may be doubted of the present form of the work, but there is no question that the book does contain for the most part traditional prayers, and it is likely that they have been selected out of a group that as a whole was not so well suited to the climate of 1568 as those that are found here. The litany especially has been brought up to date,[34] differing only in the dropping out of one of the petitions—for the strengthening of the queen in the true faith—from, for example, the litany in an edition of the *Queenes Praiers* of about the same date.[35]

Otherwise, the prayers of *The Treasure of Gladnesse* are, in the main, of a familiar type. The opening selection is from "Osee .14." and treats prayer in general; it is followed by petitions for God's hearing of the prayers offered and for mercy, and then the Lord's Prayer, and the twelve articles of the Creed.[36] "A forme of makinge a Testament" styled, "My Testament," includes a number of texts relevant to the testator's situation, and "The Confession of the penitent Sinner, conceived through faith, joyned with a strong hope in Christes merites," is really a mosaic of Scripture texts drawn from the Old Testament and the New, which sums up Christian teaching on the purpose and significance of Christ's coming into the world.[37] The theme is then taken up and carried on by "The Apostles and Prophetes." [38] The same technique of citation of relevant texts is followed in presenting "The Catholique Church," and Christ's continuing work of redemption as revealed in a series of texts from the writings of his Apostles.[39]

"The Prayer" which follows, a prayer for grace to find out and do the will of God and for the means necessary to do so, is in substance the same prayer as one of the "Godly Prayers" at the end of the restored primer of 1555.[40] There are, however, certain differences in phrasing, the most significant, perhaps, being those in the rendering of the first petition. In the primer of 1555 it runs as follows: "Graunt me merciful Lorde god, to desyre fervently, to search wisely, to know truely, to perfourme perfectly al thinges, that be pleasant to the," etc. It is unquestionably the same petition, but it is worded quite differently in the *Treasure of Gladnesse:* "O most mercifull God and loving father, I beseche thee for thy sonne Christes sake, graunt to me to covet with prudent minde, those thinges whiche may please thee. To searche them wysely, to knowe them truely, and to fulfill them perfectly," etc.[41]

The next item, an extended paraphrase of the petitions of the Lord's Prayer [42] represents a more elaborate version of the type of thing that was very popular in late medieval and early Renaissance manuals of devotion.[43] Thoroughly traditional, too, are the salutations to God and to Christ which, with a series of invocations and anthems, constitute what is substantially a cursus in honor and praise of God and Christ,

but particularly of Christ as the Redeemer.[44] The general technique
of composition of this cursus may be judged from the following so-called
"psalm":

O Lorde Jesu Christe the sonne of God, thou annointed kinge over Syon,
hear mee, and have mercie upon mee.
Thou arte my glory, O Lorde Christe, save me for thy names sake, deliver
mee by thy power.
Healthe and salutation is thine, therefore poure forthe thy mercie upon
thy people.
Oure fathers trusted in thee, and thou deliveredst them, O Lorde Christe,
my truste is in thee, O Lorde save thou mee.
O Lord let thy mercy and gentlenesse folowe mee all the daies of my life.
Glory be to the father, &c.[45]

So the book proceeds, justifying its title by a greater emphasis on
prayers of praise than is usually to be found in the devotional literature
of the time. But in spite of this the work as a whole is by no means
indifferent to the controversial preoccupations of the day. The most
striking revelation of the author's position is to be found in the meditation or expatiation upon the paternoster in the form of a dialogue, "The
Pater noster spoken of the Sinner: God aunswering him at every petition." It is always a risky thing for man to presume to put words
into the mouth of his Creator, but at first sight God's expressions of
weariness at the seeming futility of letting his word be preached to
sinners who do not obey but despise it, would seem a reasonable state
of mind for the much tried Creator contemplating the too enduring
sinner. But there is more to it than that, for the sinner has just been
praying in the characteristic fashion of the unsatisfied reformer for
priests and preachers "to feede us with the woorde of thy holy Gospell,
not with the dregges and chaffe of fables and mens doctrine." So there is
a real controversial point to God's answer:

It is not good to caste pearles before Swyne, neither to give holy thinges and
the childrens bread unto the dogges and houndes, yee sinne continually
without ceassing, and though I let my woorde be preached among you never
so muche, yet ye folowe not, neither obey, but despise it.[46]

Such a passage well illustrates the way in which the plastic treatment
of the Psalms with which we are already familiar could be extended
to parable and scriptural episode, not only for devotional but for controversial purposes as well.

Indeed, a good many of the freshest and most timely compositions of the new popular prayer books of the century are little more than sheer mosaics of Scripture. Thomas Becon is a very good example, as we shall see presently, of the sixteenth-century preacher who knew how to catch the spirit of the time and turn it to account. Yet Scripture is his basic instrument. There is a prayer in *The Flower of Godly Prayers* that illustrates his technique. It is on a classic theme of the traditional prayer books, "for a faythfull man beyng in trouble or enduraunce." [47] It begins with one of the familiar salutations of Psalter and Primer, based on 2 Corinthians 1 : 3: "O Lorde, father of mercies and God of all consolation, whiche rulest and disposest all thinges after thine unsearchable wisdom, and workest in thy creatures according to thy blessed wil," etc. It then proceeds to develop the familiar theme of the wonderful dealing of God with his creatures, citing a long list of scriptural examples. In the case of this prayer Becon (or his editor) has done a very careful job of marginal annotation, giving the appropriate references. Before he is through with a prayer in all not much over six hundred words long, he has drawn on some fifty chapters, only a few of which are in sequence, from more than a score of books in the Old and the New Testaments.

The process may be studied, also, in one of the prayers from the Bull-Middleton prayer book of 1578 to be discussed presently. It is titled, "A psalme to be saide in the time of any common plague, sicknes, or other crosse and visitation of God." It opens with two verses from Psalm 95:

O come let us humble our selves and fall downe before the Lorde with reverence and feare.

For he is the Lord our God, and we are the people of his pasture and the sheepe of his handes.

From these two verses the author proceeds to draw upon a wide variety of texts until something like twenty-one passages from a dozen different books of the Bible have been invoked for the composition of one prayer. Sometimes the transcription of the scriptural source is quite literal. For instance, the line, "For we acknowledg our faultes, and our sinnes are ever before us," is strikingly faithful to its acknowledged source in the third verse of Psalm 51.

Much freer is the handling of another petition in this same "psalm": "In deede we acknowledge that our punishmentes are lesse then our deservinges: but yet of thy mercie Lord correct us to amendment, and plague us not to our destruction." [48] Against this the following sources are noted: "Judeth.8. Job.11. Sapi.12." But when these references are checked, it becomes clear that neither the Job nor the Wisdom verses have been used in this version. They are merely other places in Scripture where the same theme is treated. The important reference is that to the words which Judith spoke to the ancients:

And therfore shuld not we undertake to be avenged, for the thyng that is done unto us: but to consydre, that all these punyshmentes are farre lesse then oure synnes and mysdedes. Belevynge also that this correccyon commeth unto us (as to the servauntes of God) for amendemente, and not for oure destruccyon.[49]

So this prayer proceeds until something like twenty-one passages from some dozen different books of the Bible have been invoked either for source or for parallels. It is typical of a process found everywhere in the books of devotion of the time, sometimes as above with marginal references, probably more often without.

One other type of direct and immediate use of scriptural material for devotional purposes should be noted, and that is a combination of meditation and prayer based upon biblical materials, or rather biblical episodes and transactions. A rather elaborate example is to be found in a work which treats the Canticle of Canticles, or Song of Solomon in a fashion in some ways reminiscent of the medieval meditation-commentaries on the Psalms, *The Canticles or Balades of Salomon, phraselyke declared in Englyshe Metres,* which William Baldwin published in 1549. Baldwin's approach to his material is the classic one, as may be seen from the core statement of an interesting preface. He tells his reader that the scriptural book "is (as it wer) a dialogue between Christ and his churche." [50] The general technique of the book may be understood from the handling of one of the shorter sentences in that by no means laconic work, the last verse of the fourth chapter:

The Texte. Let my beloved cum into hys gardeyn, and eate the swete fruites therof

The Argument

After the north and south wynde have so long blowen upon the churche that her fruites of pacience, humblenes, obedience and charitie are rype: she calleth Christe unto her his garden: desyryng hym to eat his fruites, that is to accept for good the wurkes, which she through fayth in hym hath brought furth: syngying as foloweth.

The Spouse To her Beloved .xxxiiii.

Now that I am proved
Let my best Beloved
Whome mercie hath moved,
    To make me his gardeyn:
Cum eat, and for good take
My wurkes, for his blood sake
The fruites let hym good make,
    Whiche grow in my gardeyn.[51]

But interesting as this volume is, it is still something of a curiosity.
A much more central example of the meditation-prayer type is to be
found in those prayers on the Passion of Christ which fill so much
space in the old primers. Although they were cast in the form of
prayers, they actually embodied a very considerable element of meditation. They varied, of course, greatly in the extent and character of the
meditative and contemplative element. The famous prayer of Bede
on the Seven Words which Christ spoke on the cross, for instance,
was brief and concentrated and even austere.[52] The *Fifteen Oes* of
Saint Bridget, on the contrary, was fairly elaborate, and imaginative, and
even emotional.[53] And, of course, there was a wide variety of types in
between. The motivating force behind them all was, however, the
same desire to bring that great story as close and as vividly to the mind
of the reader as possible. Plainly, the theory was that if he saw the
transaction clearly in his mind's eye, he would feel its impact the more
sharply with salutary consequences for both the heart and the will.
It is easy to see in some of these prayers the groundwork of those
famous imaginative constructions of Ignatius Loyola which were to
prove so influential in seventeenth-century Catholic devotion.

Indeed, a connecting link between the old Passion prayers and the
Ignatian meditations may be found fairly early in the sixteenth century
in such a work as *The Rosary of our Savyour Jesu,* published by
Richard Pynson, probably in 1526. In this work the story of the Passion
is elaborated in a series of meditations, one for each day of the week,
the two first dealing with Christ's incarnation and life to the last
days, the remaining five treating of the Passion from Christ's agony
in the garden to his death and descent into Limbo. The basic plan
is to present the scriptural episode in such a fashion as to evoke the
relevant emotional reactions, then to draw the appropriate moral and
spiritual lessons suggested by the transaction. The spirit of this work

is very much that of the pre-Reformation period with its development of the imaginative and emotional possibilities of the theme, and its stress on the elements of human drama presented by the scriptural materials. It is easy to see how the praise of Christ for the miracle and relic of the vernicle, or veil of Veronica, would not appeal to some of the reformers who were trying to eliminate the spirit and influence of the *Golden Legend* from the books of piety of the time. And the lively and sympathetic dwelling on the grief of Christ's mother when the body of her Son was laid on the ground [54] would seem distracting to men who had been complaining of the irrelevant fashion in which preachers had been developing the human drama of the Passion.[55]

But the type retained its appeal for Catholic writers. What is in some ways an even more advanced development of this devotional meditation is to be found in another work of approximately the same date as the *Rosary of our Savyour Jesu,* and that is *The Jesus Psalter,* which has been sometimes ascribed to Whitford. This was published in 1529 by Robert Copland under the title of *An Invocacyon Gloryous named the Psalter of Jesus.* This work apparently enjoyed considerable popularity in England on the eve of the Reformation and afterward among the recusants on the Continent, for five editions of the work survive for the sixteenth century, and it continued to be printed into the seventeenth century. The surviving mid-century edition is a rather austere little book without any pictures.

The basic pattern is quite simple. It opens with the text, Philippians 2 : 10–11, in Latin: "In nomine Iesu omne genu flectatur, celestium, terrestrium et infernorum. Et omnis lingua confiteatur quia Dominus Iesu Christus in gloria est Dei patris." Then come the ten repetitions of "Jesu. Jesu. Jesu. Mercy" of the first petition, followed by a short prayer for mercy not only for the particular sinner who is reciting these prayers, but for all sinners and for the souls in Purgatory. This first part closes with a brief petition to the Trinity and the paternoster and Ave Maria.[56] So the book runs through the fifteen petitions, "Jesu. Helpe me," "Jesu. Strength me," "Jesu. Conforte me," "Jesu. Make me constand and stable," "Jesu. Lyght me," etc. At the end the author appends a brief "admonicion" on how to resist such spiritual temptations as infidelity and desperation, a treatise of which the kernel is the sentence, "Suspend your reason, restraine all your senses, and plucke up all your spirites." And like a medieval preacher he backs up the lesson with the story of the man who saved himself from a "motion" to self-destruction by taking the "motion" for an occasion of remembrance to honour the Passion of Christ and his blessed Mother." [57] Whoever wrote it, this little "admonicion" certainly has a touch of Whitford about it.

When John Heigham brought out an edition of this "Psalter" at Douay in 1618, he dedicated it to the Fathers of the Society of Jesus,[58] certainly an appropriate dedication in view of the likeness between the type of meditational and affectional devotion presented in this new version of the old book and that which the Society of Jesus was making popular at the time of its republication. For the moment one turns to the first petition in Heigham's book, it becomes clear that this is a very different affair from the bare little sixteenth-century version. A picture has come between the old text and the first series of petitions. It gives very much the effect of an emblem with its prefatory interpretation, "In this Figure, is represented the woman of Canaan, who doubted not to intreat of Jesus, untill she obtained her request," and this scene is realized with the clear fullness and rotundity of line characteristic of the early seventeenth century.[59]

Each of the petitions that follow is embellished with a similar picture, such as "Elias resting with the Angell at his head," "Blind Tobie, stretching his hands to heaven," "Judith praying for constancy" (in a distinctly Renaissance setting), "Job on his dunghill," "Chaste Joseph tempted by his wicked mistresse," etc.,[60] all rich material for meditation and reflection on scriptural history and themes in the course of the fifteen "petitions" that make up the work. Taken all together, this series of pictures with the accompanying descriptions, brings a wide range of Old and New Testament figures and transactions before the imagination of the devout.

At first glance it would seem a far cry from the Passion prayers of the Primer to a book like this, but it is a logical development of the tendencies already implicit in their techniques of contemplation of the elements of human drama and emotion in the scriptural story.

Those techniques early evoked, as we have seen, the reprobation of some of the Protestant reformers, mainly on the ground that they distracted the reader's mind from the main didactic business of the scriptural account.[61] But there was, also, from the point of view of these men a further complication in some of the old Passion prayers, and that was the fact that a good many of them in their intimate and detailed evocation of the scenes of the Passion made a good deal of the presence and the reactions of the Mother of Christ. It was an effective way of bringing home to the reader the human aspects of the situation and of rousing human compassion, but to the anti-Marian temper of sixteenth-century Protestantism it seemed highly dangerous. That is probably why the famous prayer of Bede, the prayer of the Seven Words which Christ spoke on the cross, for instance, which was so constant a favorite of the traditional primers [62] did not survive in England.

As we shall see presently, this suspicion of the human elements suggested in the contemplation of Christ's mother was eventually to affect the treatment of the sufferings of Christ himself. But something in the nature of a half-way stage in this development can be found in such a work of the middle of the century as the "Godly Meditation upon the Passion of our Saviour Jesus Christ" which the famous Marian martyr, John Bradford, included in his *Godly Meditations on the Lord's Prayer, Belief, and Ten Commandments, with Other Exercises,* which was first published after his death, in 1562 by Rouland Hall. The spirit of Bradford's handling of the sufferings of Christ is perhaps best revealed in his treatment of the climax of the actual crucifixion:

Thy body was racked to be nailed to the tree, thy hands were bored through, and thy feet also; nails were put through them to fasten thee thereon: thou wast hanged between heaven and earth, as one spewed out of heaven, and vomited out of the earth, unworthy of any place: the high priest laughed thee to scorn, the elders blasphemed thee and said, "God hath no care for thee:" the common people laught and cry out upon thee: thirst oppressed thee, but vinegar only and gall was given to thee to drink: heaven shined not on thee, the sun gave thee no light, the earth was afraid to bear thee, Satan did sore tempt and assault thee, and thine own senses caused thee to cry out, "My God, my God, why hast thou forsaken me?" [63]

In this passage two things stand out very clearly: Bradford's rigorous concentration on the figure of Christ, and his emphasis on the physical data of the situation rather than on any imaginative effort at probing the victim's sensations and feelings. There is a moment's touching upon that aspect of the matter in the closing paragraph of the meditation, but Bradford at once passes on to what is for him the heart of the matter, and that is the consequence of this meditation for his own moral and spiritual endeavor:

O wonderful passions which thou sufferedst! In them thou teachest me, in them thou comfortest me; for by them God is my Father, my sins are forgiven: by them I should learn to fear God, to love God, to hope in God, to hate sin, to be patient, to call upon God, and never to leave him for any temptations' sake, but with thee still to cry, yea, even when very death shall approach, "Father, into thy hands I commend my spirit." [64]

In such a meditation as this we have what may be described fairly as a transitional stage. Bradford is saturated in the homely realism of the traditional prayers, but he is clearly reacting against the type of emotional and imaginative meditation which we have seen under attack, for instance, in the Byddell-Marshall primer of 1535,[65] and he is moving in the direction which meditation on such themes is going to take among men who hold his position, and that is a closer adherence to the data of Scripture, with a development of the doctrinal and moral implications of the Scripture record.

X

GUIDES TO THE DEVOUT LIFE

ONE of the most important and distinctive developments of sixteenth-century devotion was the prayer book especially designed for the devout layman living in the world. There was, as we have seen, nothing new in this effort to reach that reader. It had been the driving force behind the evolution of the Primer. But there were certain circumstances in the sixteenth century that made possible the realization of this ancient dream as never before, and there were other circumstances that made it even more urgent.

As for the first, the invention of printing and the consequent multiplication and cheapening of books made it possible to reach farther down in the social scale than ever before. Moreover, the increasing prosperity and the increasing self-consciousness of the middle classes created an ever increasing public for the books now made available. For the first time there was an economic and social base for the development of that type of prayer book addressed to the middle-class man that is represented by the book for "householders" that was to attract so much attention in this century and to flower so abundantly in the next.

On the other hand, this type of book was of peculiar interest and value to the reformers, both Catholic and Protestant. To the former, it offered a fresh way of carrying out an old evangelical purpose. And it afforded a way of satisfying those middle-class interests and ambitions to which the "English books" had been appealing with such disturbing success. But the type was of even greater importance to the Protestant reformers. The middle classes were a field of great promise for their propaganda of criticism of the established order and their suggestions of new points of view. This was true in every field of religious activity, but it was perhaps more urgent in the field of private devotion than any other. For the Protestant reformers had expressly repudiated the monastic way of life, and the premises upon which it had been erected.

They, therefore, faced with peculiar urgency the problem of organizing the life of prayer within the framework of ordinary domestic life lived in the contemporary world. There was, of course, nothing new in this endeavor of theirs. The element of novelty was in the weight now put upon that ancient Christian undertaking.

Here, as so often, the work of the reformers, both Catholic and Protestant, consisted not so much in inventing new instruments as in taking up those they found to hand in traditional writing and practice and developing them to meet new circumstances and to serve new purposes. The guide for the religious life of the layman had been one of the classic types of medieval devotional literature. This assumed various forms, of which two were to exert lasting influence throughout the sixteenth century. The more classic type which deals with the human being as the typical sinner rather than in terms of his position in life and lays more stress on meditation than on prayer is well represented by a famous English classic, *The Contemplatyon of Synners for Every Day in the Week* which Wynkyn de Worde published in 1499, and which in a "revised" version was republished as late as 1578 under the title, *A Dyall of Dayly Contemplacion*. Richard de Bury is said to have been the author of the original of this work,[1] which presented an arrangement of meditations for every day of the week, meditations based on sentences from Scripture and the Fathers, acompanied by reflections of an edifying character.

More important for the future is the type of the guide to the spiritual life designed expressly for the layman as distinct from the religious. An admirable example of this type is to be seen in that little guide which we have already encountered at the beginning of the Paris primer of 1538, between the Calendar and the prayer of the Seven Words that prefaced the usual selections from the Four Evangelists. It is "The preface and maner to lyve well," which Maister Johan Quentin, Doctor of Divinity at Paris, compiled, and Robert Copland, printer of London, translated out of French into English.[2]

This work is worth examining in some detail. For not only was it popular in its time, but it raised in that earlier period many of the problems that were to engage the attention of the authors of the later sixteenth-century guides to private devotion. Maister Quentin begins with general directions for an orderly and godly life with that combination of loftiness of principle and homely particularity of detail that is one of the characteristics of the mood and technique of that time. And then he proceeds to the problem of providing appropriate devotions for each step in the day's routine from the six-o'clock rising he recommends for all seasons. Unlike his later sixteenth-century successor, he does not attempt to provide precise and complete forms of prayer for each of these occasions, but rather contents himself simply with suggesting the theme of the prayer appropriate for each stage of the day's undertakings. Needless to say, he assumes that the Christian who takes his religion seriously will say matins, prime, and hours in his chamber or his lodging if he can before he sallies forth on the day's business. And for the man who is not pressed by business, he suggests, also, the theme of the meditations which should busy his mind during the visit to the church for "the space of a lowe masse." [3]

Here as elsewhere the themes of the meditations which Maister Quentin suggests are not very different from the themes which the makers of the later sixteenth-century prayer books are going to dwell on, thanks to God for all his benefits, especially for the benefits of creation and baptism and redemption, with salutary reminders of the sufferings of Christ in the accomplishment of this redemption so often taken lightly by the busy man of affairs. Throughout there is a recurring reminder of the sinfulness of the reader thus urged to prayer.[4] Needless to say, the most anti-Roman of Puritan preachers might in this follow the thoughts, if not always the precise terms, of Maister Quentin. The accompanying reminder of the sufferings of Christ's mother would of course be left out by the Puritan, jealous of any seeming effort to distract the attention of the Christian from his Maker and Redeemer to a fellow creature. However, Maister Quentin does not linger on this more human aspect of the matter, but hurries on to the *memento mori* with reminders of what it will be like when the lonely soul faces by itself the perils of hell and the devils and perdition. Thus much for the reflections of the pious in church.[5]

After that the devout soul was supposed to devote himself to his various businesses until dinner. But Maister Quentin reminds him here that however difficult or bothersome his affairs, the troubles of this world are nothing to take too seriously in the light of the eternal glory that awaits the faithful Christian when this life is over.[6] The modesty in eating and drinking which Maister Quentin enjoins is about what one would expect, but the rest of an hour or half an hour after dinner

suggests a care for the welfare of the body for which the late medieval
guide to the spiritual life is not always given due credit. However,
Maister Quentin makes the objective of this concession to the frailty of
the body quite clear when he bids his reader pray God that by this rest
he may serve him more effectively. For the afternoon has its devotions, too, for the interstices of business or when the day's business is
completed. Since the hours to tierce are supposed to have been said
before dinner, the remaining hours of the day should be finished before
supper. The *Dirige* should be said, too, when it can be managed, and
the Commendations for the Souls, at least on holy days, and on other
days if possible.[7]

Then follow general directions for a life of Christian observance:
weekly confession if possible, alms to the first poor soul who asks it for
that day, if it can be managed, and daily confession to God of the
particular day's faults.[8] Of a more general character is the recom-
mendation of meditation at the corresponding hours of the day on
Christ's Passion, and this is followed by a rather miscellaneous collection
of recommendations, including the choice of a sound spiritual friend and
counsellor for matters of the spirit, the cherishing of one's neighbor's
interest as one's own, the keeping of good company, the praising of God
after "all werke," the going to bed with some good thought of the
Passion of Our Lord, or of sins, or of the sufferings of the souls in
Purgatory, or some other good spiritual thought.[9] In other words, what
Maister Quentin offers is a devotional schedule for the waking hours
of the layman. It is set in the over-all context of the liturgy, but it is not
unmindful of the prospective reader's secular obligations.

If one compares this outline with the pattern of later sixteenth- and
seventeenth-century devotional books, two distinctive characteristics of
Quentin's work become apparent. The first is that almost as much
attention is paid to appropriate meditations as to prayers in this outline.
And the second is that in general the author contents himself with
suggesting the theme and objective of prayer and meditation and leaves
the development of the material to the individual reader. Part of this
confidence in the reader's capacity to carry on devotionally for himself
may be due to the fact that, by and large, the readers of such books as
this would be men and women of a fair degree of education, possessed
of an amount of leisure that would permit the cultivation of whatever
talents they might have for prayer or meditation. But part of it was

undoubtedly due to the gulf between the professional and the average even literate layman.

The magnitude of the undertaking of a systematic and extended program of prayer for the layman who was not trained for it was not easy for the professional to grasp. It is never easy for the man who has a special aptitude for a certain way of life, and who has trained himself systematically in its techniques, to remember afterwards what that field looked like to him before he achieved his mastery, and still less easy is it for him to envisage the nature of the problems it offers to the man who not only has not enjoyed his opportunities for training but has neither his impelling interest in nor his talent for the pursuit at the center of his own life.

One of the writers of this period did have some idea of the problem, for he set himself to write an elementary treatise on prayer for the benefit of the layman, and the unlearned layman at that. He is the unknown author of the *Pomander of Prayer,* which Robert Copland published in 1530. The title is a striking one, destined to be made famous by the successive editions of a book of devotions which Thomas Becon was to publish in the years between 1558 and 1578, so famous, indeed, that even this original has on occasion been attributed to him. But it is a very different type of work from Becon's, and its author is obviously a very different type of man. Outside of his work we know very little about him, simply that he was one of the devout fathers of the Charterhouse at Shene, an institution that was presently to give a very good account of its attachment to its traditions in the struggle with Henry VIII. This much we learn from "An exhortacion to the reders by a broder of Syon," which introduces the work.[10] The brother of Syon is not identified, but in view of the date and the undertaking it is tempting to think that he was Richard Whitford. The "exhortacion" certainly sounds like him.

The author's preface makes his approach very clear: "Of late tyme I have ben instantly desyred of certayne spyrytuall frendes to wryte some treatyse that myght be inductyve and also demonstratyve (to suche devout persones as lacke lernyng and knowlege of holy scrypture) howe and under what maner they myght order them selfe in prayer."[11] And the elementary fashion in which he sets about fulfilling the task he has undertaken may be gauged from the way the table of contents begins:

The dyffynycyon of prayer.

That we sholde oft tymes use prayer.

Of the profyte that cometh by prayer.

Of .iii. thynges necessary to be consydered afore the begynnynge of prayer.

How there is two maners of prayers: of the whych one is called vocall, and the other mentall, etc.[12]

The way in which the author develops these topics is an interesting one, characteristic of the time, a combination of the academic with the homely and practical. A good example is his discussion of how the man who prays may make sure that his prayer is heard by God:

Saynt Augustin sayth that who so ever wyll have his prayer fle or ascend to god, must prepare for it .ii. winges: that is to say, fasting and almes dedes. And saynt Bernard in his fourth sermon upon the epiphany of our lorde affirmeth the same, callyng these .ii. wynges afflyccion of the fleshe, and contempt or dyspysyng of the worlde.

The author further explains that alms-giving and despising of the world are the same thing.[13] And he enters no less practically into the inner labors of prayer, with, among other things an interesting discussion of the problem of distraction.[14] It is altogether a very moving effort of a broadly learned and obviously well experienced professional to write a text for beginners.

But it was by no means unique. The also unknown author of *A Dyurnall for Devoute Soules* which Robert Wyer published some time before 1533 had the same elementary public in mind and the same objective in writing his little book. But his approach to the common problem is different, something halfway between that of the Carthusian of Shene and Maister Quentin. For he offers not only a more limited guide to daily devotion but one more aware of the layman's psychological problems than that of the Paris Doctor of Divinity. Indeed, the opening remarks of the work suggest that the little book was undertaken to comply with the request of readers for whom the author would seem to have already served as the spiritual adviser and director envisaged by Maister Quentin.[15] The plan of the book is much less ambitious than the latter's, as it is limited to three offerings of advice for prayer, that is, for morning, for meat, and "before nyght," three occasions when the church had always enjoined devotion but for which, from the nature of things, the rite of church or chapel could hardly make provision.[16]

But limited as is the undertaking of this unknown master, the book is distinctive because of a certain psychological direction that reminds one not only of the Carthusian writer whom we have just been looking at but still more of the very elaborate and shrewd introspection of some of the medieval mystical writers. For the author of *A Dyurnall for Devoute Soules* advises his reader when he finds himself fully awake to note what first comes to his mind.

And y[f] ye fynde that any thynge hathe occupye[d] your herte then the rule of perfeccyon requyreth, the whiche is that our herte be at all tymes unyd and knytte unto god, eyther by actuall love and contemplacion of his good-nesse with dewe thankes gyvynge for his benefytes, or els by contynuall prayer and Confessyon of our owne evylles. Then anone with great hevynes complayne of your selfe knowlegyng that this inperfeccyon is founde in you for want of dylygente ghostly exercyse in the tyme past.[17]

There is an unmistakable hint of the psychoanalytical approach to the unconscious and the half-conscious in such a passage.

The author of *A Dyurnall* then proceeds to enjoin prayer and re-membrance of God and his mercy very much as Maister Quentin had done, but with the difference that he provides forms of prayer, print-ing in large type a brief set prayer for each occasion. Of these the basic prayer is that offered to be said first in the morning, "O beata et bene-dicta et gloriosa trinitas tibi laus et gloria et gratiarum actio ab omni creatura tua per infinita secula seculorum. Amen." This he at once translates: "O blyssed and gloryous trynyte, laude, glory and thankes be to the of all thy creatures, worlde withoute any ende. Amen." This prayer is to be said not only in the morning but "so oft as ye fele any ghostly, or elles corporall, delectacyon of god, or of his creatures."[18] Such a provision for the adequate expression of the Christian's delight in the world which his God has made is not the most common provision of the spiritual writers of the period, and this joined with the dis-tinctively psychological approach noted above makes one wonder just whom this writer has been especially reading in his studies of the spiritual life.

That question he answers for us with unusual precision when he gives the menu of the spiritual "refeccyon" which he has appointed for reading every day of the week. The dominating influence is, as one might have suspected from his approach, that of one of the great mystical writers of the high Middle Ages, Saint Bonaventura, and the work he has specifically in mind is one of the many falsely attributed to the great Franciscan but obviously composed under his inspiration, the *Vita christi,* or *Meditationes vitae Christi.* From this work a chapter is to be read each day in the week with the general direction: "These chapitres ye shal use to rede eyther in part or hole as may be suffycyent to styrre youre herte to compunccyon." [19]

Something of the humane spirit of Saint Bonaventura is to be seen especially in the advice for meal time. The admonition against greed is, of course, what one would expect, and so is the acceptance of whatever is set before you, and the constant remembrance as you eat, of God who gave it, and of the need of the poor. In the face of such an approach one wonders what sort of table companion this devotee would make, but the spirit of the Franciscan is seen in the second injunction "that youre abstynence be as secrete as ye can, standynge rather in the brekynge of your appetytes, and forberynge of those meates that ye fele your selfe moche inclyned to desyre, than in any syngularytie notable." [20]

Again, while the clientele for whom this book is obviously designed is in the elementary stages of the spiritual life, no effort is made for any more specific appeal. Obviously, the reader whom the author has in mind is a man who possesses a certain degree of leisure as well as freedom of choice and direction of his efforts, but beyond that there is no thought of any one particular social group.

Now this point is of significance because one of the most characteristic devotional developments of the second half of the sixteenth century and still more of the first part of the seventeenth is the prayer book designed to appeal to a special audience. Especially important was the book composed for that large group known as "householders." There was nothing novel in this type of book as such, for it was well known in the Middle Ages. Presently, we shall have occasion to take a look at a famous medieval example, often erroneously ascribed like so many popular prayers and devotions to the great name of Bernard of Clairvaux.[21]

But in view of the reorientation of devotional life in this period, the old type of books for householders assumes new importance. And new and contemporary compositions in the genre take on pioneer significance because they represent a fresh and quite deliberate and self-conscious effort to adapt the old type to new conditions of life. It is always rash in a field so rich as this to speak of origins or even of priorities, but there is one book which for sixteenth-century England must be pretty close to a pioneer undertaking in this field, and that is Richard Whitford's *A Werke for Housholders* published in 1530 by Wynkyn de Worde. Richard Whitford, "professed brother of Syon," is remembered today chiefly as the author of an early and very popular English translation of Thomas à Kempis' *Imitation of Christ.* That is the sort of enterprise one would expect of a devout and learned and industrious monk of Syon. But Richard Whitford seems in his own way to have been quite alive to what was going on outside his monastery walls. After all, he did not become a monk until he had had a very considerable experience of the world. For after a distinguished career at Cambridge and Paris he became a chaplain to the fourth Lord Mountjoy, an outstanding nobleman of his day, and later to Bishop Fox of Winchester, Lord Privy Seal. He had been a member of the More circle, too, before he entered Syon monastery.[22] It is not surprising, then, that Whitford showed himself profoundly concerned about the provision of practical spiritual help for men who did not enjoy his opportunities.

For in the midst of a series of suggestions for devotion, all of a very practical and even detailed nature, and many of the type in which the devotional impulse was supposed to find its issue in a gesture or act, he breaks off to meet an objection that clearly indicates the kind of audience he had in mind:

But yet some of you wyll say. Syr, this werke is good for religious persones, and for suche persones as ben solytary and done lye alone by them selfe, but we done lye .ii. or .iii. somtyme togyder and yet in one chambre dyvers beddes and so many in company, yf we shuld use these thynges in presence of our felowes, some wold laugh us to scorne and mocke us.

Of course, Whitford will not allow that excuse; he insists that men risk much more for worldly considerations, and, anyway, in such matters it is the beginning that is hard.[23] But the important thing is that Whitford is trying to envisage the circumstances of the ordinary Christian who is forced to perform his devotions under the often distracted conditions of the large and crowded household of the time. And in this he may be taken as the forerunner of a whole host of later sixteenth-

and particularly seventeenth-century writers, especially those who are going to try to make provision for the devotional needs of the emerging middle class.

This care of his audience is to be seen in the provision which he makes for the simplest devotional needs of his clientele. For he is not content like Maister Quentin to remind his reader of the occasion for devotion and to suggest merely the theme of the ensuing prayer. Rather, with the editor of *A Dyurnall* he seems to realize that prayer, like every other form of expression, requires training and practice. He does not solve the problem like the editor of *A Dyurnall* by printing set forms of prayer; rather, he outlines, almost as if allowing his reader to eavesdrop on his own devotions, a very direct and simple course of prayer that will carry the not too learned man for whom the book is clearly intended to the desired end. Indeed, the very terms of the form of confession which he provides, though not unbecoming the greatest scholar in the world in the presence of supernal Wisdom, yet emphasize that the reader for whom this book is designed, is "rude and unlerned, without wytte, wysdom and due knowlege of the and thy lawes." [24] Nor does he ever forget that reader, for when he recommends that at every meal some person be appointed to say the paternoster aloud, he carefully takes him through the prayer with a full running comment of paraphrase and of amplification in the interest of interpretation.[25] And the same thing is done with the Ave Maria, "the moost pleasaunt prayer, and of most honour unto your blessed lady," and the twelve articles of the Creed, all to be read aloud at every meal preferably, but at least once a day.[26] And with characteristic tact Whitford suggests that the constant hearing of these things read aloud will help those who, being too old, are abashed to learn openly by the book, to remember them.[27] Then he goes on at length in the same fashion with the Ten Commandments. An exposition of the seven principal sins, the seven works of mercy, and an extended form of confession complete the round of general moral and devotional material usually printed at the beginning of the traditional Primer.[28]

But in all his treatment of this thoroughly conventional material Whitford is highly immediate and practical. For instance, in his discussion of the First Commandment he takes occasion to inveigh against the popular use of "supersticyous wytchcraftes and charmes." "For good reason," says Whitford, "wyll admyt, that no sore ne sickenes may be heeled, but eyther by nature, or by medicyne, or by myracle." [29] And he proceeds to enforce his interpretations of the precepts of the Decalogue and to bring them home to the experience of the simple by a series of stories in the best manner of the popular medieval preacher, of which stories some of his liveliest concern the contemporary addiction to swearing.[30] But Whitford also anticipates some of his Puritan successors when on the subject of Sunday observance he warns the careful head of the household to keep his charges away from a considerable list of Sunday diversions, some of which will often recur in pious discussions of sports and pastimes in the coming years: "berebayting and bulbaytyng, foteball, tenesplayeng, bowlyng, nor these unlawfull games of cardynge, dycynge, closshynge, with suche other unthryfty pastymes, or rather losetymes." [31]

Whitford's Puritan successors would approve, too, of his concern that no one should miss any possible opportunity for hearing a sermon. For when he goes on to discuss the householder's general plans for the profitable use of Sunday, Whitford particularly insists that wherever the members of the household are diverting themselves, it is important that arrangements be made so that they may be summoned if there should happen to be a sermon for the day.[32]

Whitford had shown a good deal of insight into the actual circumstances of lay life in his time, but one wonders how fully he appreciated contemporary secular notions of recreation when he recommended the reading of this book "or suche other good englysshe bookes" to as large a company as could be gathered together as "a very good sure pastyme upon the holy daye." [33] It is quite apparent that the worthy monk of Syon's notions of what constitutes recreational reading are as remote from the traditions of Merry England as his attitude to the sporting life of his day.

But there is greater realism in the offering of a short compendium or outline of the main events in the life of Christ as the history of the achievement of our redemption. That is brief, to the point, each stage in the process being summed up in a single word, which is repeated again in a brief mnemonic recapitulation at the end of the summary, "Incarnacion, natyvyte, circumcision, epyphany, presentacyon, egypte, disputacyon, humiliacyon, educacyon," etc.[34] Indeed, this "table of remembraunce" is one of the most practical items in all of Whitford's offering for the busy, and doubtless too often distracted, layman.

The same practical spirit is again manifest in the little treatise which Whitford adds to his own work: "A breve or shorte monicyon or counseyle, of the cure and governaunce of a householde, accordyng unto policye, taken out of a pystle of a great lerned man called Bernarde sylvestre, and put amonge the werkes of saynt Bernarde for bycause that many done judge and thynke it was his owne werke." There is much of Whitford's own spirit in this treatise. For instance, "The best way to kepe a woman good: is gentle intreaty and never to let her knowe that she is suspected, and ever to be counseyled and informed with lovynge maner," [35] is one of Bernard's contributions to that always puzzling matter of how the stalwart Christian husband is to keep his frailer half in order. There are signs, too, in Bernard Sylvestre of the coming of the thrifty middle-class world of the future: "Make your byldynges rather for nede than for pleasure," and "Great gay horses, and lytle prety dogges: leve you unto lordes and ladyes." [36] But the voice of the old experience without regard to class or group speaks out of the classic "The most sure waye: to dye well, is well to lyve." And the translation of Bernard's work ends with the closing admonition of the whole book, "Of your charite pray for the same olde wretche of Syon Rycharde Whytforde." [37]

The importance of Whitford's book lies in the author's sympathy with the problems of the average man in family life, with his responsibilities for the behavior of his servants and children, and for the education of his children in the way they should go. The monk of Syon makes a real effort to meet some of these difficulties of the lay and secular Christian life about which the Puritans, especially, were going to have so much to say in the years ahead. As may be seen in what he had to say of the reading of English books to the household and the neighbors, and the provision for the instruction of those who would be discouraged by the labors of book-learning. Whitford had begun to understand the importance of those problems of shifting literacy which were so much to engage the attention of the Protestant reformers. In all this he showed a better grasp of the realities of the contemporary scene than did many of his fellow-defenders of the existing order.

Yet for all his realism, one wonders if Whitford were still not asking a good deal of the layman. Or perhaps it would be nearer to the facts to say that his type of manual with its suggestion of themes and lines of prayer would in any case have had a hard time to hold its own with prayer books like Thomas Becon's which would provide definite formulas of prayer for every occasion and need. Whitford's more informal type of direction with its demands on the reader's own initiative in the actual shaping of his prayers would soon give way to the new prayer books for householders in which the work of formulation would already be done, and the finished product ready for the use of the man who wished to pray heaven. From the point of view of a man trained and accustomed to the devotional life that would, of course, seem a loss, but it is clear that the advantage would be to the new types of books with their clearer appreciation of the realities of human indolence even among the aspiring and the literate.

Moreover, in its large classic lines and its sense of the immemorial patterns of personal and domestic life there is in Whitford's work a feeling of calm stability and basic reality, but there is in it little of that sense of the stir of particular groups and classes in their day-to-day business that one is going to find presently in some of Becon's books, for instance. There is less of that particular gearing to the emergencies of the moment in Whitford than in Becon. And there is less, too, of that sense of being taken into the high affairs of state for the universe at large in the earlier work. It is easy to see how the monk of Syon's book might come presently to seem a little too much of the same old thing to men and women who were being carried along on headier currents of theological and social controversy.

Two Continental contemporaries of Whitford should be mentioned here, Erasmus, who was one of his friends, and Juan Luis Vives. For both the Dutch and the Spanish humanist had intimate personal ties with England, having lived there for varying periods of their lives. And both wrote collections of prayers that enjoyed wide popularity and circulation in England, unlike Whitford's work continuing in influence through the changes of the century. They belonged, too, like Whitford to the early sixteenth-century Catholic reform movement, and like Whitford they had considerable contacts with the great world of their day. Erasmus, as a famous scholar and promoter of learning, had taken a very active part in various aspects of the several movements that led to the outbreak of the Protestant revolt, and he was long counted by the Protestants on their side, even after he had made it clear that he was loath to go as far as they went. Vives was interested in learning, too, but his interests were more in education and social problems. In spite of suspicions in some quarters he seems never to have shown any real disposition to move in the Protestant direction. But his interest in the renewal of spiritual life in the light of contemporary conditions made his work sympathetic to those of the Protestant reformers like John Bradford who were especially concerned with the life of prayer.

In spite of many and great differences in personality and habits of mind, Vives and Erasmus have a good deal in common as devotional writers. To begin with, they are both interested like Whitford in helping the average layman to deepen and enrich his daily devotional life. Both, however, go farther than Whitford in the direction which the English reformers like Becon are going to take, by providing quite specific forms of prayer for daily use. In the composition of those prayers both used traditional breviary and primer materials quite unconsciously, for both were steeped in that literature. At the same time, both had come under the influence of certain devotional currents in the Low Countries.[38] However, he might repudiate his monastic background, Erasmus was a pupil of the Brethren of the Common Life to whom Thomas à Kempis had belonged. And Vives who chose Flanders for his second country had obviously come under their influence as is shown in the delicate realism of his psychological analysis and the warmth of his human sympathy, to say nothing of his gift for stating a traditional idea in terms of the moment.

Of all the works of these prolific writers two especially entered again and again into the devotional literature of sixteenth-century England, the *Preces et Meditationes Diurnae* of Vives, and the *Precationes aliquot* of Erasmus. Both works had promptly found their way into England. The prayers of Erasmus were used in the mid-century primers, especially the primer of 1545, though it is probable that they exercised their widest influence in the more Latinate circles which used the *Preces privatae* of 1564.[39] For in their original form they enjoyed very distinguished patronage. Princess Mary translated the "Prayer for the peace of the church," leaving out a sentence which derived the royal power, under God, from the people, and the prayer "In serious illness" was recited by Thomas Cromwell when he came to his execution.[40]

But for our purposes the story of Vives' prayers is more illuminating. For they early achieved wide popularity in distinctly Protestant circles through the use which the famous Marian martyr, John Bradford, made of them in his work. His *Private Prayers and Meditations, with other Exercises* was not published until after his death, when Copland printed them for the first time in a volume dated March 15, 1559. In many ways Bradford's approach to the devotional problem is not unlike Whitford's. The lines of his devotion are classic, dealing with general matters of the universal and timeless spiritual life. The distinctive preoccupation of his time is to be discerned in the fact that he opens his little volume with a prayer "On the Wrath of God against Sin," the constant and haunting worry of sixteenth-century piety. But the prayer itself is full of quotations and echoes, not only from the Bible but from the Primer as well. In the very first sentence, for instance, there is a key phrase from the *Conditor coeli*. And as the prayer unfolds, one catches echoes of some of Saint Augustine's devotions and meditations as well as an astonishing number of direct allusions to Scripture, all put together with a good deal of organizing skill.[41]

But this scholarly allusiveness is only one side of the story. No less characteristic of this volume of Bradford's is a certain homely practicality, a concern with the perennial housekeeping problems of the individual soul, that is very like Whitford's in its simplicity and directness. This is hardly surprising, for these prayers are sometimes translations, and sometimes adaptations, of the daily prayers of Vives. There is in Vives that same homely intimacy and unpretentious practicality that is so striking a feature of Whitford's approach to the problem of providing the effective instruments of popular devotion. Like Whitford, Vives appreciates the minutiae of daily routine, and their importance for the creation of a prayerful approach to ordinary life. Like Whitford he takes hold of the aspiring, but perhaps not too dependable, Christian when he wakes from sleep in the morning. Like Whitford he suggests themes for reflection and meditation as he begins the day. Indeed, he quite frankly calls his suggestions, compact and incisive, "Occasions to meditate." For instance, after the prayer to be said while the reader is dressing, he goes on to suggest the following reflections on the basic indebtedness of the Christian to Christ: "Call to mind a little how we are incorporate into Christ; again, how he doth clothe us, nourish us under his wings, protection, and providence, preserve us, &c." [42] In the same way the other spiritual landmarks of the daily routine are marked and furnished with appropriate prayers:

When you go forth of the doors . . . When you are going any journey . . . When you are about to receive your meat . . . In the meal-time . . . After your meat . . . Cogitations for about the mid-day time . . . When you come home again . . . At the sun going down . . . When the candles be light . . . When you make yourself unready . . . When you enter into your bed . . . When you feel sleep to be coming.

So Vives develops with further ramifications the analysis of the day which we have already met in Whitford.

Typical, likewise, of the monk of Syon is the technique of suggestion and brief definition of a devotional core as a solution for the problem of teaching the layman to pray. But Vives seems to have been less optimistic as to the capacity of the average man to elaborate his own prayers without more help than a suggested theme and outline. For he gives a complete and relevant prayer to be recited on each occasion: "When you awake out of your sleep . . . So soon as you behold the daylight . . . When you arise . . . When you apparel yourself . . . When you are made ready to begin the day withal——," so it goes, each time with a substantial and fully developed prayer. And this tendency of Vives to make quite specific devotional provision is reënforced by Bradford's own disposition to explain and to amplify. Indeed, Bradford goes so far in "Cogitations meet to begin the day with," as to set before his reader a fully developed meditation, thoroughly explicit and complete, as to the path which the thoughts of the devout man should take as he faces the opportunities of a new day.[43]

In these "cogitations" Bradford takes up the theme of man's own weakness and reliance on God which Vives suggests in his prayer for setting forth for the day and elaborates it with his general review of fallen man's relation to God and the Christian's obligation to "take the most profitable things in hand." The sixteenth-century Protestant leader had high hopes of the possibilities of the ordinary man, but he was clearly not disposed to be over-optimistic about the likelihood of his realizing those capacities unaided, and he was not disposed to leave the business to chance. Moreover, the taste of the sixteenth century in devotion was not so much for the vague and the suggestive as for the explicit and the comprehensive. There is something almost baroque in its love of drawing out its cogitations about the most abstruse and elusive of themes until they stand complete and in the round like a seventeenth-century emblem. By and large it is not disposed to take much for granted. It rather prefers to have the matter canvassed precisely and set forth substantially in detail.

It is characteristic, therefore, that Bradford was not satisfied with Vives' suggestion of a theme for the beginning of the day: "Think first that man consisteth of soul and body, and that the soul is from heaven, heavenly, firm, and immortal; but the body is from the earth, earthly, frail, and mortal." For he at once takes up the burden afresh for himself with an insistence that is characteristic of the time:

Again, think that though by reason of sin, wherein you are conceived and born, the parts of the soul which do understand and desire be so corrupt that, without special grace to both parts, you can neither know nor love any good thing in God's sight, much less then do that is good; yet this notwithstanding think that you are regenerate by Christ's resurrection, (which your baptism requireth you to believe;) and therefore have both those parts something reformed both to know and to love; and therefore to do also some good in the sight of God through Christ, for whose sake our poor doings are accepted for good, the evil and infirmity cleaving thereunto not being imputed through faith.

So Bradford went on to remind the Christian of the happy destiny appointed for him and to urge him to try to live to God's pleasure in the vocation and state of life to which he had been called by God.[44]

The volume is completed by two prayers of Bradford's own of much the same character and technique as the opening prayer, prayers for "Divine Protection," and "A Thanksgiving, being a godly prayer to be read at all times." Both prayers have the same wide-ranging scriptural and liturgical allusiveness already noted; yet both have to an extraordinary degree a logical and emotional integrity of their own, for they are fused in the crucible of Bradford's own moral and spiritual earnestness. They, also, reflect admirably the orientation of their author with regard to the religious issues and interests of his own day. The first sentence of the second prayer sums that up with an extraordinary inclusiveness and representativeness:

Honour and praise be given to thee, O Lord God Almighty, most dear Father of heaven, for all thy mercies and loving-kindness shewed unto us, in that it hath pleased thy gracious goodness, freely and of thine own accord, to elect and choose us to salvation before the beginning of the world: and even like continual thanks be given to thee, for creating of us after thine own image; for redeeming us with the precious blood of thy dear Son, when we were utterly lost; for sanctifying us with thy holy Spirit in the revelation and

knowledge of thy holy word; for helping and succouring us in all our needs
and necessities; for saving us from all dangers of body and soul; for comforting us so fatherly in all our tribulations and persecutions; for sparing us
so long, and giving us so large a time of repentance.[45]

In other words, Bradford does not hesitate to adapt both to his
devotional purposes and to his theological principles the prayers of
Vives. But in doing so he gave currency to Vives' prayers in quarters
which in the normal course of events they would hardly have reached.
And, still, more important, it was an example which, as we shall see
presently, was to be followed with significant results. But, for the
present, the important thing about these books of roughly the first
half of the sixteenth century is that in them well-established traditions of
form and type of prayer book were adapted to other points of view
and developed in the direction of greater explicitness and fullness of
provision for the layman's needs.

But more than that was to come. By and large these early sixteenth-
century prayer books had preserved the generality of spiritual provision
characteristic of the older books. For it had been the basic premise of
the medieval prayer books that the fundamental spiritual needs of all
men are pretty much alike. If one looks at a collection like that of the
Regnault *Hore* of 1527, it is apparent that, by and large, it is occasion
and spiritual circumstance not personal status or identity that deter-
mines the nature of the prayers. They are inspired by regard for general
and unstratified humanity. Of course, it is true that the very circumstances of the origin and spread of the Primer had restricted the sections
of society to whom the editors of such compilations could appeal. But
whatever the ultimate importance of that factor of social limitation, it
remains true that the question of social reference hardly arose in the old
books of private devotion.

But it did arise in the mid-century prayer books, interestingly enough
in some of the collections of prayers that most abundantly preserved
the traditional materials. This is demonstrated especially in the work
of the man who after Bradford may be regarded as the most important
and influential, to say nothing of prolific, of the devotional writers of
the time. He is said to have written more than forty books on religious
subjects in the years between 1541 and 1566. The first of his devotional
works, *The Pathwai unto Prayer,* appeared in 1542, and a fragment of
a copy of *The Flower of Godly Prayers* survives from 1551. But the

first of his books to achieve a wide popularity, *The Pomander of Prayer,* did not appear until 1558. By 1578 that book had run through at least five editions. But the most popular of all was *The Sycke Mans Salve,* which, first published in 1561, had run through ten editions before the end of the century. By 1632 the total number had risen to seventeen. Obviously, these were among the most popular of sixteenth-century devotional books.

We shall presently have occasion to examine Becon's *Pomander of Prayer* in some detail when we come to the general prayer books which carry on in a modified form the Primer tradition. For the present study of more specialized types of devotional provision for the layman the most interesting element in this remarkably extensive collection of prayers is a very considerable group pretty close to the beginning of the book. In this Becon provides prayers to be said by the magistrates, the ministers of God's word, subjects or commons, fathers and mothers, children, masters, servants, maids, single men, husbands, wives, women with child, householders, and, finally, all Christians.[46] In other words all the different orders of society are provided with prayers for their special functions and needs.

But this innovation, striking as it is in so highly traditional a book as the *Pomander of Prayer* is but the beginning of a development of socially specific prayers which Becon was to carry to its full-blown perfection in a later work, *The Flower of Godly Prayers.* The very title page of this book suggests the growing consciousness of social degree in religious life; for the work is offered as "very necessarye to be used of the faythfull Chrystians in these our dayes for the safegarde, health and comfort of all degrees and estates." [47] The dedication of the work to the Lady Anne, Duchess of Somerset, is conventional enough and means little, for Becon had been chaplain to the Duke of Somerset about 1549.[48] But in the provision of prayers for special classes of men, there is abundant evidence of a practical and constant awareness of the various classes of men that make up an active society. In the list of the groups of men for whom these prayers are designed, one finds what is substantially Becon's chart of the social structure of his day. He begins at the top with the King, and from him moves down the social hierarchy with the usual wavering of the Elizabethan catalogue, to the King's council, the judges, all magistrates, bishops and ministers of God's word, gentlemen, landlords, merchants, lawyers, "laborers and men of occupacions," rich men, poor people, the commons, the unmarried, the married, women with child (with an appropriate thanksgiving for safe delivery), fathers and mothers, children, masters and servants, the sick, soldiers, mariners, travellers by land, and then he switches from the specific to the general with a prayer for "a faythfull man beyng in trouble or enduraunce," a "thanksgevyng to God for hys delyveraunce," and, a fitting conclusion to what is substantially a grand division of the volume, "A general prayer that al Men may walke in theyr vocacion and callyng." [49] This stress on the calling is certainly the most distinctive note of this work. But it should be noted that there is in this volume as a whole more stress on the social aspects of religion than in the *Pomander*. It is evidenced by the inclusion, right after the above, of such comprehensive prayers as that "for the adversaries of gods truth, and that all men mai come to the true knowledge of gods blessed worde," and a "praier for one uniforme and perfect agrement in matters of Chrysten religion." [50]

The orientation of Becon's work is, as the above suggests, clearly middle-class, as was the orientation of most of the books of this type. But there were, of course, exceptions to this middle-class approach. One of the most interesting of these is a little book which William Seres published in 1574, *A Tablet for Gentlewomen*. In external form it is a distinctly miniature performance, obviously designed to be kept in a capacious Elizabethan pocket or to be dangled with the keys and other housewifely appurtenances from an elegant girdle. The main lines of this guide for the feminine half of the world are classic, as indicated in the opening of "A prayer for Maydes": "There is nothing that becommeth a maid better than silence." [51] One wonders a little what the high-spirited ladies who inspired Shakespeare's Rosalind thought as they prayed that prayer!

But the provision of help for householders still continued to be the most popular of these special devotional books throughout the sixteenth century. One of the most notable of the later writers who exploited the type was Edward Dering. The first of his offerings for the householder was a catechism, *A Brief and Necessary Instruction,* first published in 1572, a book which ran through four editions between that time and 1606. His second effort was *Godly Private Praiers for Householders to Meditate Upon, and to say in their Families,* published in 1576, and this was even more successful, running through half a dozen editions by 1624. But in 1582 he apparently decided to combine these two popular approaches to the problem, for in that year, he published *A Shorte Catechisme for Housholders, with Prayers to the same adjoyning,* and this ran through some fourteen editions by 1631.

As in most of the collections which we have been studying, the prayers which Dering provides are for general spiritual needs, prayers before and after meals, prayers for constant perseverance, prayers for morning and evening, for mortification, after the sacrament, for patience, and so on.[52] But there is a touch of originality and of first-hand immediacy in Dering. It is suggested in the titles of prayers like "A thanksgiving when one hath received some comfort, but not fully delivered," and "A prayer against the secret venim, and great danger of prosperitie." [53] But it is revealed most fully in "A prayer for constant Perseverance," in a passage of honest puzzlement and even wonder, that seems to come straight from the heart:

> O Lord God, most merciful, kind, and loving Father, according to thy commaundement, in my afflictions and necessities, I seeke unto thee for succour by continuall prayer, and calling upon thy holy Name, I call upon thee in the day time, and in the night season doe I poure out prayers unto thee, and yet for all that I feele mee nothing released, but oftentimes worse and worse, which maketh me oftentimes deere Father, almost to doubt of thy goodnesse, that thou doost reject my prayers, and givest no heed unto them, whereby I doe almost think, that it is no booke for mee to pray, seeing I feele no release, but (O Lorde) this is my weaknesse in mee, and the frailtie of my flesh, which wil not willingly be subdued unto the Spirit: which my frailtie, I beseech thee, O lord forgive mee. For thou doost, O Lord God, see my conflicts, and lookest upon my continuall sighes and peticions, but thou doost defer and prolong thine helpe the longer: and doost not at the first helpe mee, to this end, that I may se fully mine owne weaknesse, learne by little and little to subdue my rebellious will, to thy good will, who knoweth better what is meet for me then I my selfe.[54]

There is in such a prayer a candor, a directness, and an independence of spirit that is eminently characteristic of the man who in his famous sermon of 1569 did not hesitate to defy Queen Elizabeth herself when conviction demanded.[55]

But by and large that is not the usual tone and temper of these collections of prayers. And that for obvious reasons. Their purpose is not to give the writer a chance for Donne-like expression of his own inner struggles but a more pedagogical one, to give help and guidance to those laymen, ordinary citizens, as it were, who are looking to the

preacher for guidance, or for whom the preacher is volunteering direction as to what they should be wanting to do. For the problem of the
spiritual guidance of the devout and aspiring layman did not become
any simpler as the conscience-troubled and controversy-tossed sixteenth
century drew to its far from quiet close. However secure his official
position, the religious leader and adviser was often hard put to it to
keep the attention of his wavering and distracted and indifferent
charges on the central spiritual business of translating precept and principle into attitude and behavior, that the professed Christian might
in thought and feeling and action be, indeed, a Christian. It is not surprising, therefore, that the English devotional writer continued to be
on the alert for any reënforcement he might turn to his purpose.

Even when the lines between Catholic and Protestant had been
clearly drawn, and the controversial battle joined on scores of issues,
English devotional writers still went on translating and adapting Continental works of devotion from Catholic as well as Protestant sources.
Perhaps the most striking example of this continuing use of Continental
devotional literature is to be found in the history of one of the most
popular guides for the Christian life published in the second half of
the sixteenth century, the famous *Booke of Christian Exercise, appertaining to Resolution*. The book was in the beginning the work of an
Italian Jesuit, Gaspare Loarte, and in its original form it was very
much the sort of thing which we have been studying, devotional
materials so organized and arranged as to provide suitable meditations
and prayers for every day in the week, and devotional aid for all the
pious needs of the average Christian. It was not only popular on the
Continent, but it was translated into English, an "improved" version
by James Sancer being published in Paris in 1579.

Its history for us begins when Robert Parsons, the famous Jesuit
missionary and controversialist, came across it. To judge from the
preface he prefixed to his version of 1585, Parsons had been exercised
over the religious indifference and even scepticism that was growing out
of the confusion of controversy besetting the English layman on every
side in those years. In this concern of his he was anticipating by only a
few years the very widespread anxiety over the devastating effects of
too much religious controversy from the spiritual and devotional point
of view that was to be so striking a feature of English devotional writing
at the opening of the next century.[56] It seemed to him that here in

Loarte's book was a possible remedy. So he took it for his foundation, and with the free hand of the sixteenth-century editor he proceeded to make it over to his purpose, eventually expanding the original work to between three and four times its size with not only devotional but theological and ethical materials that would afford the confused and perhaps wavering Christian the instruction he needed, ranging from assurance as to the existence of God and the proofs of the Christian religion to help with the more intimately psychological problems of despair of God's mercy and fear of persecution. The result was a very impressive compendium of Christian doctrine and ethics as well as a guide to the Christian life.

The first edition of this expanded *Booke of Christian Exercise* was published by Parsons in 1582 somewhere abroad, probably at Rouen. It very speedily found its way into England where it came into the hands of a zealous minister of the Church of England, who doubtless had been encountering in his more secure ministry some of the psychological phenomena that had been worrying Parsons and his colleagues on the English Mission. At any rate, Edmund Bunny undertook to make the book available to his flock with a series of changes that outraged Parsons when he saw them, but which were the standard procedure of sixteenth-century editors engaged in such a pious undertaking. Bunny was quite frank as to his editorial techniques of omission of certain, from his point of view, unassimilable ideas, substitution of harmless, or what he considered doctrinally correct, expressions for objectionable terms in the original, correction of certain, again from his point of view, glaring errors, and so on.[57] The story of the resulting controversy between Bunny and Parsons over the result of these labors is an entertaining one, and for the student of the controversies of the time, an instructive one,[58] but it lies outside our immediate business. The point is that this Anglican adaptation of the Jesuit's guide to the devout life enjoyed wide favor in Protestant circles in England and continued to exert an influence well into the next century. Indeed, Richard Baxter, the great Presbyterian leader and devotional writer of the Civil War period was to attribute his conversion to the reading of an old torn copy of what was popularly known as *Bunny's Resolution*.[59]

This remarkably enduring popularity of the guides for the devout layman was on the whole, well deserved. It was not the eloquence with which they expressed their own spiritual experience that enabled the authors of these books for the average man to win such a wide and appreciative audience in the latter years of the sixteenth century. It was the shrewdness with which they appraised the devotional interests and needs of their potential readers, and the informed resourcefulness and alert practicality with which they met them. And, not least, it was the instinctive sense with which they tempered their faith in their readers' spiritual potentialities with a working awareness of the limitations of their present capacities.

XI

THE GENERAL PRAYER BOOKS

GREAT as was the success of the more specialized prayer books, the Primer-like collections of prayers still held their own. True, the name "Primer" went out of use as a title for such books, as was to be expected in view of its association with the rejected and outlawed books of the ancient order. But the collections of prayers for various occasions and for various needs that had sprouted so steadily and finally so lushly between its covers continued under various names. And, particularly in the early years, they appeared under very distinguished auspices. For the reformers had soon discovered that successful as they had been in the very complex business of destroying the ancient religious order and establishing a regime that assured them support, ranging from conformity to conviction, for the theological positions they advocated, they still faced the basic problem of all religious leaders: that of imparting inner meaning and actuality to profession in the private day-to-day devotional life of the individual soul.

In the nature of things, that was a problem much harder of solution. For difficult as it is to establish a desired position in a period of religious conflict, it is still more difficult to make sure that those who accept that position adhere to it in practice, to say nothing of making the most of its moral and spiritual possibilities. It is in this realm, therefore, that the religious reformer, whether he is instituting a new system or renewing an existing order, meets his most exacting challenge. For now he is not trying to persuade the average human being to consent to a change of ideas, difficult as that is, but to do something even more repugnant to human inertia, namely to change himself. For that is the indispensable prerequisite to the life of prayer. If it is easy for public devotion to become formal and conventional, it is still easier for the private devotion of unaroused average humanity to remain routine and perfunctory and sterile.

Every movement of religious change in every age has run into this fact; and the movements of the sixteenth century were no exception. For the life of prayer, like any other way of life, presents those problems of time and place which must be solved if the humblest of intentions is to be realized in sustained endeavor. For all its faith in the possibilities of the human spirit, it was not the habit of the sixteenth century to leave their realization to chance. In fact, there seems to have been something of a special effort to inculcate an appreciation of private, personal prayer in some of the prayer books and books on prayer that appeared in and about the middle of the century. Particularly revealing is the dedication of Becon's *The Pathwai unto Prayer,* which was first published in London in 1542. In this Becon complains with characteristic vigor of the neglect of private prayer:

We can not excuse our self by ignorancy, in asmuch as we have plenty of prayers prepared for us in the Englishe tonge both in the holy Bible, and in other godly treatises, which are now in this moost florishyng Realme of Englande published universally unto the great glory of God, and the exceadynge consolacion of all true Christen men . . . . I have therfore in this my treatise folowing declared what praier is, wherfore it serveth, and unto what ende we shoulde use it . . . . And for, asmuch as som men ar of so scrupulous, I had almost said, supersticious conscience, that they thinke no prayer to be hard, but that onely whiche is praied in the chirche or some other sacred place, as they call it, I have declared both by Scriptures and auncient Doctoures in what place it is lawfull to praye.[1]

It was certainly not the way of Becon to understate the shortcomings of his age at any point at which he had quarrel with it, nor was it to be expected that such a very accomplished purveyor of popular religious literature would underestimate any spiritual need which he was prepared to supply. But one on reading Becon's words is reminded of those complaints of the way devotion has been sacrificed to controversy that are to be such a common prelude to devotional books at the turn of the century, and that were to constitute the stock prelude to devotional writing through the first half of the seventeenth century.

Nor was he the only reformer of those middle years to be concerned about the neglect of private prayer in that century in which so much attention had gone to the controversies on public prayer. Something over a dozen years after the publication of Becon's complaint, John

Bradford translated a treatise on prayer by Philip Melanchthon and published it in London, apparently in 1556–57. Bradford's preface to this work exhibits something of the same downright temper and determination to get down to fundamentals that is so striking in Becon's approach to the teaching of the techniques of prayer; for he commends Melanchthon's treatise to the prospective reader in these terms:

It teacheth thee what GOD thou shouldeste call upon, it teacheth thee wherefore he heareth thee, it teacheth thee wherefore thou shouldeste call upon him: it teacheth thee what thinges thou shalte aske, and in what order, it teacheth thee howe to honoure the Saynctes, and what is theyr worshyppe, it teacheth thee to be thankefull yf thou wylte reade it, waye it, carye it awaye, and practyse that which it teacheth.[2]

This treatise thus prefaced is controversial enough, but it also gives expression to a real and at times even eloquent appreciation of prayer as in the following key sentence: "Prayer oughte to be made in spyryte, that is to saye, not in hypocrisye, not in the multitude of woordes, and bablinge, but in the godly affections of the heart." [3] As we shall see presently, Melanchthon's translator, Bradford, also was to do his share of fulfilling these devotional needs.

An early, and in many ways rudimentary effort, to make general provision for the life of prayer is to be seen in a work which we have already had occasion to refer to for its incidental use of the Psalms, and that is the collection of prayers known as *The Queenes Praiers*, first published in 1545 by Thomas Berthelet as *Queen Catharine's Prayers* (Catharine Parr's) and reprinted at London by H. Wykes in 1568, as *The Queenes Praiers or Meditations* with the added description: "wherein the mynde is stirred to suffer all afflictions here." At first sight, this collection seems a rather miscellaneous one, for it consists of a scarcely organized series of sentences or paragraphs of petition. But as one goes through the series, he soon finds certain recurring themes emerging and imparting a kind of unity to otherwise heterogeneous elements. For instance, the opening theme of prayer for grace to embrace the will of God is pursued through a good many component petitions until it issues finally in a prayer for what may be described as spiritual courage. That in turn leads to a prayer for the contentment of humility, and that to a prayer for strength to throw off all worldly liens that might entangle the aspiring spirit, and so on.[4] In this fashion, out of a process which at first sight seems to be nothing more than one thought or impulse borrowing another, presently emerges something like an order of logical progression.

As for the contents of these prayers, not only the Psalms but the prayers of the Primer are here used with a good deal of freedom as the stuff out of which the devotional writer constructs his supplications. The opening prayers are directed to the Son rather than the Father. The beginning of the first of these prayers is typical both in form and spirit:

Moste benyng Lorde Jesu, graunte me thy grace, that it maie alwaie woorke in me, and persevere with me unto thende.

Graunte me, that I maie ever desire and will that, whiche is most pleasaunte, and moste acceptable to thee.

Thy will bee my will, and my will be to folowe alwaie thy will.

Or take a paragraph from the middle of the same prayer:

O Jesu, king of everlaking glorie, the joye and comforte of all Christian people, that are wandring as pilgrimes, in the wildernesse of this world my harte crieth to thee by still desires, and my silence speaketh unto thee, and saieth: how long tarieth my Lorde God to come to me.[5]

The very address to Jesu, the stress on the graciousness of Christ, the theme of conformity of the worshiper's will to the will of God, these are elements that recall the Jesu prayers of the primers, especially such prayers as those of the *Fifteen Oes* with their stress on the tenderer aspects of Christ's personality, and their emphasis, by and large, not so much on the more aggressive and militant aspects of the life of the spirit as on resignation and submission. The language, in its very simplicity, its intimate, even colloquial quality as compared with the more firmly stylized diction of the psalm-derived prayers, is striking evidence of a quite different provenience.

Nothing could be in sharper contrast to the somewhat amorphous character of the *Queenes Praiers* than the always clear-cut and consciously directed work of Thomas Becon. Becon was easily one of the most prolific of sixteenth-century writers on religious themes, and one of the most indefatigable collectors of other men's prayers and devotions. While *The Sycke Mannes Salve,* a specialized book for the ill and dying, was unquestionably his most popular publication, probably his most influential was the *Pomander of Prayer.* As we have seen, a book by that name appeared as early as 1530. That book has sometimes been attributed to Becon, but it is quite impossible to believe that a youth under twenty (Becon was born in 1511 or 1512) would have been able to produce so seasoned and mature a work, or would have wanted to write a book of a type already distinctly old-fashioned by 1530. As for Becon's *Pomander of Prayer,* there is no evidence of any publication of that book before 1558.

That publication in itself is interesting enough. At the time, the author was on the Continent, where he had taken refuge, and where he made a great name for himself as a preacher and a writer for the Protestant exiles. That did not, however, prevent the appearance of a quite Catholic book complete with the *Fifteen Oes.* This work was republished soon after by John Day, probably in 1560, without the *Fifteen Oes,* but it was still to a striking degree a traditional book.

This edition opens in the classic fashion with prayers for morning and evening, a prayer for the forgiveness of sins, and a group of three prayers, one to each of the three persons of the Trinity.[6] This is all standard material. Indeed, that is true of the major proportion of the contents. There is, for instance, a long series of prayers for specific spiritual needs regardless of social place or function, such as prayers for the grace and favor of God, for the gift of the Holy Ghost, "for the true knowledge of ourselves," "for a pure and cleane hart," "for a quiet conscience," for faith, and for charity.[7] Two of this series would seem perhaps to strain the general classification of "spiritual" unduly, unless one remembers the close connection between fortune and desert often taken for granted at this time. They are the petitions for a good name and for "a competent living," [8] both on familiar themes of the Primer but, as we shall see presently, quite different from the traditional prayers. Then comes a series of more specific prayers, this time for souls in particular situations or predicaments, called "Meditations for the soule." But again the situations involved are independent of rank or place in society, such as these: "The godly beeing troubled by the wicked, complayneth unto God," "The godly beeing thus greeved, desireth God to be delivered," "That God would dismay their enemies, by his promises," [9] this a rather embattled-sounding series, reminiscent of some of the introductions to the devotions from the Psalms. But these give way presently to more peaceful thanksgivings,[10] and the traditional character of the book is quite explicitly resumed with the classic *Conditor coeli et terrae,* as we have seen, one of the most enduringly popular of all the prayers of the Primer. Of a traditional type, too, as far as theme is concerned, though often enough of fresh content, are the prayers that follow, such as prayers for the dying, the litany and suffrages, the general collects, etc.[11]

As suggested above, the contents of the *Pomander of Prayer* vary from edition to edition. For instance, the edition which John Day published in 1561, adds to the core of the book described above, a group of meditations. This time, however, they are not by Hierom of Ferrara but by the most popular of all sixteenth-century devotional survivals, Saint Augustine, or to be more precise, Saint Augustine including the various works ascribed to him. The selection is significant, meditations in the form of prayers on the commemoration of Christ's Passion, with stress on the relation of that passion to man's sin.[12] Then there are more prayers, to the Holy Ghost, to the Trinity, "An acknowledgyng of almightie God and his Majesty," "After what sorte God the Father vouchedsafe to helpe mankinde, and of the incarnation of the Ward, whiche is Christe, and of the geving of thankes," "of the trust whiche a soule ought to have in our Lorde Jesu and in his Passion," and so on.[13] It is, in short, a fairly comprehensive, even if brief, survey of the fundamental Christian teachings on the redemption of man.

But even without these meditations, the *Pomander of Prayer* in itself presents a remarkable variety of prayers for almost every human occasion. And that very variety of prayers crammed into so brief a compass points to what is one of the most traditional characteristics of this collection, and that is the brevity of the individual prayer. By and large, the sixteenth-century prayer designed for popular use is usually more extended than the medieval prayer for the same public. If one looks through the hundreds of individual prayers in a collection like that of the Regnault *Hore* of 1527, he is at once struck by the fact that, though often enough the prayers are organized into a rather extensive and elaborate cursus, the individual prayer is fairly short. There are, of course, exceptions, but they are relatively few.

The typical late medieval prayer for the layman is a prose lyric with one central idea or theme focusing and giving force to the jet of feeling that inspired its creation. By and large, the sixteenth-century prayer is more of a short essay, with a much more elaborate and involved development of the theme. That is not surprising in view of the fact that so many of the sixteenth-century writers felt it necessary to steer the mind as well as the heart of the devout into what they considered the direction they should go.

But there is another reason for this difference, and that is that very often the sixteenth-century prayer performed the function of a meditation as well as of a prayer. This is particularly clear in the titles of some of the prayers named above. They represent a very careful analysis of the significance of some theme of sixteenth-century reflection with a very careful, even if brief, development of its implications as discovered in such detailed reflection upon it. Indeed, in some cases, one can discern in the sequence of certain prayers a marking of the stages in the elaboration of one fundamental consideration. Sometimes the analysis seems rather to break down, but the break is more a matter of form than of substance in the development of the theme of the complete devotional life. And it should never be forgotten that a cavalier disregard of straight-ahead development and consistency of classification is a very frequent characteristic of the Elizabethan catalogue.

In this sense this collection moves out of the old medieval pattern. But the number of old prayers or adaptations of old prayers is so large that they impart to the book as a whole a remarkable impression of continuity. Becon was thoroughly alert to the needs of his day from the point of view of the reform, to which he was devoted. It is significant that it was to the traditional materials of the Primer that he went so largely for the devotions that would satisfy those needs.

One is at once struck by something of the same traditional character in a very different type of book by one of Becon's most distinguished contemporaries in this field of popular devotional writing, John Bradford. We have already seen something of Bradford's devotional work in our consideration of the guides to the devout life, especially his *Private Prayers and Meditations, with Other Exercises,* which William Copland first printed after his death in 1559. But that was not the only aspect of Bradford's devotional effort that was to be appreciated by his successors. His meditations were to play no less a part in his contributions to other men's collections of prayers later in the century.

Especially popular was his *Godly Meditations on the Lord's Prayer, Belief, and Ten Commandments, with Other Exercises,* first printed by Rouland Hall in London, again after the author's death, in 1562. A facet of the situation, not always appreciated by the modern student, is suggested by the preface to the reader which Thomas Lever contributed to the 1567 edition of this work:

> And for that everie man can not have all scriptures, and no man ought to be without the ten commaundementes, the articles of the beliefe, and the Lordes prayer, to meditate in hys minde: therfore the meditation of them shoulde be in such sorte, as we might best finde and feele the sicknes and daunger of our sinne, by the commaundements: then see the remedie and salve for sinne, which is the goodnes of God confessed in the articles of the beliefe: and so, as followeth in the Lords prayer, use the maner and forme of desiring and joyning the medicine and salve of Gods mercifull goodnes, unto the sicknes and sores of mans sinful wretchednes.[14]

In other words, the free circulation of the Scriptures in English had not even by that date so covered the ground as to make entirely obsolete the old elementary instruction in the Christian fundamentals that was the familiar opening of the Primer.

As we have seen, the meditation on the Lord's Prayer, in particular, was a favorite undertaking with the old devotional writers. Whitford gave what was substantially an outline of such a meditation in his *A Werke for Housholders*.[15] But Bradford's meditation differs from Whitford's in its extensiveness and its comprehensiveness. It supplies its reader with a brief survey of the creation and the redemption and a guide to the Christian life, all in one.[16] It is the mid-century reformer at his most instructive, and not far from his most exhaustive; yet the whole thing is alive with the vigor and color characteristic of Bradford.

But there is, of course, a good deal more to Bradford's work even in this particular volume. For these elementary meditations are followed by a number of others on a variety of themes, for instance, on prayer, on the coming of Christ to judgment and the reward and punishment to follow, on the pleasures of this life, on the presence of God, on the passion of Christ, to name just a few.[17] And Bradford can write very finely on these high themes, as witness the opening of the "Meditation concerning Prayer": "The mind of man hath so large room to receive good things, that nothing indeed can fully fill it but only God." [18]

In the prayer books of the sixteenth century, meditation and prayer were pretty much intermixed, and sometimes even confused, as we shall see presently in the Bull-Middleton and the Day prayer books. But characteristically Bradford preserved the distinction between meditation and prayer, although he usually opened a meditation with something in the nature of a petition, and closed it with a definite prayer for the keeping in mind or the application of the lesson to be extracted from the meditation. And, equally characteristically, Bradford here as in his prayers did not hesitate to take the work of an author like Vives and adapt it to his purposes. His general method may be well illustrated by his "Meditation of the Blessed State and Felicity of the Life to Come." The key idea of this meditation is to be found in a prayer of Vives, *Pro desiderio alterius vitae,* which in a somewhat condensed form found its way into a very conspicuous position in the primer of 1545 as the closing prayer of the series at the end of the volume under the title, "For the desire of the life to come." [19] It is also found in a fuller form near the end of the Day *Christian Prayers* of 1578.[20]

Like the version of the primer of 1545, Bradford opens with what is really the middle of Vives' prayer, translated in the 1578 version of the *Christian Prayers* as follows:

This body of mine is but a prison to my soul; yea, and that a most dark and loathsome one. This world is but a banishment, and this life but sorrow and wretchedness. But where as thou art, there is our home, our freedom, and our endless bliss.[21]

The first two sentences of this passage give the theme for the first paragraph of Bradford's meditation:

This body is but a prison, wherein the soul is kept; and that verily not beautiful nor bright, but most foul and dark, disquiet, frail, and filled up with much vermin and venemous vipers (I mean it concerning our affections), standing in an air most unwholesome, and prospect most loathsome, if a man consider the excrements of it by the eyes, nose, mouth, ears, hands, feet, and all the other parts: so that no Bocardo, no little-ease, no dungeon, no bishop's prison, no gatehouse, no sink, no pit, may be compared in any point to be so evil a prison for the body, as the body is for and of the soul; wherethrough the children of God have been occasioned to cry and lament their long being in it. "O," saith David, "how long shall I lie in this prison?" "O wretch that I am!" saith Paul, "who shall deliver me out of this body of sin?" which is "an heavy burden to the soul," as the wise man saith. And therefore the godly cry, "Now let thy servant depart in peace." O that I were dissolved, and had put off this earthly and frail tabernacle! Take me unto thee, and "bring my soul out of this prison, that it may give thanks unto thee," O Lord! For so long as we be in this body, we cannot see the Lord: yea, it is as an heavy habitation, and depresseth down sore the spirit from the familiarity which else it should have with God.[22]

So this runs for between a quarter and a third of its extent, enough to give a notion of the technique. The prayer of Vives furnishes the outline of the theme, and then Bradford fills in this outline in two ways. The first is the citation of apposite passages from Scripture, to reënforce with the authority of Old and New Testament notables the basic idea. The second is the addition of homely and practical detail that gives descriptive body to the main concept. The result is distinctive and characteristic of the period. There is an atmosphere of scriptural majesty and eternal consequence that invests the individual effort with great and urgent significance, and yet the classic meanings are spelled out in the most familiar terms of the immediate environment and the immediate situation. That, I think, is the secret of the great magnetism which the writings of Bradford and men like him exerted on so many of the earnest and aspiring minds of their generation. It is, also, the secret of the personal impress which Bradford like Becon was able to make on his fairly far-ranging borrowings.

It is that personal accent which one misses in what are probably the most influential of the devotional collections of the middle decades of the century. There is, rather, a return of the classic Primer impersonality in the collection of *Christian Praiers and Holi Meditations, as well for Private as Publique exercise* which Henry Bull made and the printer Middleton first printed in 1566. It is a more extensive collection even than that of Becon, and in many ways more comprehensive. It begins very much in the fashion of Bradford and Vives, but in a manner more self-conscious and deliberate than either, for it opens with a formal "Introduction to Prayer," [23] with a stress on the helplessness of man and the mercy of God that is characteristic of the thinking and feeling of these years in which so much attention was given to the doctrine of justification by faith. This is followed by a meditation concerning prayer, of a rather more practical devotional character,[24] taken, in fact, from John Bradford, as so many of the materials of this book are presently discovered to be. The choice of these two little essays to introduce the collection, as it were, suggests that its compiler is a careful and systematic scholar, who approaches his field in a spirit not only hortatory and pastoral but also philosophic, with a serious interest in the theory as well as the practice of the art with which he deals. This impression is confirmed by the extended meditation upon the Lord's

Prayer which follows, again from the pen of John Bradford, indeed, the same composition which we have already noted.

Then, when the prospective reader is properly prepared for the use of the ensuing book, Bull plunges into the scheme for the day's devotion with which we are now already well acquainted from the work of Whitford, Vives, Becon, and Bradford. There are the usual prayers for the morning, for going on a journey, and rather more than the usual variety of prayers for meals. There are, also, prayers for midday, indeed for all the various stages of the day, especially that crucial period from sunset to sleep.[25] In his main title Bull disclaims any pretense at originality. So one is not surprised to recognize in these occasional prayers the old prayers of Vives translated by Bradford. Even those elaborations on Vives which Bradford made in some of the accompanying meditations are retained.[26]

Indeed, the core of the book is made up for the most part of prayers from Bradford, with just the initials I. B. after them.[27] These are of the prayer-meditation type of which Bradford composed so many, such as "A meditation of the comming of Christ to judgement, and of the reward both of the faithfull and unfaithfull," "A meditation of the life everlasting, the place where it is, and the incomparable joyes thereof," "A meditation of the presence of God," "A meditation concerning the sober usage of the bodie, that it may be subject and obedient to the soule," "A meditation upon the passion of our Saviour Jesus Christ," etc.[28]

But these prayers from Bradford do not proceed without interruption. Interspersed among them are a number of non-Bradford prayers without any indication of their authorship and provenience. These include general confessions, more petitions for morning and evening, prayers for the remission of sins, and "for the true knowledge of the mysterie of our redemption in Christ," thanksgiving prayers, prayers on mortification, etc.[29] These are all traditional types of prayers, very much on the classic Primer order. Some meditation-type prayers that follow these are more of the sort of thing Bradford specialized in, but they are not ascribed to him: "A meditation upon the passion of our Saviour Jesus Christ," and another beginning dramatically, "Thou Lord didest put away Marie Magdalen from the kissing of they feete."[30]

Then Bull returns to Bradford for such prayers as "for the true sense and feeling of Gods favour and mercie in Christe" and "A prayer of the afflicted for the profession of Gods worde." [31] But, again, with the curious oscillation that characterizes the book, more non-Bradford prayers are scattered among them, prayers to help in temptation, prayers for those in affliction, prayers to the Trinity, and before and after Communion, and prayers for the sick and the dying, and so forth.[32] Most of these prayers if not from the Primer are at least in the Primer tradition.

Then, just as at the beginning of the book Bull took over bodily Bradford's version of Vives, so toward the end of the book in the third edition, that of 1578, he reprinted a group of prayers which he described as "Prayers, commonly called Lydley's Prayers," followed by what he calls, "certaine godly additions." [33] These are very substantial and, as compared with either Vives' or Becon's prayers, very extensive prayers, mainly of confession of the sinner's unworthiness and of petition for forgiveness and for grace to lead a new life. As so often happens in this period, the titles are significant of the range of intellectual and spiritual content, such as "A confession of sinnes and a prayer for the remission thereof," and "A prayer for the leading of a godly life." [34]

These prayers abound in scriptural echoes, especially the first prayer in the series, an untitled confession, of which the theme and spirit are clearly indicated in the opening sentence: "O Almightie and moste mercifull father, I thy poor creature and worke of thy handes, acknowledg and confesse unto thee my manifoulde sinnes and offences." [35] Another prayer, "for deliverance from sin, and to be restored to God's grace and favour again," bears the familiar signature "I. B.," John Bradford.[36] And still another is a somewhat modified version of the famous prayer of the primers, "O Bountiful Lord Jesu!" [37] of which we shall have occasion to say more presently.

As for the rest of the volume, the litany and the suffrages, the latter to the number of fifteen,[38] constitute a substantial portion. And appropriately, in view of the general pedagogical purpose of the editor, the book ends with John Bradford's "A Godly Instruction, conteining the summe of all the divinitie necessarie for a Christian conscience." [39]

In general, then, these prayers are of the universal type. They are prayers for the continuing needs of the human spirit with emphasis, of course, on those themes that most engaged the interest of the time. Since so large a proportion of the materials of this book was caught up into the Day prayer books, it will be best to defer the consideration of the history of those prayers which came from the Primer until we have taken account of what may for this century be regarded as the culminating example of the transformation of traditional materials. For the present, it is enough simply to stress the extraordinarily rich character of this Bull-Middleton collection, and the breadth of its representation of the devotional materials of the time, including, as it does, traditional material, almost contemporary Catholic material as passed through translation, like Bradford's version of the prayers of Vives, and of course, contemporary materials from some of the Protestant reformers.

There was no question of the public response to a book of so traditional a character. It is attested by the number of editions through which it ran in the years that followed, of which at least half a dozen still survive. This success must have emboldened the publisher, Middleton, to try an even more traditional book some eight years later in 1574. This time no editor was named for a work bearing the title reminiscent of the *Hortulus animae,* "A godly Garden out of the which most comfortable herbs may be gathered for the health of the wounded conscience of all penitent sinners." The opening with the full calendar, including Thomas Becket for November twenty-eighth,[40] is significant of the unknown editor's approach.

As in the earlier Bull-Middleton book, the devotional contents are prefaced with a formal account of prayer, of which the tone may be judged by the following pithy yet elevated definition: "There is no man but hee knoweth that praer is the chiefest thing that we maye present God withall, for it is the head fountaine, the spring of all goodnes, and a meane to attaine eternall life." [41] Then after a confession to be recited before morning prayer and the Our Father, followed by a little rhymed prayer on the same theme, come a series of morning prayers in what has come to be the established fashion of this type of book.[42]

But it is the content of these morning prayers that is significant for the rather mixed character of the first part of the book. The first one begins in the traditional fashion of matins, "O Lord open thou my lippes, that my mouth may speak and shewe forth, that which is to thy glorie and prayse," etc. And this familiar opening is followed by a group of psalms in matins fashion, ending with the traditional "Glory be," [43] but the psalms are quite different from those usually found in the matins of the Little Office. And pretty much the same is true of the Evening Prayer which begins, "Convert us (God our Saviour) and turne thy wrath awaye from us," in the traditional fashion, but soon take a very different course.[44] Of the same mixed character are the prayers that follow the morning prayers on various Primer themes and patterns, including the reformed litany and its accompanying prayers.[45]

But the most interesting section of this book is that headed, "Garden," with a prefatory note on "The right use of this Garden." [46] Among other devotional provisions this affords prayers for every morning in the week, very much in the fashion of the Marian primer of 1555. Indeed, many of the prayers are the same, for they are either traditional prayers or more recent compositions in the traditional style. For example, the Sunday morning prayer, "I render unto thee (O heavenly Father) most harty thanks by thy deare Sonne Jesus Christ, that this night thou hast vouchsaved of thy Fatherly goodnes to preserve me from all evil, and to give my body rest and slepe," shows obvious indebtedness to a traditional prayer found in the Jehannot *Horae* of 1498 and the Regnault *Hore* of 1527: [47] "Piissime deus et clementissime pater laudes et gratias ago tibi domine iesu christe omnipotens eterne deus: qui me indignum famulum tuum in hac nocte custodisti." The prayer for Wednesday morning, "All possible thanks that I am able, I render unto thee O Lord Jesus Christ," has an equally obvious indebtedness to a morning prayer of Vives which Bradford translated. This prayer was carried over with slight verbal changes into the Marian primer of 1555.[48] And it clearly inspired a fresh prayer on the same lines in the Bull-Middleton *Christian Praiers,* that was taken over into the Day *Christian Prayers* of 1569.[49]

These various morning prayers are followed by a whole series of prayers from the Primer, "A prayer unto God the Father"; "Omnipotent, and mercifull God the Father eternall"; the *Conditor coeli:* "O maker of heaven and earth, king of kinges"; "O Bountifull Jesu, O sweete Saviour"; "A prayer of Manasses King of Juda"; "O Lord almightie, God of our Fathers Abraham Isaac and Jacob, and of the just seede of them." [50] But of all these traditional prayers perhaps the most notable inclusion is that of a free expansion of Thomas Aquinas' great Communion prayer, *Omnipotens sempiterne Deus, ecce accedo ad sacramentum unigeniti Filii,* a prayer not usually found in sixteenth-century primers, but often found in present-day Missals for the use of the laity. The relation of this version to the original may be illustrated by a comparison of the opening sentences. In Dom Cabrol's version the prayer begins as follows:

Almighty and eternal God, I draw near to the sacrament of thine only-begotten Son, our Lord Jesus Christ. As a sick man I approach the physician of life; as unclean I come to the fountain of mercy; blind, to the light of eternal brightness; poor and needy to the Lord of heaven and earth.[51]

In Middleton's version the prayer opens with the familiar Communion petition of the Mass[52] and then swings presently into the prayer of Thomas Aquinas:

O Lord although I be not worthy to receive thee into the house of my soule, for mine innumerable offences and sinnes done against thy great goodnesse, yet trustinge (good Lord) in thy great pitie and infinite mercye; I come to receive thy blessed bodye, as a sicke creature to thee that art the health of life, uncleane too thee that art the wel of mercy, blinde by ignorance too thee that art the light everlasting, needy of grace and power in vertue to thee that art the king of heaven and earth, naked of good works to thee that art the authour of grace.[53]

In this revival of old prayers Middleton (or his unknown editor) was ministering to what seems to have been a very real revival of interest in ancient devotion in this third quarter of the sixteenth century. It may have been a by-product of that solicitude for the testimony of antiquity that is so marked a feature of the defense of the Elizabethan Settlement in these years, evidenced very dramatically, for instance, by the publication of a sermon of Ælfric on the Sacrament of the Body and Blood of the Lord with a certificate from some thirteen bishops as to the authenticity of this "Testimonie of Antiquitie" as to the continuity of the position of the Church of England on that much controverted issue.[54] But it is more probable that we have here fresh proof of that tenderness for tradition and antiquity that has often manifested itself in the aesthetic and religious life of the English. We have already encountered that antiquarian interest on the title page of another devotional production of these years, the 1568 edition of *The Treasure of Gladnesse:* "This Booke is called the Treasure of Gladnesse, and semeth by the Copie, beinge a very little Manuell, and written in Velam, to be made above .CC. yeares past at the least."[55]

But the most impressive evidence of this appreciation of the traditional in devotional literature is to be seen in the Day prayer books, of which the first appeared not long after the *Treasure of Gladnesse* and a few years before the Middleton *Godly Garden*. It is that prayer book which John Day published at London in 1569, *Christian Prayers and Meditations in English, French, Italian, Spanish, Greeke, and Latine*. This work is often referred to as "Queen Elizabeth's Prayer Book," partly because the picture on the back of the title page portrays Queen Elizabeth at prayer in a chamber hung with brocades as rich and ornate as her dress,[56] and partly because a number of the prayers such as the "Prayer for wisedome to governe the Realme," [57] are put in the first person.

The very first glance at this book to a striking degree recalls the ancient primers. The title page is emblazoned with a Tree of Jesse, in which the protagonists are portrayed with that degree of bearded venerableness at that time deemed appropriate for Old Testament worthies, and the whole surmounted by a Madonna and Child that even though little more than an outline gives a certain effect of graciousness. The decoration of the pages, too, recalls the page of the old Primer, for instance, that of the Jehannot *Horae* of 1498 already referred to. Indeed, the same formula for the border decoration is used, three little scenes in the left-hand margin of the left page, and three similar scenes in the right-hand margin of the right. Each of these pictures presents an episode from the life of Christ, beginning with the birth of his mother, and the series is linked together with a running explanation from Scripture. A couple of Old Testament figures, also with appropriate texts between them, fill in the bottom of the pages, and conventionalized designs of various sorts with animals and fruits and human figures and urns and scrolls and other motifs of classical decoration popular in that period take up the other two margins. That these pictures are from old designs would seem clear from the costumes worn by two cowled figures in the concluding scene of the series.[58]

Although the series of pictures from Christ's life is repeated a number of times, it is presently supplanted by a series of designs illustrating the Dance of Death, with a very lively skeleton Death leading off with appropriate gestures various representatives of the social classes of the day. The type of this series of illustrations is an ancient one, very popular with the French printers of the *Horae* like Pigouchet, Kerver, and Regnault.[59] So far, then, as the appearance of the book goes, Day's

Christian Prayers of 1569 must have looked to any informed reader like a resurrection of the old Primer. And though in the next edition that has survived, that of 1578, the ornament was enriched with the addition of certain allegorical figures and scenes representing the five senses and the virtues trampling upon corresponding vices, in place of the repetition of the foregoing motifs,[60] the series representing the life of Christ and the Dance of Death remained constant through all the succeeding editions that have survived.

As for the contents of the edition of 1569, the first thing to catch the eye is the linguistic versatility implied by the inclusion of standard prayers in various languages. It is interesting that by the next edition of the book in 1578 the foreign-language prayers had disappeared; nor did they reappear in later editions. But it was not these prayers which opened the book and set the tone of it. Rather, it was the prayers for the various basic movements of the day from the first waking to the prayer to be said "When you enter *into your bed*." [61] These included prayers for the first waking, for the first sight of the daylight, for arising, for beginning the day when the preparations noted above were completed, and prayers to be said at the going down of the sun, at the lighting of candles, at the making of oneself unready, at the entering into bed, all interspersed with meditations. In other words, it was what had become the standard Primer–Prayer-Book approach of the time. The prayers themselves are the same prayers which Bradford had translated and which the Bull-Middleton *Christian Praiers and Holie Meditations* had taken over from Bradford, Vives' *Preces et Meditationes Diurnae,* but this time in a different translation.[62]

Of the prayers which follow in Day's book [63] all but three are taken from Bull's book, and reprinted in his order. Not all of Bull's prayers have been taken by any means, for he often provided two or more prayers for the same general occasion or topic. Sometimes the Day book omits a whole topic or category of Bull's prayers, but in spite of that the basic ground of the layman's devotional life is covered pretty well, in fact, with more economy and efficiency than in the Bull-Middleton book. One has a sense of a fairly direct and orderly progression through the main themes of prayer for the devout Christian of the time: "A prayer to God the Father, for the true knowledge of the mystery of our redemption in Christ," "A forme of thanksgeving for our redemption, and prayer for strength and encrease of faith," "A meditation for the exercise of true mortification," "A meditation of the comming of Christ to judgement, and of the rewarde both of the faithful and unfaithful," [64] and so on. There are some striking omissions from the earlier series, notably "A prayer for the true sense and feeling of Gods favour and mercie in Christe," and "A prayer against our spirituall enemies, the divel, the worlde, and the flesh." [65] But, in general, one feels that the objectives of the selection are clear, the elimination of duplication and the sharpening of the organization of the book.

As for the sources of the prayers, Bull had already attributed some of them to Bradford, with the initials "*I.B.*" Conspicuous among these are "A meditation of the comming of Christ to judgement, and of the rewarde both of the faithfull and unfaithfull," "A meditation concerning the lyfe everlasting, the place where it is, and the incomparable joyes thereof," and "A meditation of the presence of God," [66] to use the titles of the Day book. As for the three prayers in this general devotional section of the volume not to be found in the Bull-Middleton collection, two of them, "A meditation concerning the sober usage of the body, and pleasures in this life," and "A meditation of Gods power, beautie, goodnes," are also from Bradford, this time from his *Godly Meditations on the Lord's Prayer, Belief and Ten Command-ments, with other Exercises.*[67] The third, "A Prayer for wisedome to gouverne the Realme," beginning, "Almightie God and King of all Kinges, Lorde of heaven and earth, by whose ordinaunce Princes have governance of mortal men," though put into the mouth of Queen Elizabeth with a good deal of circumstantial personal detail, quite explicitly takes off, as it were, from that prayer of Solomon's for wisdom to govern that is so frequently found both in the primers and the prayer books of the time.[68]

As for the rest of the book, the most notable thing about it is its traditional character. This is apparent at once in the printing of the Seven Penitential Psalms of the primers.[69] Characteristically, these psalms are handled with some freedom. The first one, for instance, "O Lorde rebuke me not in thine indignation," has been cut a little. Then, too, each psalm is immediately followed by one and sometimes two prayers, "taken out" of it,[70] drawing, as it were, the theological or spiritual consequences of the reflections suggested by the Psalmist. Then come the Litany and Suffrages as in the traditional Primer. They are followed by three prayers to be said in sickness, and a very lengthy one "to be sayd after sicknes or any other kinde of crosse or affliction." [71] The remainder of the English section of the book (actually all but a very small portion of the total) is made up of prayers drawn from Scripture [72] in the fashion with which we are already familiar in the *Praiers of Holi Fathers.*

All in all, while this is unmistakably a Protestant book, it is still strikingly reminiscent of the Primer. Some elements are clearly taken out of the old primers; a good many others which are not to be found in the primers were, as we have seen, quite obviously composed as substitutions for traditional Primer elements.

In many ways this basic formula of the first edition of the *Christian Prayers* becomes even more apparent in the form which the book assumed when it appeared again some nine years later, under the title of *A Booke of Christian Prayers,* with the unusually appropriate title-page description:

. . . collected out of the auncient writers, and best learned in our tyme, worthy to be read with an earnest mynde of all Christians, in these daungerous and troublesome dayes, that God for Christes sake will yet still be mercyfull unto us.

At first this book of 1578 looks like nothing more than another edition of the *Christian Prayers* of 1569. The format is much the same, with the same Tree-of-Jesse title-page illumination and the same ornamental page border. There is, however, some change in the illustrations that make up the border, the most significant being the dropping of the Pietà, the picture of Mary with the dead Christ in her arms, that is one of the common elements in the designs of the first edition of 1569.[73] For this are substituted in the edition of 1578 scenes depicting the laying of Christ in the tomb and the women going to the sepulchre.[74] The explanation of this change is not far to seek in the continuing suspicion of the time with regard to any recognition of the Blessed Virgin.[75]

There are still other changes in the border illuminations. For instance, after several repetitions of the Life of Christ series there suddenly appears in the middle of the book a series of single female figures of a rather baroque type, posed in dramatic positions appropriate to the allegorical significance of the Five Senses, with the Virtues trampling upon the corresponding Vices.[76] At the foot of these pages now appear pictures illustrating the church life of the new order, with the new minister in the new clerical costume of the time performing the new rites, for instance, distributing the bread of the Communion to a group kneeling around an oblong-shaped table. And in some of the margins at both the sides and the foot of the page, there are new scenes illustrating scriptural texts. One, for instance, shows the sun being darkened, and the moon losing her light, and the stars falling from the sky.[77]

However curious and interesting, these changes are of minor significance compared with the changes that have been made in the contents of the book. These are so considerable as to make this new edition to a very large extent a new book. This is apparent from the beginning. Where the book of 1569 opens directly with "Prayers to be sayd in the mornyng," the version of 1578 begins with an address to the Christian Reader, the work of Richard Day. This is a systematic exhortation to prayer, each of its prescriptions and explanations bolstered by the relevant scriptural example or text. In the course of this exhortation, certain supposed objections to the value of prayer are met. The most interesting of these is that of the supposed superfluity of prayer in the light of the orthodox doctrine of predestination. It was a real enough issue which, if we may judge from the preachers of this century and the opening years of the next, much engaged the attention of casuists, amateur and professional, in the England of the time.[78]

Richard Day faces the problem boldly:

But yet here remaineth a farther question, how it may stand with God's immutable wil, and decree, that our prayers should be of such strength and force to alter the threatenings which are decreed, and therfore of force must come to passe. I aunswere God never promysed any thing in scripture, for the most part, except it were the absolute promises concerning *Messias* and such like) [*sic*] but it hath a condition annexed unto it, ether expressly, or to be understood. Likewise, he never threatneth (for the most part) but a condition is added thereunto. As for example. Adam was created of God that he should have lived continually in blessed estate, if he would so remayne: this was the condition, and the decree. . . . And thus very well our prayers have strength to stay Gods wrath, his decree remayning immutable, because it is threatned but upon a condition, if we repent not.[79]

In other words, like the preachers, this editor is determined that no lazy Christian shall find in predestination any excuse for his refusal to embrace the strenuous life.

The book thus prefaced begins in a fashion with which we are already quite familiar in the Bull-Middleton books and the Day volume of 1569, that is with prayers for the various stages of the day's routine. They are on the whole quite different prayers from those that open the edition of 1569, but they are of the same type. Indeed, most of them come from the same source, the famous *Preces et Meditationes Diurnae* of Vives.[80] But a number of non-Vives prayers intrude into this series, notably a second "uprising" prayer from Erasmus' *Precationes aliquot,* and one for "putting on of our Clothes," found, according to Clay, not only in the primer of Germany, the *Hortulus animae,* but also in a collection of traditional prayers which the noted Protestant divine, Musculus published at Leipsic in 1570.[81] But Erasmus was a contemporary of Vives, and though his position was mistaken more often than that of his Spanish colleague, he belonged to the same general spiritual movement, seeking to make tradition available to the needs of his day.

So far, the devotional pattern of the second edition of the Day collection seems to follow closely that of the first. But at this point there is a sharp break. For where the earlier edition had, as we have seen, turned from the Vives prayers to a series of prayer-meditations, mostly by Bradford, this after a couple of prefatory pieces plunges into a succession of rather miscellaneous prayers which may be roughly gathered up into a relatively few groups. First, come what might be called general and basic prayers, to each of the persons of the Trinity. Then there is a prayer for grace to pray "effectively," followed by what might be called a series of official prayers, for the realm and for the church and the members thereof in their various degrees, followed by several for the church, the last of which is uncommonly long for this volume. Then come prayers for the Queen (to the number of three), for the ministers of God's word, for all magistrates, for children to say for their parents, and for charity or love towards our neighbors. Appropriately enough, these last give way to prayers for the afflicted and persecuted, for the poor, culminating in a couple for "our Evilwillers." A new section of a generally more penitential character opens with a confession of sins, followed by a series of fifteen prayers on the general theme of the forgiveness of sins, and then several prayers dealing with various facets of the sinner's experience of comfort and discouragement. The penitential horizon is then widened and lifted by a series of fifteen prayers on the general theme of "the minding of Christes passion," followed by prayers on Christ's resurrection and ascension.[82] That rounds out a series obviously devoted to the foundations of religion.

It is succeeded in turn by another series of a somewhat more practical character, such as prayers for hearing a sermon, a series of Communion prayers, and a long series of prayers for various spiritual gifts, such as God's grace, trust in God, fear of God, etc.[83] Then, again without any sign of division, come a series of prayers for special circumstances and needs, such as prayers in sickness, and in affliction, and in temptation.[84] After these come the litany and the suffrages, followed by a prayer for the visitation of the sick, reënforcing the somewhat liturgical effect of this section, and then a couple of prayers looking to the spiritual future, the second, on the fear of the Judge and the Judgment Day, not a prayer but a meditation. Then the book ends as a good Elizabethan book should end with a prayer for the Queen, the magistrates, and the nation.[85]

At first glance, this book would seem even more miscellaneous and encyclopedic than the edition of 1569. It is better organized, but the organization is still a rather loose and general one with prayers clustered together according to theme. There is very little evidence, outside of the litany and the suffrages, of the old liturgical character of the Primer. It is, as with most of these post–Book-of-Common-Prayer works that we have been studying, quite literally a collection of prayers for various private devotional needs and occasions, supplemented by an obvious effort of the editor to widen the reader's horizons beyond his own personal preoccupations.

In other words, the contents of this book would at first sight seem pretty completely to bely the Primer appearance. But nothing could be farther from the truth than this first superficial impression. For the great bulk of these prayers are either from the Primer and the Primer tradition, or from later writers who wrote in that tradition, as may be seen from Clay's study of their sources. True, the leaders of the Protestant reform are well represented by prayers from Calvin, Knox, Foxe, and Bradford. But the number of prayers so contributed is small, two from Calvin, one from Knox, one from Foxe, and two from Bradford, of which only one is his own composition. And even more significant is the character of these contributions. The Bradford prayer "For true mortification" is of the private devotion type.[86] But the first borrowing from Calvin, a prayer "for the whole Realm, and the body of the Church, with the members therof, according to their estates, and degrees," was formed, according to Clay, on the model of a prayer in Valerandus Pollanus' translation of Calvin's liturgy for the Strassburg congregation, a version which Pollanus in turn translated into English and published in London in 1552.[87] The other Calvin selection, "A confession of our sinnes," is a translation from the *Confessio Peccatorum* at the beginning of the Latin version of Calvin's French liturgy.[88]

The Knox contribution is, also, a liturgical one, a Communion prayer from "The Administration of the Lord's Supper" in Knox' *Book of Common Order*.[89] The John Foxe prayer, following the Calvin prayer on the same theme noted above, "Another prayer for the church, and all the states thereof," [90] but, unlike the Calvin prayer, inscribed with the author's name (one of the few in the book so inscribed), is of the same kind. In other words, specifically Protestant prayers are mainly of the liturgical type, from the orders of public worship which the reformers had been composing to take the place of the repudiated liturgies.

But for the bulk of the private prayers the editors of this book relied upon the traditional prayers of the Primer type. Something over a third of all the prayers in the book come directly or indirectly from Vives, the great Spanish devotional writer, and something less than half as many from Vives' rival in this field, Erasmus. The remainder come from the Primer or its cognates such as the *Hortulus animae,* or from collections of traditional Primer-type prayers like the *Precationes ex veteribus orthodoxis Doctoribus* of Musculus, the famous Public Reader of Divinity of Berne. So this book may very well be regarded as the culmination of that process of adaptation of traditional materials to the devotional needs of the sixteenth century which we have been studying.

Indeed, that is the key to the whole devotional development of the sixteenth century. The early reformers like Whitford, who had no thought of breaking with tradition, were troubled by the ignorance of the common man of the riches of his tradition. They sought to bring them to him, to put him in active possession of them. To that end, they tried to adapt them to the circumstances and needs of his life. In so doing they set a pattern which the reformers who felt they must break with tradition out of the very necessities of the case turned to.

Inevitably, the main energies of those reformers who had dedicated themselves to the establishment of a new religious order went in those first post-Reformation decades to the establishment of their position politically and socially as well as religiously, and to the working out of the forms of public worship and church government and discipline that would make the theoretical position a living reality. But there was more to it than simple expediency. There are many evidences in Elizabethan cultural history of the strong appeal which the traditional, the humanly seasoned and enriched, held for the English temperament. For all their criticisms, the leaders of English spiritual life in the second half of the sixteenth century were too much aware of the value of the traditional devotional literature to throw away its resources. Indeed, if one remembers that in the changes of the century, the victory was at last to those who did not wish to change more than they regarded as absolutely necessary in prayer and rite, it is not surprising that such a large proportion of the treasures of the Primer was carried over into the prayer books that succeeded it.

XII

THE ADAPTATION OF
TRADITIONAL MATERIALS

STRIKING as is their dependence on traditional materials, there is nothing antiquarian about these books. They were prepared for the current devotional life of their time. Their context is that of the Church of England as defined in the Elizabethan Settlement. The litanies printed in them, for instance, are the official litanies. And the central Protestant rejections of prayers for the Pope, prayers to saints, and prayers to the Virgin are maintained. The over-all effect of these books is clearly Protestant. If there had been any doubt of it, they would certainly not have been suffered to run through edition after edition. Finally, there is no reason to believe that the makers of these books were anything but convinced members of the Church of England, zealous to serve and to enrich the devotional life of that institution.

The explanation of this situation is, of course, that these traditional materials which we have been studying were handled with the freedom characteristic of sixteenth-century literary habit in all fields. If the traditional prayer suited the editor as it was, he kept it in its traditional form, subject, of course, to the normal vicissitudes of Elizabethan editing and printing. If it did not, he did not hesitate to adapt it to his purposes. In this work of adaptation he suffered none of the inhibitions that dog the efforts of his modern successors in this footnote-ridden age. If a prayer of the fourteenth century, for instance, contained elements which seemed to the sixteenth-century mind superstitious, idolatrous, or out-moded, the sixteenth-century editor, as we have seen, held it the part of charity to free his predecessor's work of blemishes which he would doubtless have repudiated if he had been privileged to live in a more enlightened age. Moreover, such a correction made the ancient prayer safe for good work beyond the dreams of its creator. If the sixteenth-century editor felt any qualms about the literary rights of the original author, he was sure that the latter would have been grateful if he could know how his work had been purified from the inevitable errors of his time.

There were, of course, some prayers that would seem to have offered no problem, prayers that passed from decade to decade and editor to editor as they had done for centuries. It is not always easy to tell just why some prayers survived all the shifts in point of view and taste of the time, while others did not. There is an unmistakable element of individual taste and purpose involved, and probably, too, some element of what is nothing much more than chance. Anyone who has ever had a hand in the making of an anthology knows how uncertain are the processes by which one passage is taken and another rejected. The desire to furnish what other people will want and need is at constant tension with one's own tenderness for certain works and passages. Not only the demands of the time, then, but the patterns of personal preference are to be reckoned with in this matter of choice.

But whatever the cause, the fact remains that some prayers do continue through the vicissitudes of the sixteenth century with surprisingly little change. Perhaps the most dramatic of these survivals is that prayer which the editor of the Regnault *Hore* of 1527 described as follows:

Oratio sancti Bernardi de senis ordinis minorum. This moost devoutly prayer sayd the holy father saint Bernard dayly knelying in the worshyp of the moost holy name Jesus. And it is well to beleve that through the invocation of the moost excellent name of Jesu saint bernard obteyned a syngulare warde of perpetuall consolacion of our lorde Jesu criste. And thys prayer is wryttem in a thabell that haunged at rome in saint Peters chyrche nere to the hye awter there as our holy fader the pope evely is wounte to saye the office of the masse, and who that devoutly wyth a contrite herte dayly say thys oryson yf he be that day in the state of eternall damnacyon than thys eternall payne shall be chaunged hym in temporall payne of purgatory than yf he hath deserved the payne of purgatory it shall be forgotten and forgyven throwe the infinyte mercy of god.[1]

Needless to say, in view of the sixteenth-century criticisms of that type of promise, this introduction did not share the prayer's powers of survival.

The temper of the prayer itself may be judged from the opening petitions, from the first of which it takes its name: "O bone iesu. O dulcis iesu. O iesu fili marie virginis marie plenus misericordia et veritate. O dulcis iesu miserere mei secundum magnam misericordiam tuam." Or, as the English of the Paris primer of 1538 ran:

O bountyfull Jesu o swete Jesu, o Jesu the sonne of the pure virgyne mary, full of mercy and truthe. O swete Jesu after thy great mercye have pyte upon me. O benigne Jesu I praye the by the same precyous blode, whiche for us myserable sinners, thou were content to shede in the aulter of the crosse that thou vouchsave clene to avoyde all my wyckednes, and nat to despyse me, humbly this requyryng, and upon thy moste holy name Jesus callyng. This name Jesus is the name of helthe what is Jesus but a savyour. O good Jesus that hast me created, and with thy precyous blode redcmyd. Suffer me nat to be dampned, whom of nought thou hast made. O good Jesu, let nat my wyckednes destroye me, that thy almyghty goodnes made and fourmed. O good Jesu reknowlege that is thyne in me and wype clene awaye, that eloyneth me from the. O good Jesu, whan tyme of mercy is have mercy upon me. Nor confounde me nat in tyme of thy terryble judgement. O good Jesu yf I wretched synner for my moste grevous offences have by thy very justice deserved eternall payne, yet I appell from thy very ryghtuousnes, and stedfastly truste in thyne ineffable mercy: so as a mylde father and mercyful lorde ought, take pyte on me O good Jesu what profyte is in my blode, syns that I muste descende into eternal corrupcyon. Certaynly they that ben deade shal nat magnyfye thee, nor lykewyse all they that go to hell. O moste mercyfull Jesu, have mercy upon me O most swete Jesu delyver me. O most meke Jesu, be unto me confortable O Jesu accepte me a wretchyd synner, into the nombre of them that shal be saved. O Jesu the helth of them that beleve in the, have mercy upon me. O Jesu the swete forgyvenes of all my synnes. O Jesu the sone of the pure virgyn Mary: Endewe me with thy grace wysdome, charyte, chastite, and humilitie: ye, and in al myne adversyties, stedfast pacyens, so that I may perfytely love the, and in thee to be gloryfied and have my only delite in the world without cnde. So be it.[2]

This prayer held its own through all the changes of the sixteenth century. It is found in Latin and English not only in the Paris primer of 1538, but in Bishop Hilsey's primer of 1539, the Toye primer of 1542, and the official Marian primer of 1555, and in English only, in the Byddell-Marshall primer of 1535, the official Henrician primer of 1545, and the Day *Christian Prayers* of 1578, and in a modified but still recognizable version in Lidley's prayers in the Bull-Middleton *Christian Praiers* of 1578.[3] Bishop Hilsey's version of 1539 is practically the same as that of the Paris primer of 1538 with one or two slight changes in wording of no importance. The Toye version of 1542 has been cut somewhat, but it is without question the same prayer. The version of the official primer of 1545 is the same with some minor changes, as if the editor of 1545 had corrected the Paris English version of 1538 with its own accompanying Latin. For instance, a sentence of praise that was in the beginning of the prayer in the Latin of the Regnault *Hore* of 1527 and the Paris primer of 1538 but apparently fell out of the English translation of the latter, is translated in the 1545 primer as well as in the Marian primer of 1555.

The version of the Day *Christian Prayers* of 1578 is characteristically a fresh try at the Latin but also a faithful translation, more complete where something had accidentally dropped out of the Paris primer of 1538, and more up to date, and also, perhaps a little more precise, if not more literal at times. There is some gain in suavity of style, too. The opening sentences of Day's version will suffice to show something of its spirit as compared with that of the Paris primer of 1538 above:

O Good Jesu, O sweet Jesu, the sonne of the virgine Mary, full of mercie and truth, O sweet Jesu have pitie upon me according to thy great mercy. O loving Jesu, I beseech thee by that precious bloud of thine, which thou didst vouchsafe to shed for us wretched sinners upon the altar of the crosse, put away all my sinnes and despise me not in myne humble sute calling upon this thy most holy name of Jesus.

Clearly the change in language so far is in the interest of that smoothness of style which seems to have been one of the outstanding interests of the editor of the *Christian Prayers* of 1578. But in the closing petition of the prayer there is a rather significant change, an insertion of a phrase that suggests a wish to enhance the worshiper's desire to enter as intimately as possible into the human experience of his Redeemer:

O Jesu the sweete remission of all my sinnes, O Jesu the sonne of the virgine Mary, poure thy grace, wisedome, lovingnes, charity, and humility into me: and in all mine adversityes geve me holy patience, that I may be able to beare thy crosse with thee, to love thee, and to glory and delight in thee for ever and ever. Amen.[4]

But in spite of any gain in fidelity or grace, the Day prayer of 1578 is still pretty much the prayer of the Paris primer of 1538. This is not true of the version in Lidley's prayers reprinted in the Bull-Middleton *Christian Praiers and Holie Meditations* of 1578. It is labeled "a prayer necessarie to be saide at all times." Since it is a good deal longer than the original, it is not worth quoting in its entirety, but even a selection (the beginning and the end) will show the difference in technique and spirit:

O Bountiful Lord Jesu, O sweete saviour, O Christ the sonne of God, have
pittie upon mee, mercifully heare mee, and despise not my prayers. Thou hast
created me of nothing, thou hast redeemed me from the bondage of sinne,
death, and hel, neither with Gould nor Silver, but with thy moste precious
bodie once offered upon the crosse, and thine owne blood shedde once for all
for a ransome. Therefore cast me not away, whom thou by thy great wisedome hast made.

.   .   .   .

Accept me (O Lord) among the number of them whom thou hast in Christ
elected and chosen to salvation. Forgive me my sinnes: give me grace to leade
a godly and innocent life: graunt me thy heavenly wisedome: inspire my
hart with faith, hope, and charitie: give me grace to bee humble in prosperitie,
patiente in adversitie, obedient to my rulers, in all my doinges faithfull,
dealing truely with all men, to live chastly in wedlock, to abhorre adulterie,
fornication and all uncleanes, to doe good after my power unto all men, to
hurt no man: that thy name may be glorified in mee during this present life,
and that I afterwarde may atteine everlasting life, through thy mercie, and
the merites of thy death and passion. Amen.[5]

The note of argument with the Lord that gives a quaintly human
flavor to the old prayer has here yielded to greater stress on self-
exhortation, to a greater particularization of the sins to be repented of,
in short to the greater explicitness and greater didacticism of a later time.
Yet even here the main lines of the old prayer are to be discerned. It
is not difficult to see why Saint Bernardine of Siena's prayer continued
to be printed. In spite of the somewhat emotional character of the
invocations, the prayer as a whole is concerned with one of the dearest
preoccupations of the sixteenth century, the pleading of the frightened
sinner with his Maker for forgiveness. The very argument that there
is nothing possible in the way of satisfaction for the God who damns
the sinner is one that would appeal to the sixteenth-century despair of
man's unaided efforts, and strengthen its conviction that only in Christ's
sacrifice was relief to be had.

With the exception of the Bull-Middleton version, the transcription
of the *O bone Jesu* was notably faithful and constant throughout. More
often the old prayer was altered to some extent. Sometimes the change
was not much more than a matter of rhetoric, involving little beyond
considerations of time and space. An example of such a condensation
is to be seen in the history of one of the diurnal prayers, *Oratio dicenda
dormituro,* given as follows in the *Enchiridion* which Thielman Kerver's widow printed in Paris in 1528:

O Iesu dulcissime: iesu patris dilectissime: tu mecum queso maneas: hac nocte mecum dormias: ut corpus somnum capiat: et nunquam cor obdormiat: sed semper tecum vigilet: te corde mente cupiat presentem absens videat: quo malum omne caveat: me angelus custodiat: et signo crucis muniat: hic sathan procul fugiat: et iesus solus maneat: quos amo tecum colligas, in lecto cordis foveas: nec me nec ipsos deferas: sed benedicens protegas, et in evum custodias. Amen.

A slightly condensed and slightly modified version of this prayer is to be found in the Bull-Middleton book of *Christian Praiers* in a prayer titled "When you feele sleepe to be comming, pray":

O Lord Jesus Christ, my watchman and keeper, take me into thy protection. Graunt that my body sleeping, my minde may watch in thee, and be made merrie by some sight of that celestiall and heavenly life, wherein thou art the king and prince, together with the father and the holie Ghost, where the Angels and holy soules be most happie citizens. Oh purifie my soule, keepe cleane my bodie, that in both I may please thee, sleeping and waking for ever. Amen.

As so often happens, this version is carried over into the Day *Christian Prayers* of 1569. Still another version, even more condensed, is found in "A Prayer when we be redy to sleep," in the Day *Christian Prayers* of 1578:

Take me into thy protection, O Lord Jesu Christ our defender: and graunt that while my body slepeth my soul may wake in thee, and cheerefully, and joyfully behold the happy, and gladsome heavenly life, wherein thou art soveraine with the Father and the holy Ghost: and the Angels, and holy soules of men are most blessed fellow Citizens for ever and ever, Amen.[6]

In this case the result of the process of condensation is not entirely fortunate. The resulting prayer is more compact and even smoother, but it has lost much of the dramatic quality of the original, and most of its pictorial vigor.

Such condensation is, on the whole, comparatively rare. The general habit of the sixteenth century in the devotional field is to expand rather than to cut. A good example is to be seen in "A prayer agaynst the devel," printed in the official primer of 1545 as follows:

Jesu Christ (our Lorde) whiche by the mouth of the holy Apostle seinte Peter, moost truely diddest say that oure adversary the devyll goeth about like a roaryinge Lyon, sekyng whome he may devour: he is busy and fyerse, and breaketh in upon us, so that if thou helpe not, he wyl sone deceive us, with his craft overturn us, with his might and with his cruelnes teare us in peces. But yf thou whiche hast vanquished him wilt appere, but as it were a far of, thou wilt make him afraid, and with thy onely loke put him to flight. Vouchesafe (o lorde) to receive us into thy garde, beyng but infantes, weke feble, and unskylfull, least the fyers and cruell beast all to teare us. We beare before us and shewe furth in this our fight the crosse thy banner, the crosse thy tryumph and victory, that our enemy may well know that we do oure busynes by thy counsaile, ayde, and strength: to the bee glory for ever. Amen.[7]

That prayer is not, of course, original with the editors of 1545. It is a close and faithful translation of a prayer of Vives.[8] Except for the omission of one phrase of emphasis, "most truely," in the invocation, "Jesu Christ our lorde, whiche by the mouth of the holye Apostle saynct Peter, most truely diddest saye," the Marian primer of 1555 very exactly reproduces the phrasing of the official Henrician primer of 1545.[9] But in the Day *Christian Prayers* of 1578 the main lines of the old prayer have been expanded, and the implications developed, as may be seen in the following version of the first part of the prayer:

Jesus Christ, our Lord God, our shield, our fortres, our strong rock, our only defence, thou knowest, and it greeveth us to feel, with how great force, and perilous pollicie, that olde enemy of oures the wily serpent, that beguiled our first parents in paradise, the roaring Lyon that goeth about night and day, seeking whom he may devoure. That destroyer, waster, and accuser of the saynts, the devill, commeth upon us to assayle us, thou knowest how small, or rather no power at al we have of our selves to withstand him, so that unlesse thou succour us, he will easely deceave us by his craftynes, overthrow us by his mightynes, and rend us in peeces by his cruelty. But we know that if thou doe but shewe thy selfe to him aloof, thou shalt drive him away with thine only looke. For thou hast overcome him by thy death, thou hast bound him, disarmed him, and spoyled his house, thou hast bereft him of all lordship and power, thou hast crushed his head, thou hast cast down hys throne, and dispossessed him of hys kingdome, thou hast led away captivity captive, thou hast cancelled the obligation that he had of oures, and nayled it to thy crosse: and finally, thou hast tryumphed over him in our nature, to our benefite and behoofe.[10]

The motive of such an expansion as the foregoing is, of course, to make the theological conceptions that underlie the prayer as clear and as moving as possible. That is, indeed, one of the commonest causes of change in this literature. But sometimes there is more to it than this desire for clarification. Sometimes the alterations are due to a change in basic orientation as may be seen in the history of another prayer of Vives, *Initium ruinae hominis, sibi fidere,* published in the famous *Preces* of 1539. An English version of this prayer was printed in the official primers of 1545 and 1555 under the title, "A prayer for to trust in God." But the Day *Christian Prayers* of 1578 produced a fresh translation of the old prayer.[11] There is no doctrinal significance in the change. There could hardly be. After all, the original prayer of Vives had already passed through the editorial processes of the official primer of 1545. But a comparison of the two versions reveals a difference in emphasis that, however slight, is still suggestive of an important change in attitude and feeling. In the primer of 1545 the prayer runs as follows:

The beginnyng of the fal of man was trust in him self. The beginnyng of the restoring of man was distrust in him self and trust in God. O most gratious and most wise guide our saviour Christ, whiche doest leade them the right way to immortall blessednes, whiche truely and unfaynedly trusting in the, commit them selfe to the. Graunt us that like as we be blinde and feble in dede, so we may take and repute our selfes, that we presume not of our selfes, to se our selfes, but so farre to se, that alway we maye have the before oure eyes to folowe the, beying our guyde, to be redy at thi cal most obediently, and to commit our selfes wholy unto the, that thou which onely knowest the way, mayst leade us the same way unto oure heavenly desires. To the with the father and the holy gost be glory for ever. Amen.

This becomes in the Day version of 1578:

The ground of mans decay was his trusting of himselfe: and the beginning of his rysing agayne, was his distrusting of him selfe, and his trusting to god.
O most excellent and singular wise guid, which leadest all them the rightest and nearest way to everlasting blessednes, which trust thee truely and unfaynedly. Graunt that as we be blind, and weak in very deed, so we may take our selves so to be, that we take not up on us to shift for our selves: but let our looking be to see thee alone: and let our inabling of our selves be no further, but to desire to follow thee going afore us: to come to thee when thou callest us: to obay thee as thou guydest us: and to betake our selves wholy unto thee, that thou who only knowest what way to goe, mayst lead us to the attaynement of our desires that way which we wold never have set foote into of our own accord, Amen.

The difference in style is of course the most striking difference between the two versions. The earlier is more compact, perhaps sharper, the later easier, more flexible. One may measure something of the progress which English prose had made in fluidity, if not in strength, in the years between. But there is, also, a difference in temper and atmosphere between the two. The element of man's helplessness is underlined in the second as it is not in the first. And that is in keeping with the emphasis on man's dependence on his God which was characteristic of the preaching on justification in this period.

And yet, as we have had occasion to see before, this sense of man's helplessness when it came to the matter of saving his soul was perfectly compatible with a very complete confidence in himself when he was sure that he was of the elect. This other facet of the doctrine of justification is apparent in what happened to the first of a group of prayers for the dying which were published in the famous *Precationes Erasmi* in 1537.[12] In the generally traditional Toye primer of 1542 this prayer is presented in a version which begins as follows:

> O Lorde Jesu, whych arte the onelye healthe of all men lyvynge. And the everlastinge lyfe of them whych dye in thy fayth. I wretched synner geve and submytte my selfe holye unto thy mooste blyssed wyll.

The same prayer is found in the official primer of 1545. The changes are slight, but there is one which is suggestive. The first sentence after the passage quoted above, runs as follows:

> And I beinge sure that the thyng cannot peryshe whych is commytted unto thy mercye O Lorde geve me grace that wyllynglye I maye leave thys frayle and wyked fleshe: in hoope of the resurrectyon, whyche in betterwyse shall restoore it to me agayne.

It is unquestionably the same prayer in the primer of 1545, but there is a slight change that raises interesting possibilities:

> And I beyng sure that the thyng cannot perysh, whiche is commytted unto thy mercy: wyllingly now I leave this frail and wicked flesh in hope of the resurreccion whiche in better wyse shall restore it to me againe.[13]

In other words, the first version prays that the dying Christian may have the proper attitude; the second assumes that he has it, perhaps a reflection of the emphasis which the theological thinking of the time put upon firmness of faith in the redemptive promises of Christ.

Becon's *Pommaunder of Prayers* of about 1560 reprints the Toye version of 1542, here, as so often, following the traditional pattern, but the Bull-Middleton *Christian Praiers* substantially follows the primer of 1545, and so does the Day *Christian Prayers* of 1578 in a version which, though different from that of the primer of 1545, develops along the same lines and is basically the same prayer.[14] The most interesting of the changes which it makes in the earlier version is the addition of a brief allusion to the martyrs of old time, doubtless with an eye to the remembrance of more recent martyrs.

Sometimes the change in the phrasing of a prayer is not so much a matter of theological position or premise, as of mood and temper. The change in language may be so slight that any attempt at evaluation runs the risk of exaggeration. And yet it remains teasingly suggestive. There is an especially interesting example of such a slight but possibly significant change in one of the scriptural prayers so characteristic of all the prayer books of the time. It is that "prayer to obtayne wysdome Sapyence the .ix. Chapitre," which in the English of the Paris primer of 1538 ran as follows:

O the god of our fathers, god of mercy whiche hast made al with thy worde, and with thy wysedome hast constitute man, to have domynyon upon the creature whiche was made of the, to order the worlde with equitie and justice and in the direction of harte to judge judgementes, gyve me the assistent wysedome of thy seates and reprove me nat from thy chyldren.[15]

This prayer proved to be a very popular one, for it is found in a good many of the devotional collections of the next years, for example, the Toye primer of 1542, the official primers of 1545 and 1555, the *Praiers of Holi Fathers,* and the Day *Christian Prayers* of 1569.[16] The Toye primer, as usual, reprints the version found in the 1538 Paris primer; the 1545 primer makes certain verbal changes which persist in the primer of 1555 and the Day *Christian Prayers* of 1569. Of these, the most suggestive is found at the very beginning of the prayer. In the initial description of the function of man in the creation, the phrase of the Paris primer of 1538, describing the way he is to order the world, "with equitie and justice," becomes in the primer of 1545, "according to equitie and righteousnes," and in the Day book, "according to holines and righteousnes." That dangerous substitution of "holiness and righteousnes" for the more objective "equitie and justice," is a striking one, probably not to be emphasized unduly, but still a straw to show in what way the wind was blowing in certain quarters.

It is difficult to find any temporal order in these adaptations. Indeed, what might be called a chronological teetering back and forth is one of the most interesting characteristics of the whole process. Very often a later prayer book, especially the Day *Christian Prayers,* will go back over the changes of years to pick up again an earlier version of a prayer. A good example is to be seen in the history of one of the classic morning prayers, a thanksgiving for safe-keeping through the night. It is to be found in the 1498 Jehannot *Horae:*

Piissime deus et clementissime pater laudes et gratias ago tibi domine iesu criste omnipotens eterne deus qui me indignum famulum tuum. N. in hac nocte custodisti, protexisti visitasti sanum et incolumen ad principium huius diei me pervenire fecisti et pro aliis beneficiis tuis que tua sola bonitate michi contulisti deprecor clementiam tuam misericors deus ut concedas michi diem venturum sic peragere in tuo sancto servitio cum humilitate discretione devotione et dilectione benigna . . . .[17]

The same prayer was reprinted in Latin alone in the Regnault *Hore* of 1527. Bishop Hilsey's primer somewhat condensed it.[18] The primer of 1555 printed for its Friday morning prayer an English prayer that begins like this and follows its main lines but which often differs considerably in detail.[19] The Bull-Middleton *Christian Praiers* translated the Latin prayer of 1498 with great fidelity as may be seen in the opening sentence:

We humblie and heartily give thankes unto thee (O heavenly father) through thy dearely beloved sonne Jesus Christ, that to thy innumerable benefites, hitherto powred upon our soules and upon our bodies, thou hast kept us this night past from many evils . . . .[20]

The Day *Christian Prayers* of 1578, on the other hand, yields a version not quite like any of the foregoing, but still clearly an adaptation of the prayer of 1498, as may be seen from the opening petition:

I thank thee O holy Lord, father almighty, and everlasting God, that thou hast vouchsafed to keepe me this night through thy great mercy. And I beseech thee of thine unmeasurable clemency, to geve me grace so to pas this day now comming, in all lowlynesse, meeknes, chastity, charitie, patience, goodnes, feare, and warynesse, as my servise may please thee, through him which shall come to judge both the quick and the dead, and the world by fire.[21]

This process of adaptation is not by any means confined to Scripture and Primer. It is applied in much the same way to other collections of prayers, like those of the pseudo-Augustine. For instance, "A prayer upon the minding of Christes resurrection and ascention," in the Day *Christian Prayers* of 1578 is a faithful rendering of roughly the first fifth of the thirty-sixth chapter of *A Right Christian Treatise, entituled S. Augustine's Praiers,* headed, "A verie effectual praier to the stirring up of the mind unto godlines being zelouslie uttered." A comparison of the opening sentences in the two versions will briefly suggest the technique of adaptation. The S. *Augustines Praiers* version opens:

O lord Jesus, o pitiful Jesus, o good Jesus, who both hast voutsafed to suffer death for our sinnes, and art risen againe for our justification.

I humblie beseech thee by thy glorious resurrection, raise me out of the sepulchre of my sins, and of al my vices, and give me dailie a part in the first resurrection, that trulie I may receave a portion in the resurrection at the last daie.

But, though only a little briefer, the version of the Day *Christian Prayers* of 1578 does seem a good deal more compact:

O Lord Jesu, O good Jesu, which diddest vouchsafe to die for my sinnes, and rosest agayn for my justification: I beseech thee by thy glorious resurrection, raise me up from the grave of al my vices and sinnes, and geve me part daily in the first resurrection, that I may be made partaker of the second resurrection also.[22]

Not all of the adaptations of traditional materials are by any means so easy to follow. More often at first sight the later Primer- or prayer-book prayer seems to be an entirely new approach to an ancient theme, and yet there is that constant and persistent sense of familiarity. Even in many of the substitute prayers one has that haunting sense of the already known, not always by any means tangible, but nevertheless ineluctable.

One reads over a prayer of the middle to the end of the century and feels sure that it is something he has already met in one of the earlier Primer collections. But still there is something different about it. It does not go quite as one expected. In a good many cases it is like following a will-o'-the-wisp through a bog to try to run down the teasing echo, and yet there is no question of the relation. Very often it is, of course, no more than the fact that the ultimate source of the prayers is the same, the Bible. Under the circumstances of the time, when men mastered Scripture so painstakingly, and so constantly had its phrases as well as its themes and ideas on their lips, it is not surprising that there should be this constant sense of familiarity. For the language of their expression was a common instrument upon which the changing modulations of translation had very little effect. It would be a Herculean undertaking, therefore, to try to run down all these quotations and echoes and imitations, and it is doubtful, even if an exhaustive identification were possible, that it would add very much to the general impression of traditional elements persisting with remarkable tenacity through all sorts of conscious and unconscious changes.

But from the consideration of a few cases, of course an infinitesimally small proportion of the total involved, it is possible to see something of how the thing worked. And it seems worth doing even to that limited and qualified extent because of the light it throws on the persistence and vitality of certain group patterns of thought and feeling. Moreover, it is in such continuities that the real effects of the changes of the times are seen most impressively and significantly.

In a certain number of cases the explanation is quite simple. The editor has used the traditional Psalter and Primer materials, but in selecting just what he wants from his sources, he has merely run two or three prayers together. An interesting example of this is to be seen in "The prayer for the Morning," that opens Becon's *Pommaunder of Prayers*. It begins like the familiar *Piissime deus et clementissime pater laudes et gratias ago tibi domine iesu christe* prayer of the Jehannot *Horae* of 1498, the first sentence of which the Bull-Middleton *Christian Praiers* translated:

We humblie and heartily give thankes unto thee (O heavenly father) through thy dearly beloved sonne Jesus Christ, that to thy innumerable benefites, hitherto powred upon our soules and upon our bodies, thou hast kept us this night past from many evils . . . .

Then Becon picks up still another prayer found also in the Bull-Middleton volume, this time based on a well-known morning prayer of Erasmus, and beginning:

Most mercifull God and Father of our Saviour Jesus Christ, I most humbly thanke thee for the sweete sleepe and comfortable rest which thou hast given me this night past: beseeching thee, that like as thou hast nowe awaked my bodie from sleepe, so thou wouldest awake my soule from the sleepe of sinne and darkenesse of this world. . . .

And yet in spite of this diversity of source, the resulting composition of Becon's is a fairly compact and thoroughly integral prayer:

I render unto thee, (O heavenly Father,) most harty thankes by thy deare Sonne Jesus Christ, that this night past, thou hast vouchedsafe of thy fatherly goodnesse, to preserve mee from all evill, and to geve my body rest and sleepe: I now most entirelye beseeche thee that as thou hast raysed up this my body from sleepe: so likewese, thou wilt deliver my mind from the sleepe of sinne, and from the darkenes of this world, that I walkyng in the

lyght of thy blessed worde may onely do that is pleasaunt in thy sight
profitable to my neighbour and healthful to my soule. Amen.[23]

An even more elaborate mosaic of elements is to be found in Edward
Dering's "A fourme of Morning prayer necessarie for this present time
for Godly Christians, to use in their houses and families":

We moste humbly thanke thee (O Heavenly Father) for the sweete and
quiet rest that we have had this night, for the loving and favorable deliverance
out of all daungers bothe of bodie and soule, which we justly deserve to be
throwne into for our manifolde sinnes: for that thou hast raised us upp this
morning, we pray thee to go before us: and for as muche as thou seest our
sluggishnesse and drowsines, it would please thee (good Lord) to pull us after
thee, and to shewe us those wayes, whiche thou hast appointed us to walke
in. And as thou renuest this morning, so renue thy mercies: and as thou
causest the Sunne comfortably to shine to our bodily eyes, so vouchesafe (we
pray thee) to be Sun unto our bodies and to our soules, by the beames of thy
holy Spirit, and Starr of thy blessed Word, shining into the middes of our
hartes, to drive away all the night and darkenesse of all prophanenesse . . . .[24]

This is less than half of Dering's prayer, but even in this much of
it one may find unmistakable echoes of a number of now very familiar
morning prayers. The first is that "sweet sleep and comfortable rest"
prayer of Erasmus which is found in so many of the devotional books of
the time. Then comes the familiar Primer prayer of thanks to God for
safe-keeping through the night. And this is followed by a rather elaborate development of the theme of another of Erasmus' prayers which
is often found in the devotional books of this period, for instance, in the
official primer of 1545, "O Lorde Jesu Chryst, which art the verye
bright sonne of the worlde." [25]

What all this adds up to is simply that the prayer-book makers of this
period used the materials of the Primer very much as they used the
Psalms as a quarry from which to take the raw materials for their own
compositions. Again, as with the Psalms, the prayers of the Primer had
become so much a part of their consciousness that their most fervent
and spontaneous devotional impulses would tend to find expression in
the familiar images and even phrases of the prayers of daily use. Sometimes the derivation would be direct and immediate, and this would be
truer earlier in the century perhaps than later. But when one remembers
the chain character of sixteenth-century devotional literature, it is not
surprising that even men who did not use the Primer in any direct form

would be drawing on it unconsciously through the various intervening collections which we have been surveying.

Perhaps the most dramatic evidence of this process of adaptation which we have been studying is the way in which these editors turned to the traditional materials even when for some reason they felt compelled to reject an established prayer and provide a substitute. This is particularly striking in the case of some of those prayers for the universal and enduring everyday needs of humanity. In such cases what they had to do was to substitute for the old prayer that seemed misleading or sometimes simply out of date what they considered a sound and adequate prayer. A very good example is to be seen in the provision of a prayer for a woman with child. The Regnault *Hore* of 1527 with classic universality and impersonality provides a psalm, to which is added the comforting reminder of the common lot in terms of scriptural and sanctoral motherhoods, beginning with the greatest of all:

Beatus vir qui non abiit in consilio impiorum, et in via peccatorum non stetit et in cathedra pestilentie non sedit.

Sed in lege domini voluntas eius: et in lege eius meditabitur die ac nocti.

. . . .

Quoniam novit dominus viam iustorum: et iter impiorum peribit. Gloria patri et filio. Sicut erat in principio. ✠ Maria peperit christum. ✠ Anna mariam. ✠ Elizabeth iohannem. ✠ Cecilia remigium. ✠ Sic me feliciter parere concedat omnipotens deus in perfecto maturitatis tempore. Amen.[26]

For all the traditional elements which Becon took over in *The Flower of Godly Prayers,* this prayer he did not take over, and that for quite obvious reasons. The scriptural opening would, of course, appeal to him, but the emphasis on the Virgin and her mother, to say nothing of the accompanying saints would encourage sentiments and reflections of a kind which Becon and his colleagues were eager to extirpate from English devotion. The prayer which he printed, therefore, was of a very different character.[27] This prayer begins with praise for the wonderful works of the Creator and then proceeds to a lengthy reminder of the primal curse upon Eve. Then it goes on to pray for ease of pain and for the successful delivery of the child and the joyous restoration of the mother. Throughout there is a characteristic emphasis on the intellectual elements of devotion, and yet at the end there is a particular, personal touch that points to the original source of this prayer. For Becon did not compose this prayer. It is a modified version of a well-known prayer of Vives.[28]

The same version was used in the Bull-Middleton *Christian Praiers*.[29] But the 1578 edition of the Day *Christian Prayers* went back to the Latin of Vives' prayer for a much more faithful translation,[30] one of many characteristic revivals of traditional elements in that book. As one would expect, there is much less of the fall of Eve in the original, and in the final petition as it appears in the Day book one catches that note of tender compassion that is characteristic of Vives:

O most gracious workman, let thy pitifulnes amend the thing which our sinfulnes hath marred, and eyther abate my payne, that I may not have neede of so great strength, tendance, and cunning: or els increase my strength, power, and courage, that I may be able to overcome all the payne of my travell, Amen.

But interesting as is this use of traditional materials for the continuing needs of humanity, still more illuminating is the way in which traditional materials were used to meet the evolving needs of the sixteenth-century situation. Probably the most striking example of this, as well as the most consequential, is to be seen in the development of those prayers for royal authority that came to play an ever larger part in the English prayer books of the century.

The Regnault *Hore* of 1527 included a prayer for the king, the classic *Deus regnorum et Christiane maxime protector,* in a highly miscellaneous series of prayers, all in Latin, between the prayers "Ayenst evyll thoughtes" and "For thy frende lyvyng." [31] Such a position hardly suggests much attention to this prayer. The Paris primer of 1538 gives a rather more conspicuous position to the subject, but even less space in one of the petitions of the Litany, "That thou gyve peace and concorde to our kynge and prynces, and also victorye, We praye the to heare us." [32] That is followed by petitions for the bishops and for all congregations of saints. But in the prayers at the end of the Litany although there are more prayers for bishops and congregations and for all the faithful as well, there is none for the king.[33] Indeed, the only other prayer for the king in the book is "The prayer of Salomon for wysdome to the entente to governe the people ryghtly to be daydly [*sic*] pronunced of al prynces whiche be set authoritie" from 1 Kings 3, given in both Latin and English.[34]

But the Rouen primer of the same year, whose relationship to this Paris primer we have already studied, does print in the prayers at the end of the Litany a substantial prayer "For the kynge," the old prayer of the Regnault *Hore* of 1527, this time with an English version:

Lorde of god hostes, kynge most myghtye and stronge, by whom kynges do reigne, and in whose handes are the hertes of all kynges: graunte unto thy wel beloved servaunt, H. our kynge continuall helthe of body and soule, that his herte always enclynynge to holsome and godly counselles: and the enemyes of the common welthe beinge vanquished we may longe enjoye under hym perpetuall peace, and brotherly concorde.[35]

The Henrician primer of 1545, as one would expect, gives more attention to this theme, for it provides three prayers for Henry, and one each for Catharine and Edward, in the petitions of the litany itself, but there is still no sign of any special prayer for the king among the prayers at the end of the litany.[36] But the Marian primer of 1555 provides a prayer with the legend "For the kinge" in rubric red with "And Quene," added in black, in the prayers at the end of the litany,[37] and the prayer itself is in both the Latin and the English version of the Rouen primer of 1538 with the exception of the necessary adaptation to the two persons, the king and queen. This is fresh evidence of the distinctly eclectic character of the primer of 1555.

But this prayer was apparently too bare and perhaps even a little too forthright for the taste of the editor of *Psalmes or Prayers taken out of Holie Scripture* of 1544. For there the bare outline of the traditional prayer was richly embroidered with phrases from Scripture and the Primer, as may be seen from the opening petition:

O LORDE Jesu Christe most hygh, most mightye, kynge of kynges, lorde of lordes, the onely rular of princis, the very sonne of god, on whose ryght hand syttyng, dooeste frome thy throne beholde all the dwellers upon earth: with moste lowly hertes we beseche the, vouchesafe with favourable regarde, to beholde our most gratious soveraygne lorde, kynge HENRY the eight, and so replenyshe hym with the grace of thy holye spyrite, that he alway inclyne to thy wyll, and walke in thy waye.[38]

But, as usual, in *The Pommaunder of Prayers* Becon returned to a version closer to the traditional one, this time, of course, in a prayer for the queen.[39] Except for one or two minor changes this version of Becon's reappeared in *The Queenes Praiers* of about 1568, the Bull-Middleton *Christian Praiers,* and the Day prayer books, both that of 1569 and that of 1578.[40] But this single prayer is no longer enough.

In the Day book of 1578,[41] for instance, there are three other very substantial prayers for the queen, to say nothing of allusions to her in still other prayers. There is no question of the relative position of the ruler in this prayer book and in earlier primers. Indeed, this prayer for the ruler becomes one of the most important constituents of the sixteenth-century prayer book. And it is easy to see why. It was a prime instrument for the encouragement of that loyalty to the established order in Church and State that was so much desired by those responsible for the peace of the realm.

But it could on occasion work in the opposite direction as well. It could be used as a form of moral pressure on the government to go farther in the direction of desired changes than it seemed of itself disposed to go. Becon shows what could be done with this instrument entirely within the accepted bounds of patriotism and piety alike in a prayer for King Edward in *The Flower of Godly Prayers:*

O Almyghtye god kyng of kynges and Lord of Lords, which by thy devyne ordynaunce hast appoynted temporall rulers to governe thy people accordyng to equyty and justyce, and to lyve amonge them as a loving father among his natural children, unto the avauncement of the good, and punyshmente of the evyll, we most humbly besech the favorably to be holde Edward thy servaunte oure kynge and Governoure, and to breath into hys hert through thy holy spirit that wysdome, that is ever about the trone of thy Majestye, whereby he may be provoked, moved and styrred to love, feare and serve the, to seke thy glorye, to banyshe Idolatry, supersticion and hipocrysye out of thys hys realme, and unfaynedly to avaunce thy holy and pure religion amonge us his subjects unto the example of other forren nacions.[42]

But once things were firmly in hand, this type of prayer did not have much chance. There is a prayer in the first of the Day prayer books that betrays something of the same desire to make sure that the ruler is of the right mind, but it disappeared by the next edition. And it is not hard to see why when one reads it. For "A Prayer for wisedome to governe the Realme," is one of the most interesting prayers in all these books. It is a prayer put into the lips of Queen Elizabeth, alluding specifically to that prayer of Solomon's for wisdom to rule well that was one of the continuing favorites of all the primers and prayer books of the time. But the interest of this prayer lies in its particular references to the circumstances of Queen Elizabeth herself:

Almightie God and King of all Kinges, Lorde of heaven and earth, by whose ordinaunce Princes have governance of mortal men, wheras the

wisest King Salomon plainly confesseth him self unable to governe his kingdome without thy helpe and assistance: how much lesse shall I thy hand-
maide, being by kinde a weake woman, have sufficient abilitie to rule these
thy kingdomes of England and Ireland, an innumerable and warlike nation,
or how shall I possibly be able to beare the infinite weight of so great a burden,
unlesse thou (O most mercifull Father) as thou hast of thine own liberalitie,
without my deserving and agaynst the expectation of many, geven me a
kingdome and made me to reigne, doe also in my reigning endue and helpe
me with thy heavenly grace, without which, none, even the wisest among the
children of men, can once thinke a right thought.[43]

However edifying in the abstract the humility expressed in this prayer
may be, it well might seem a bit overdone as a lasting prescription to a
more patient woman than Queen Elizabeth. At any rate it was not to
be found in the second version of the Day prayer books in 1578. But in
the appeal to the prayer of Solomon, it well illustrates the way in which
even in the response to new occasions, the instinct for the traditional
still persisted in the devotional books of the sixteenth century.

XIII

THE FIFTEEN OES

UT illuminating even in scattered examples as this study of the techniques of adaptation is, it does not give such a sense of an organic process as would the study of these techniques at work in the handling of a single unified group of prayers. Fortunately, we have such a group of prayers to study in a variety of transformations in what is perhaps the most remarkable example of the process of survival through modification and adaptation which we have been studying. It is that famous series of prayers, known as the *Fifteen Oes,* probably first printed in an English version in that separate edition which William Caxton printed about 1490, at the commandment of the Princess Elizabeth, Queen of England and of France, and also of the Princess Margaret, mother of King Henry VII.[1]

So fervent and tender are these prayers that a nineteenth-century editor of Caxton's, Stephen Ayling, was moved to suggest that they must owe their origin to some of Wyclif's followers.[2] They are, however, thoroughly orthodox classics of the traditional Primer as may well be seen in the little prefatory note in English which the editor of the Regnault *Hore* of 1527 prefixed to his text: "These be the .xv. oos the whyche the holy virgyn saint brygitta was wounte to say dayly before the holy rode in saint Paules chyrche at Rome." Such was the potency of this series of prayers according to the editor of this quite unreformed volume that

who so say this a hole yere he shall delever .xv. soules out of purgatory of hys next kyndreed: and converte other .xv. synners to gode lyf and other .xv. ryghtuouse men of hys kynde shall persever in gode lyfe. And what ye desyre of god ye shall have yt, yf it be to the salvacyon of your sowle.[3]

But in spite of these rash and circumstantial promises, the prayers in themselves were sound and edifying even to the critical eye of the sixteenth-century English reforming editors, as Bishop Hilsey readily admitted in an equally characteristic note of explanation in his primer of 1539:

These .xv. prayers folowing called commonly the .xv. Ooes are set forth in divers laten primers with goodly printed prefaces, promisinge to the sayers therof many thinges both folyshe and false, as the deliveraunce of .xv. soules out of purgatory, with other lyke vanities: yet are the prayers selfe right good and vertuous, yf they be sayd without any suche supersticious truste or blynde confidence. And for as much as these prayers are a goodly and godly meditacion of Christes passion, we have not thoughte it nether to us grevous, nether to thys primer superfluous to set them in thys place.[4]

They are, as Bishop Hilsey said, "a goodly and godly meditation of Christ's passion," but they are something more, and it is that something more that makes their history in English devotional books of this century so interesting and so significant. For they are just the type of prayer that one would expect to see disappear from the devotional books of the middle of the sixteenth century on. Their approach to the basic transaction of Christian history is characteristic of the age in which they were composed. The Passion and Death of Christ is viewed not as something past, to be commemorated for its theological significance, to be honored for its redemptive efficacy, but rather as a continuing spiritual reality into which the worshiper aspires to enter as directly and as immediately as possible. The whole contemplative effort, therefore, is animated by a desire not only to appreciate intellectually a great transaction but to participate as fully as possible in the experience of it, with every resource of the human being. What is sought, in other words, is no passive effect, but a very active response of love, and compunction, and gratitude. In this the imaginative and affective elements of human experience have their due part, just as do the moral and intellectual.

Moreover, this series of prayers belongs to that late development of medieval devotion which concentrated especially on the humanity of Christ. That leads in the contemplation of the Passion to an exploration of the human elements of Christ's suffering, and a development not only of the physical appearance of pain, but of the feeling and suffering of pain, developed with a great deal of graphic sense detail and emotional reaction. The result is an unmistakable emotional glow, a warmth of enthusiasm, in general rather different from the gravity of temper of men like Bradford. A few passages will make clear this peculiar emotional tenderness and intimacy of feeling. The beginning of the first of the *Fifteen Oes* in Caxton's version sets the emotional tone very well:

O Jhesu endles swetnes of lovyng soules, O Jhesu gostly joye passing and excedyng all gladnes and desires. O Jhesu helthe and tendre lover of al repentaunt sinners that likest to dwelle as thou saydest thy selfe with the children of men. For that was the cause why thou were incarnate, and made man in the ende of the worlde.[5]

That tender intimacy of invocation, that assurance not of divine approval but of divine tenderness, is not the characteristic note of sixteenth-century English devotion.

The very technique of reminding Christ of the grief of his Passion is more like the highly anthropomorphic devotion of the fourteenth century, say, than the highly theological and analytic and forensic devotion of the sixteenth century:

O blessid Jhesu maker of al the worlde, that of a man may not be mesured, whiche closest in thy honde all the erthe. Have mynde of thy bitter sorow . . . .

O Jhesu hevenly leche have mynde of thy langour and blewnes of thy woundes and sorowe that thou suffredest in the heyght of the crosse . . . .

O Jhesu very fredom of aungellys, paradys of all gostly delites. Have mynde of the drede and hideous ferfulnesse that thou suffredest whan all thyne enmyes stode abowte the and clipped the as wode lions smytyng the and spittynge the, cratchyng the and many other grevous paynes puttyng to the . . . .

O Blessed Jhesu lovable kyng, and frende in all thyng. Have mynde of the sorowes that thou haddest whan thou hengest naked dispitously upon the cros. And all thy frendes and knowlege stode ayenst the, of whom thou fondest noo comforte, but oonly of thi blessed mother . . . .[6]

So from prayer to prayer the reminders proceed with an emphasis upon the human pain and loneliness of Christ that is more in the temper of the pre-Reformation period than of the sixteenth century.

True, there are prayers in this group that put as much stress as any reforming composition on the theological conceptions involved, but one feels that the theological conceptions are the basis, the statement of the premises on which the prayer is based, and not the objective of the prayer. A good example is to be seen in the fifth of the series:

O Jhesu blessyd myrrour of endles clerenes. Have mynde of thy blessyd memoryall recorde, whan thou beheldest in the myrrour of thy ryght clere mageste in predestynacion of all thy chosen soules that sholde be saved by the merite of thy passyon. For mynde of the depnes of thy grete mercy whyche thou haddest upon us lost desperate sinners, and namely for the grete mercy whiche thou shewdeste to the theef that henge on thy ryght side sayenge to hym thus. This day thou shalt be wyth me in paradyse. I praye the benygne Jhesu to shewe thy merci to me in the hour of my deth. Amen.[7]

Still more is this true of what is probably the highest flight of the series in the theological realm, and that is the beginning of the fourteenth prayer:

O Blessid Jhesu the oncly begoten sone of almyghty god thy fader and shinyng likenes of his fygural substaunce. Have mynde of thy meke commendyng, whan thou commendest thy spiryte in to the handes of thy fader. And soo thou lostest thy bodely life with a grete cryeng and with a torne body and broken hert shewyng to us for our raunson the bowellis of thy mercy.[8]

That these prayers were widely appreciated in England is indicated by their history. In the Jehannot *Horae* of 1498 they were printed in Latin alone, but they were given in both English and Latin in the *Hore* which Christopher of Endhoven printed at Antwerp in 1525, the Regnault *Hore* of 1527, the Rouen primers of 1536 and 1538, the Paris primer of 1538, Bishop Hilsey's primer of 1539, the Toye primer of 1542, and the official Marian primer of 1555,[9] to name the most notable among the books we have studied. Something of the value set upon them is apparent in the fact that though the Christopher of Endhoven *Hore* contains after the opening materials no other English prayers, these prayers are given in full in an English version, set in the midst of the Latin prayers, between the so-called *Versus sancti Bernardi* and the *Vigilie mortuorum*.

In general the text of the Latin is, as one would expect, the same, but there is one notable exception. That exception is a curious confusion between the fifth and sixth prayers that goes back as far at least as the Jehannot *Horae* of 1498 but which in view of the presence of the English translation on the same page is best illustrated in the Paris primer of 1538. In the latter edition the English version of the fifth prayer opens as follows:

O Blessyd Jesu myrroure of the divyne clerenesse, Have mynde of the drede and hevynes whan thou hangest naked and myserable on the crosse, and all thy fryndes and acquoyntaunce stode agaynst the, and founded com-

fort of none but onely thy most lovyng mother faytfully standynge by the
with great bytternes of harte.

And the sixth begins thus:

O Blessyd Jesu, kynge moost worthy to be lovyd, and frende moste to be
desyred have mynde of that sorowe that thou haddest whan thou beheldest
in the myrrour of thy ryght clere magestie in predestinacyon of al thy chosen
soules that shulde be saved by the meryte of thy passyon.[10]

The confusion of initial images and immediately ensuing petitions is
obvious. In the version which Caxton gives, the relations are logical, with
the appropriate petition developing out of the basic image:

V. O Jhesu blessyd myrrour of endles clerenes. Have mynde of thy blessyd
memoryall record, whan thou beheldest in the myrrour of thy ryght clere
mageste in predestynacion of all thy chosen soules that sholde be saved by the
merite of thy passyon.

VI. O Blessed Jhesu lovable kyng, and frende in all thyng. Have mynde of
the sorowes that thou haddest whan thou hengest naked despitously upon
the cros. And all thy frendes and knowlege stode ayenst the, of whom thou
fondest noo comforte, but oonly of thi blessed moder standyng wyth the
feythfully and truly al the tyme of thy bitter passion? [11]

Now the interesting thing is that the Latin versions of these two prayers are mixed up in this fashion in the Jehannot *Horae* of 1498, the
Christopher of Endhoven *Hore* of 1525, and the Regnault *Hore of*
1527,[12] but the English versions are straight as in Caxton in both the
Christopher of Endhoven *Hore* and the Regnault *Hore*.[13] In the Rouen
primers of 1536 and 1538 [14] both the Latin and the English are mixed
up alike as they are in the Paris primer of 1538. And the same is true of
Bishop Hilsey's primer of 1539, the Toye primer of 1542, and the Marian
primer of 1555.[15] This is fresh confirmation of the relations already suggested for these versions of the traditional primer.

Still more interesting is the fact that in all these books the English
version comes from the same source, Caxton. True, there are changes
from time to time. As one would expect, there is a tendency to emotional elaboration in the Regnault primer of 1527. In the second prayer,
for instance, with regard to the piercing of Christ's feet by the nails,
Caxton's phrase is "thy blessed tendre feet," but in 1527, it has been
intensified to "thy blessyd, tender and swete fete." [16] Likewise in the
seventh prayer, Caxton's "the cros of thy passion" becomes in the Regnault version "the tree of the holy crosse at thy bytter passyon." [17] As

one would expect, the Paris primer of 1538 returns to the emotionally simpler form of Caxton, with "thy tender fete" in the second prayer and "the crosse of thy passyon" in the seventh,[18] and it keeps to it with a good deal of fidelity, with the exception of the confusion already noted between the fifth and sixth prayers, it will be remembered, a confusion carried over from the Latin.

The Marian primer of 1555 prints a version under the less traditional title, "The .xv. prayers of sainct Brygyde," [19] between a couple of miscellaneous prayers after Compline and the Seven Penitential Psalms. The very first prayer begins quite differently from Caxton's, almost as if a fresh translation were being assayed, but soon lapses into what is basically his version.[20] There are deviations, however, not to be found in the Paris primer of 1538. The most striking is the interpolation of a passage on the grief in Christ's mind when he gave his body and blood to his disciples at the Last Supper,[21] a passage to be found in the Latin of the Regnault *Hore* of 1527 but not in the English version,[22] for the simple reason that the latter is Caxton's. There are some changes in the wording of other prayers, sometimes cutting down on emotional intensity, sometimes heightening it, altogether making it very risky to generalize on the total effect.[23] There are, on the whole, a good many changes from Caxton's version, but it is still undeniably his.

Such was the history of this famous series when the Day *Christian Prayers* of 1578 took them over. From the very start a difference in approach is apparent, as one would expect, more like that of, say, the Hilsey primer of 1539 than the Regnault *Hore* of 1527. To begin with, there is no mention of Saint Bridget or any other author. The *Fifteen Oes* appear without warning in a series of prayers introduced by "A Prayer upon the minding of Christes passion," [24] each labeled simply "Another," with no hint that they are more than a series of Passion prayers. Only ten out of the fifteen prayers, with the addition of the beginning of the otherwise omitted fifth prayer transposed to the beginning of the seventh, are used. The first of the original series comes first here, and the fifteenth last, but otherwise the order is different. For the first time the basic version is not Caxton's but a fresh translation, apparently made directly from the current Latin version in which, as we have seen, the fifth and sixth prayers were already mixed up.

When it comes to the selection of these prayers, it is almost more interesting to note what is omitted than what is kept. For, on the whole,

the omissions mark the major differences between the point of view of
Caxton's time and that of 1578. There is one possible exception where
the reasons for the omission are not by any means entirely clear. It is the
fifth prayer, which is omitted but for the striking invocation: "O Jhesu
blessyd myrrour of endles clerenes. Have mynde of thy blessyd memoryall recorde." [25] This is the invocation which in the confusion of
Latin texts noted above was transferred to the opening of the sixth
prayer. This time it is not transferred to the sixth prayer, for that was
omitted, as we shall see in a moment, but to the seventh. It is not easy
to see just why the remainder of the fifth prayer was omitted unless that
phrase about predestination, "whan thou beheldest in the myrour of
thy ryght clere mageste in predestynacion of all thy chosen soules that
sholde be saved by the merite of thy passyon," [26] applied to Christ hanging on the cross seemed, when coupled with the pardoning of the thief,
a bit too vague for an age that was especially clear in its theory about
predestination.

And it is not easy, either, to see why the opening of the fifth prayer
is transferred to the opening of the seventh prayer. The result is that
the prayer which runs as follows in Caxton,

O Blessed Jhesu welle of endles pyte, that saydest on the cros of thy passion by inwardely affection of love, I thurst, that is to saye, the helthe of
mannys soule. For mynde of this blessid desire, I beseche the benigne Jhesu
take hede to my desire, that it maye be parfight in all good werkes. And
quenche in me the thirste of all fleshly love and lust Amen.

becomes in the Day *Christian Prayers* of 1578:

O Jesu the mirror of eternall brightnes, and fountayn of unconsumeable
goodnes, which hanging upon the crosse, didst thirst for the salvation of
man [*sic*] mankind, I beseech thee kindle in us the desire of all good works,
and quench in us the thirst of all fleshly lustes, and both coole and kill in us
the love of all worldly delighte, Amen. [27]

The result of this change is a somewhat incongruous pairing of
images with not entirely happy results for the logic. And it does violence,
also, to what is in general the rather exact congruity between opening
image and theme. Certainly the well figure is a much happier one than
the mirror figure in view of the emphasis on the thirst of the cross in
the prayer that follows. One wonders if the emphasis on the pity and
solicitude of Christ in the original seemed perhaps to the editor of 1578
less bracing and edifying than the emphasis on Christ's goodness.

There is no such uncertainty about the motives for the omission of the sixth prayer. The main idea of this prayer is, as we have seen, that Christ found human comfort on the Cross only in the presence of his mother. With tender and awed sympathy the author of the prayer watches him give her to the care of Saint John.[28] In view of the contemporary suspicions of any attention to Mary, it is easy to see why this prayer was left out by the editor of 1578.

In similar fashion the eighth prayer [29] disappears in the Day book. It is a sacramental prayer that we may receive the Body and Blood of the Lord for the remedy of our sins. It clearly runs counter to the commemorative view of the Sacrament held by so many English Protestants of the time, and to many it might suggest an infringement upon the unique redemptive potency of Christ's suffering on the cross. In general temper and tone this prayer is very different from the English Communion prayers of the third quarter of the sixteenth century; so it is easy to understand its omission. But, again it is not so easy to see why the thirteenth prayer, devoted to the commemoration of Christ's exhaustion on the cross and the final words of consummation,[30] should be omitted. It might be because of a certain fear of emphasizing the human suffering at the expense of the redemptive significance of the whole sacrifice. That, as we have seen, was one of the important changes in point of view inspiring alterations in the Primer materials at that time.

But dramatic as this process of selection is in its implications, it is not by any means the whole story of the adaptation of these prayers to new times and feelings. For even where the old prayers are kept in their entirety, there is a good deal of more or less quiet modification of effect if not content.

Some notion of the variations possible between the different versions of these prayers may be obtained from a comparison of a few passages. We shall take the opening of the first prayer, for that not only comes first in both the traditional series and the abbreviated series of Day's *Christian Prayers* of 1578, but this section has probably undergone more experimentation than any other in the entire series. In the opening invocation and petition, we shall find no overt changes, but a progressive sharpening of the statement so that the final effect is less emotional and intellectually more insistent.

In Caxton's version it runs:

O Jhesu endles swetnes of lovyng soules. O Jhesu gostly joye passing and excedyng all gladnes and desires. O Jhesu helthe and tendre lover of al repentaunt sinners that likest to dwelle as thou saydest thy selfe with the children of men. For that was the cause why thou were incarnate, and made man in the ende of the worlde. Have mynde blessed Jhesu of all the sorowes that thou suffredest in thy manhode drawynge nyghe to thy blessed passion. In the whiche most holsom passion was ordeyned to be in thy devyne herte, by counseyle of al the hole trynyte, for the raunson of al mankynde.

In the Marian primer of 1555 this becomes:

O Jesu, endles swetnes to al that love thee: a joye passyng and excedynge all gladnes and desire, The saviour and lover of all repentaunte synners, that lykest to dwell (as thou sayedst thy selfe) wyth the children of men, for that was the cause why thou wast incarnate, and made man in the ende of the worlde. Have mind blessed Jesu, of al the sorowes that thou sufferedst in thy manhode, drawyng nigh to thy blessed passion, the which moste holsome passyon was ordeyned to bee in thy divine hearte, by counsaile of the holye Trinitie, for the raunsome of all mankynde.

The version of the *Christian Prayers* of 1578 begins:

O Lord Jesu Christ, the everlasting sweetnesse and triumph of them that love thee, exceeding all joy, and all longing, thou saver and lover of repentant sinners, which avowest that thy delight is to be among the children of men: and therfore in the end of times, becamest man for mennes sakes: remember all the foretast and greefe of sorrow, which thou didst indure even from the instant of thy conception in the humain nature, forth on: but most of all when the time of thy most healthfull passion was at hand, according to the eternall ordinance which God had purposd in his mind before al worlds.[31]

So far the persistence of the traditional phrasing is striking, but now at the conclusion of the first petition, there is a sharp divergence. The Caxton version and most of the versions following it proceed from the above opening to a reminder of the betrayal by Judas, but the Marian primer of 1555 inserts between the opening and the betrayal passage the following:

Have mynd of the bytter grefe and heavines whiche (as thou thy selfe dyddest saye) was in thy mynde whan at thy laste supper thou gavest thy bodye and bloud to thy disciples, diddest wash their fete: and swetelye comfortynge them, dyddest forshewe unto them that thy passyon was at hande.[32]

Now there is a Latin version of this passage on the same page of the 1555 primer, as there was in the Regnault *Hore* and in the Paris primer of 1538,[33] but there is no English translation of the Latin in either. The explanation is simple. These earlier versions, on the whole, kept pretty faithfully to the Caxton translation. But once the passage was restored in the Marian primer of 1555, it was carried over into the *Christian Prayers* of 1578:

Remember the greefe and bitternesse which thou feltst in thy hart, even by thine own record, when thou saydst: *my soule is heavy even unto the death.* And at such time as thou gavest thy body and bloud to thy disciples at thy last supper, didst wash their feete, and comforting them sweetly, toldst them of thy passion that was at hand.[34]

Then the 1578 editor returns to the traditional theme of the prayer, the suffering of Jesus before the cross, especially the bloody sweat and the betrayal. On the whole, these themes are developed in the traditional fashion, but in more general terms than usual. And a considerable passage of general penitence and contrition for sin, not found in the other versions, is added to the foregoing materials.[35] This underscoring of the penitential motive probably reflects the sixteenth-century reformer's preoccupation with conscience. But it may also be somewhat in the nature of an offset to the emphasis on the human elements in the situation, characteristic of the foregoing portions of the prayer.

It may, also, have been inserted in anticipation of the difficulties of the traditional ending. For in Caxton the final petition runs as follows: "For mynde of this blessed passion, I beseche the benygne Jhesu graunte me afore my deth very contricyon, trew confessyon, and worthy satysfaction. And of al my sinnes plener remyssion, amen." [36]. The primer of 1555 kept the same petition with the exception that the adjective, "plener" dropped out before the word "remission." [37] This may be sheer accident, by no means unique in sixteenth-century printing. But it may, also, be further evidence of a certain tendency to accommodation to the times already suggested by other changes made in that book.

For there is no doubt of the intention of the editor of 1578 in what he does with this petition. All reference to confession drops out, and the occasion is improved to remind the pious reader of the source of his salvation in the merits of his redeemer:

Wherefore I beseech thee graunt me true repentance, amendment of life, perseverance in all goodnes, a stedfast fayth, and a happy death, through the merites of thy sufferings, that I may also be made partaker of thy blessed resurrection. Amen.[38]

In general, the remaining prayers are reproduced in their traditional form with very few changes of any great importance. Now and then, however, a seemingly slight alteration is seen upon closer scrutiny to reflect a really significant difference in point of view.

One of the most interesting of these is to be found in the concluding petition of what in Caxton is the eleventh prayer and in the *Booke of Christian Prayers* of 1578 the seventh. The Caxton version addresses the prayer to Christ: ". . . that thou vouchesauf to draw me oute of sinne, and hide me ever after in the holes of thy woundes fro the face of thy wrath unto the tyme lorde that thy dredeful dome be passed. Amen"— a petition that rather assumes the whole Trinity in each member thereof. But in the version of 1578 there is a careful discrimination between the Son sacrificed and the Father whose wrath is appeased: ". . . hide me in the holes of thy wounds, from the sight of thy Fathers just wrath, untill his displeasure be overpast, Amen." [39]

These examples are but a few among many that might be instanced of alterations and adaptations that reflect profound changes in the religious thought and feeling of the sixteenth century. The sum total of their effect pretty much confirms what we have observed already in the adaptation of other primer materials. At first glance, the most striking of these changes are obviously the omissions. These result mainly from the fear of giving honor to the Virgin and the saints, even when as in the rejected sixth prayer of the *Fifteen Oes,* the source is clearly a record in Scripture. They result, too, from a changed attitude toward the Eucharist and the sacrament of confession, and these in turn involve some of the profoundest changes in the thinking of the time, the tendency to the attenuation of supernaturalism, and the resolution of the ancient argument as to the roles of predestination and free will in favor of predestination, and of the dispute as to the relative parts of faith and works in favor of faith.

In various of these changes, may be seen, too, the shift in emphasis from God the Son to God the Father, and from the humanity to the divinity of Christ, or to be more exact, from the human implications to the redemptive function of Christ's life on earth. And from this comes, of course, a change in the approach to the Saviour which results in less stress on the sense details of the human experience, and more on the theological significance of the scriptural transaction. Now the Protestant devotional writers were no less concerned about the reader's receiving the full impact of that story. But in general they put their trust in the efficacy of theological reminder. They stressed, therefore, the significance of the process of the redemption, and appealed more directly and perhaps more abstractly, certainly less sensuously and emotionally, to the reader's awareness of the meaning of what he was considering and to the conclusions he should draw as to his own obligations.

Possibly, this tendency, like so many other new developments in the intellectual life of the time, was reënforced by the invention of printing and the resulting cheapening and greater availability of reading matter. If the printed page is the principal medium of communication after speech, it is not surprising that the abstract formulation should impinge rather heavily upon other forms of representation. It would be rash to oversimplify in so complicated and obscure a matter as this, and assume a direct connection between the facilitation of the appeal through reading by the invention of printing and the iconoclastic attack so often found in this period upon the other forms of communication and representation of religious ideas. For that iconoclastic attack goes back much further than this period. But there can be no doubt that the invention of printing gave the iconoclast a tool which he could use himself with a clear conscience and could urge upon other people to the disparagement and neglect of other methods of communication.

But whatever the truth about this complicated matter of underlying psychology, the fact remains that the handling of scriptural narrative was for the sixteenth-century devotional writer not only a means of satisfying perennial spiritual needs, but also of reënforcing what he held to be the right doctrinal positions and attitudes.

Whatever the cause, the effect is striking as in this case, on the handling of the Passion, for now the desire of the worshiper is not to enter into the experience of the Passion through contemplation, but rather to draw its theological lessons and to take them more closely and efficaciously to heart. And this tendency is reënforced by the highly penitential mood of sixteenth-century religion in general, perhaps the inevitable mood of a century of such self-conscious and deliberate moral and religious reform.

It is these changes in fundamental religious orientation that lead to what may be called the rhetorical changes in the text of these prayers. To take the most obvious example, the expansion of the penitential theme in the first prayer, there was no need for Caxton to labor the implications of "very contricyon, trew confessyon, and worthy satysfaction and . . . plener remyssion." They were familiar to all in the accepted teachings of the sacrament of penance. There was no need, either, to explain the premises on which these conceptions rested, for they were taken for granted. But the situation was very different when this established system was rejected. It became necessary, then, to explain the ideas upon which that overturn of established custom had been predicated, and in the beginning, at least, to explain them as persuasively as possible, as we saw in the changing primers. By 1578 the new order was established and, so far as we can tell, generally accepted, or at least acquiesced in. The need, now, was not for the establishment of a new point of view, but for the enforcement of significance and the development of implications. But the old impulse to careful elaboration remained to impart that general effect of systematic theological explication and exhortation characteristic of the devotion of the time.

But against this, on the positive stylistic side should be set the disposition of the editor of the *Christian Prayers* of 1578 to blunt a little the rough edges of the often homely realism of the traditional prayers. It is apparent in many passages ranging from the all but insignificant to the all-pervasive. A good example may be found in a comparison between the two versions of what in the Caxton edition is the fifteenth prayer and in the 1578 version the tenth. The Caxton version describes the Crucifixion thus: "Thenne at last as a bundell of myrre thou hengest on the crosse on high, where thy tendre flesshe chaunged his colour by cause the licour of thy bowellis, and the mary of thy bones was dryed up." This becomes in the 1578 book, "But finally thou wast as a bundle of mirhe hanged up aloft, thy tender flesh shrunke, the moysture of thy bowels dried up, and the marow of thy bones wasted away." [40]

Indeed, the whole stylistic tendency of 1578 is, with few exceptions, in the direction of something smoother and more elegant. There are some very lovely passages in this volume, examples of a style not only serious and vigorous, but also polished and gracious. The following, the last petition of this same tenth prayer, is by no means exceptional:

Turn thou me wholy unto thee, that my hart may dwell with thee continually, and my conversation be acceptable unto thee. And let my life be such, through thy goodnes, as I may prayse thee for ever with al thy Saints in the life to come, Amen.[41]

All of these changes, whether of substance or form, are interesting in themselves and significant for the religious history of the time. Yet

when one sets what has been changed beside what has been kept, the
surprising thing is that so much has been kept relatively unaltered.
Especially is it astonishing that prayers of so emotional a character could
yet, with whatever modifications, have weathered the storms of the
times in what is after all the most brittle of the religious categories, the
field of feeling and taste. It affords fresh confirmation of the extraordinary substratum of continuity through all the changes of the period.

In many quarters the alterations in traditional ideas and attitudes
implicit in the modifications noted above, were, of course, carried much
farther than they were in this Day book of 1578, and they were to develop
to an extent and to have consequences, clearly not envisaged in this
book. But the fact remains that the very presence of these prayers of
the *Fifteen Oes* in a collection of private devotions that was to run
through at least four editions, being republished as late as 1608, bears
witness to the existence in a considerable portion of the devout public
of the third quarter of the sixteenth century of a temper and tone of
feeling not nearly so remote from that of the end of the fifteenth century and the beginning of the sixteenth as one might expect from what
some of the controversialists like Foxe had to say. If Caxton could
have read Day's series of prayers of 1578, he would have been sorry to
see the prayer honoring Christ's mother's part in the scene of the
Crucifixion omitted, and he would have missed the Communion
prayer. But otherwise in the prayers included, he would have found
little to disturb him.

And that may fairly be said of this Day prayer book in general. There
are evidences enough of the Protestant commitments of the time, but
there is little of the revolutionary and militant spirit of the controversialists of the time. Perhaps there is less controversy anyhow when
men pray to their Maker rather than talk about him. Certainly, the
spirit of these private prayer books is ampler and easier than that of
most of the religious literature of the time. In no small measure this is
due, I think, to the fact that in general the iconoclast did not have so
much to do with this type of composition as the man who appreciated
the riches of the Christian devotional tradition and was eager to make
them available to the continuing needs of the human spirit.

XIV

CONCLUSION

*T*HIS literature of private devotion is, of course, but a portion of the whole wide field of sixteenth-century religious literature. Like the rest of the field it came under the influence of those many forces, economic, social, political, and even personal, that complicated the specifically religious situation. And yet it does have its own organic character and life, emerging from a continuing past and leading into a by no means entirely discontinuous future. In the presence of changes so dramatic as those of the sixteenth century in England it is easy to miss this fundamental character of whatever comes out of the inner life of man, and to set the shifting scene of the revolutionary present against the static uniformity of a rejected past. And it is the easier to do this because of the controversial temper of this period and the highly partisan character of so many of its own self-assessments. Even if one takes a more evolutionary view of the devotional life that flowed on through the vast changes of the time, it is still all too easy to think of the past as something fairly homogeneous, suddenly beginning in the heady climate of this period to put forth unprecedented shoots of variation.

But even a cursory survey of the history of Christian devotional literature reveals a plasticity and a flexibility that reflects the responsiveness of the life of prayer to the intellectual and spiritual pressures of changing times. It may seem frivolous to suggest that devotion has its fashions, its moods, and tempers like the arts. But it is true here as in other aspects of the life of the spirit that the wind bloweth where it listeth, and the life of devotion, however fixed and immutable its center, in its responses veers in value and emphasis. For it is something living in organic relation to its context and environment.

And then there is the influence not only of the age, but for Christian devotion, of personality filtering and coloring the impersonal suggestions of changing circumstance. One needs but to recall the influence of

Saint Paul or Saint Augustine on popular piety, private as well as public, to appreciate this. And when as in the growing influence of monachism on the definition of popular devotion, the personal influence takes institutional shape in the religious order, then one perceives the life-giving as well as living quality of the personal achievement and spirit. The ordered balance of the Benedictine, clear and rational, and self-transcending, the emotional and imaginative flowering of the Cistercian spirit, the humanistic broadening and warming of the rational in Dominican contemplation, all of these are examples of vital changes and developments within the continuing life of Christian devotion. Broadly, it is all the same prayer to the same God, whether, it is Augustine praising the Triune God, with the integrations of Platonic speculation, or Benedict making a veritable liturgy of the familiar labors of daily life, or Bernard of Clairvaux warming his asceticism with the glow of the Divine Humanity and tenderness for the Virgin-Mother so inseparably bound up with that humanity.

And persistently threading all these personal accidents is the basic Christian aspiration toward perfection with its recurring goad of self-reform. Reform—that is the oldest of Christian enterprises; its attenuation and lapse the most recurrent of Christian failures, its revival the surest pledge of Christian vitality. And yet even in the desire for perfection there is always the danger of exaggeration, of excess. So no less striking in the history of Christian devotion is the instinct for adjustment, for balance, for harmony.

And yet there is something cumulative in the process. The constant reference to Scripture and the church fathers, and the unremitting adjustment to the continuing life of the church, invest the whole development of Christian devotion with a genuinely organic character. Even in the revolutionary changes of the sixteenth century certain works of both ancient and more recent provenience, held their place in popular favor. Perhaps in view of the tremendous prestige of Saint Augustine at this time, there is nothing surprising in the fact that works by him or ascribed to him continued to be printed, but the popularity of the *Imitation of Christ,* in which so many strands of medieval devotion were twisted into the psychological-pedagogical analysis dear to the age just preceding this, even more strikingly illustrates this cumulative tendency. True, these surviving masterpieces were "purified" and "corrected" in keeping with the editorial habits of the reformer, but the really surprising fact is that they were preserved, and so carried into sixteenth-century English devotional life more of the traditional than has usually been appreciated.

It is important to remember this organic character of Christian devotion because it explains a good many of the things that happened when men who little valued tradition attempted to begin all over again. Their rejection of the authority of the church and the relevance of the experience of the centuries that followed the first primitive age of Christianity led some of the Protestant reformers of the time to hope that the reading of the Bible alone would satisfy the devotional needs of the faithful. And the circulation of the Scriptures which the development of the invention of printing facilitated made that dream seem possible of realization. And yet, as it proved in the event, with what many of these leaders hoped would be a quite fresh start, some of the past experience of devotional history was strikingly recapitulated.

The Psalter, the earliest book of Christian devotion, by its very nature offered resources for personal expression which soon made clear that its age-long primacy was no accident. The English Psalter had been caught in the maelstrom of the language controversy of the fourteenth and fifteenth centuries. Quite apart from the language issue, its usefulness for the inculcation of new emphases, new points of view, had already been demonstrated. And the present possibilities of expanded circulation together with the heightened appeal of the scriptural, assured the Psalter a prominent place among the "English books" of the sixteenth century. The headings or introductory notes, from antiquity prefixed to the Psalms, were admirably suited to the influence of thought and feeling. Especially characteristic were those sixteenth-century headings which suggested a psychology of crisis, for they did not so much raise issues as assume attitudes. On the other hand, the marginal comments were usually more explicit, and occasionally they were used to good effect for the suggestion of desired changes in point of view.

But in spite of the heightened scripturalism of the time, the development of the Psalter in these years was highly reminiscent of its earlier history. Its ancient tendency to expand with various provisions, pedagogical and devotional, to take care of the daily occasions of its lay user was stronger than the prevailing suspicion of "human inventions" even in reforming circles. And the passion of that great age of English music for singing and the reformer's desire to center even the layman's recreation in Scripture combined to transform the expanded psalter into the psalter to music of Sternhold and Hopkins, and gave the Psalms a popular vogue beyond anything they had ever known.

But like their predecessors in antiquity and the Middle Ages the devotional writers of the sixteenth century began to make their selections from the Psalms and to arrange and rearrange them in new contexts and compositions. So again the text of Scripture became the springboard for fresh devotional creation. And the themes and the phrases of the Psalms were handled with increasing freedom until they came to furnish not so much the source as the very language and idiom of fresh creation. Presently, the process was extended to include other sections of Scripture, such as the prayers of Christ and his disciples in the New Testament. This use of the Bible must sometimes have troubled the more austere scripturalist who believed that all needs could be satisfied in the Word of God itself, but the ancient habit of Christian devotion, here as elsewhere, proved too strong for him.

There was no such restraining factor in the case of the Primer, that already fecund off-shoot of the Psalter which in the later Middle Ages had so strikingly surpassed its parent in popularity as the layman's prayer book. One element in its complex nature might have been expected to make it less congenial to the sixteenth-century Protestant reformer, and that was the liturgical element of the Hours of the Blessed Virgin Mary, obviously an off-shoot of the canonical hours. But this was, though the core of the Primer, still only a part of it. For the fully-developed Primer offered a broad and practical scheme of provision for the day-to-day needs and for the special occasions of the ordinary Christian, quite apart from any lay ambition to emulate monastic observance. At the peak of its development the Primer offered an instrument of popular influence so rich and so persuasive that it is no wonder that the temptations which it had offered to the reformer even within the limitations of medieval circulation should be magnified many times with the new opportunities opened by the revolution in the making and circulation of books.

There is evidence in the series of primers that emanated from Paris and Rouen in the years between 1536 and 1538 that the desirability of making the resources of the Primer more widely available in the vernacular was quite apparent to men who in the main would seem to have been anxious to preserve as much of the tradition of Christian devotion as possible even though in church government they had already yielded to Erastian influences, and shown some signs of readiness to compromise on certain of the doctrinal controversies of the time. The development of the revolution under way was to make their position untenable, but their efforts were unquestionably to count in the preservation of traditional elements in works that would go much farther in the direction of change than they would seem ever to have envisaged.

And for the reformers who wished to go farther, the very plasticity and adaptability of the Primer made it an ideal instrument for suggesting and insinuating new points of view. It had, to begin with, taken form in a period when the lack of any effective censorship gave editors and writers a good deal of latitude. Its shaping principles were customary rather than authoritative, and its obvious motive to provide for the practical day-to-day needs of the layman made adjustment and adaptation, however leisurely from our point of view, the very law of its being. It was intended for private use, too. So the possibility of fresh modification was always there. The way in which that possibility was realized in the sixteenth century is a revelation of the skillful techniques of propaganda of the time.

The Godfray primer of 1534–35 is one example of the way in which this was accomplished. At first sight this looks like a traditional primer, and the man who picked it up would have no warning from the first inspection of his new acquisition that here was anything but the usual thing. Closer acquaintance with the book would, however, reveal various symptoms of change, notably in the attenuation of the Marian elements. Doubtless, some readers would at once recognize and approve this modification. Probably more would recognize and object to it. But there would be a good many who would hardly notice it, or, if they did, would not perceive its full significance. After all, there was plenty of evidence in the volume that the author paid reverence and tribute to the Mother of Christ. Probably very few of the readers of such a work would relate these changes to others going on at the time.

Sometimes of course, the author went too far. The editor of the first of the Byddell-Marshall primers of early 1535 clearly did on his own showing. The more radical purposes back of his ostensible improving and purifying were clearly perceived and identified. And the editor in his next effort, apparently following hard on the heels of the first, was loud in his protests of injured innocence. But he had to retreat. His first primer had been too drastic in its omissions and its modifications to escape attention. So he was forced to explain that he had meant no harm to traditional beliefs and practices, and this he did in a rather ingenious preface that actually carried the attack a little farther into his critics' territory. He obviously knew his business. He knew how at one and the same time to load with enormity something he objected to and to make the protests of his critics seem mere cavilling at trifles while they shut their eyes to real abuses.

But he was also master of some of the finer techniques of adaptation. It is quite clear that he was glad to keep the devotional classic when it laid stress on the score of the sinner and his dependence on Christ for forgiveness. But he was skillful, also, in insinuating into the long-established and familiar text a new emphasis or a fresh application, and in giving a new turn to the development of an old prayer. And he knew how to take up the reader, perhaps for a moment hesitating over an unexpected turn to a familiar prayer, and make him feel that he was here becoming a part of a significant advance in current religious life, that he was keeping up with the times. This was a new type of appeal in devotional literature, but it must have had its exhilarating temptations for some at least of his readers. And, finally, with what we have no reason to doubt was complete sincerity but was nonetheless sound strategy, he reminded the reader how fortunate he was to be living in the reign of a king like Henry VIII, who had brought about what this editor clearly deemed very desirable changes in the religious situation.

Altogether, these experiments in adapting the Primer to a variety of purposes within the traditional forms of the book must have done a good deal to familiarize many readers with new points of view and perhaps even—and this was the most important of all—to accustom them to the idea that times were changing and they should keep up with them.

One might be sure that the apparent success of these primers, especially of the Byddell-Marshall series, would not be lost on a government as alert to the possibilities of propaganda as that of Henry VIII. The evidence that they were not is to be seen in the series of quasi-official and official primers that begins with the primer of Bishop Hilsey in 1539. Indeed, these books may be taken as an index to the by no means steady or uniform development of the religious position of the Henrician government. The proved value of the Primer as a pedagogical instrument was recognized in the pains to which Bishop Hilsey went in reorganizing its materials so as to get the maximum practical use from them. The traditional prefatory notes were used to inculcate the desired attitudes on what had now become such controversial matters as the praying for the dead and the honoring of the Virgin and the saints. With these historically very important exceptions, there was no question that Hilsey wished to keep as much as possible of the materials of the book which had so long enjoyed such a unique position in popular devotion.

When the first of the official primers was published by Grafton in 1545, the government of Henry VIII was either clearer in its mind or readier to go further in such matters as the honoring of the dead. The title and the opening psalm of the *Dirige,* for instance, were kept, but the office was cut by nearly two-thirds, and for the traditional psalms of penance and mercy, psalms of thanksgiving and praise were substituted. The prayers of the Passion were modified, too, so as to draw attention away from the emotional and imaginative contemplation of the experience of the Passion to profitable meditation on the lessons to be drawn therefrom, especially with regard to Christ's satisfaction for sins, a change important for the new teachings on penance. Likewise, the hymns in the Little Hours were changed from praise of the Blessed Virgin to praise of Christ, with greater emphasis on his role as the redeemer. And much of the old litany with its honoring of the saints was swept away. The occasion was taken, too, to promote hostility to Rome, and an effort made to disarm potential objections to these changes with a plea for peace and order. And yet where these central points were not at issue, there was evidently a very considerable effort to preserve the familiar prayers in the accustomed forms. In other words, while what might be called the liturgical aspect of the primer suffered, on the personal-occasional side the traditional was, if anything, underscored.

In a sense, the story of the Henrician primer is a preview of the later history of the sixteenth-century primer. The Edwardian primer of 1553, though hardly to be classified as a primer, for it was really a combination of Book of Common Prayer and Primer, still preserved many of the features of the primer. But in such matters as the calendar, for example, they had been closely assimilated to the Book of Common Prayer of 1552. As regards the portions of the book devoted to private devotion, the development was, as one would expect from the in-fluences dominant at that time, away from the liturgical and firmly in the direction of the practical and the occasional. It is in these occasional prayers that one of the tendencies which was going to prove most important for the future became apparent in this body of literature, and that was the shift from the general spiritual provision for all sorts of men in one situation to the special prayers for particular classes and conditions of men. This was an important foreshadowing of that special group and class orientation and appeal that was destined to play so great a part in later sixteenth- and seventeenth-century devotion.

The Marian restoration of the traditional Primer was not only short-lived, but bore in the book of 1555 the marks of haste and improvisation. The restoration of the traditional pattern of the Primer was to be ex-pected and was effected. What is remarkable about this restoration was its concession to recent events and its use of recent developments. For instance, it fell short of complete restoration when it came to prayers honoring the saints and the traditional Marian prayers. It used the English version of the Paris-Rouen primer of 1538 in spite of the compromises of the series to which that work belonged. And it kept the occasional prayers from the large collection at the end of the Henrician primer of 1545, including not only the traditional prayers but the Henrician borrowings from the contemporary reforming Catholic writer, Vives. And still more remarkably it preserved some of the work of a man who was by that time recognized as a leader of the Protestant reform, Becon. While the possibilities should not be over-looked of haste and of a feeling that it would be wise not to force some issues, still the total impression of this restoration is a confirmation of the general impression already noted, of something very flexible in the whole genre.

And much the same is to be said of the first Elizabethan primer of 1559. For that Queen Elizabeth went back to the Henrician primer of 1545. True, there was a further attenuation of the Marian elements, and certain modifications of what might be termed the liturgical sec-tions of the book, but otherwise Queen Elizabeth restored the primer of her father rather than of her brother, a fact significant for her whole religious orientation. But it was, also, characteristic of the Elizabethan Settlement that while this primer was reprinted several times, in the next year, 1560, came the first of another series going back to the

Edwardian primer, with its tendency away from the liturgical in its provisions for private devotion and its adaptation to the spiritual needs of specific groups and classes of readers.

All in all, the history of the sixteenth-century primer is a striking illustration of the way in which a traditional form might be used in a confused period for the moulding of thought and feeling. It is not surprising that the men who wished to change the old order were so successful, for a fair share of the time a large number of those who used these books must have been hardly aware of what was happening at any one moment.

Both the expanded Psalter and the Primer in their ultimate origins came out of the Bible, out of the Psalms, however far from their sources the developments which we have studied may seem to have carried them. But as the history of both books makes clear, this process of quarrying fresh prayers out of Scripture had never been confined to the Psalms. It is not surprising, therefore, that in this period, too, the process continued. Indeed, as one would expect from the increased emphasis upon Scripture it may even be said to have been accelerated. A work like the famous *Praiers of Holi Fathers* specialized in taking prayers directly from the Old and the New Testaments. Sometimes the headings and introductory notes quite specifically and explicitly applied these borrowings to contemporary occasions. With a good deal of imaginative adroitness the dramatic exhilaration of many of the Old Testament prayers was brought to reënforce that psychology of crisis which we have already had occasion to note in the editing of the Psalms.

Many of these prayers had, of course, already found their way into the Primer; indeed, it is apparent that the editor of the above work had drawn heavily upon the selection and arrangement of the Primer. But the general handling of the text keeps closer to Scripture, for in cases where earlier editors had not hesitated to expand or apply the scriptural passage with nonscriptural devotional additions, the latter-day editor tended to omit the addition. Clearly, he made a point of hewing as close to the scriptural line as possible. Yet he apparently found no difficulty in keeping that selection and rearrangement of the Psalms known as the *Canticle* or *Song* of Saints Ambrose and Augustine. Perhaps the antiquity of that composition and the great reputation at this time of the second of those two names exorcised that particular composition of the suspicion attaching to "human inventions."

Most of the scriptural prayers in the older devotional books had come from the Old Testament, and in the New they continued to do so. But in a collection like *Certayne Other Devout Prayers* the traditional Old Testament prayers were reënforced by prayers from the New Testament, especially a number of Christ's prayers. Obviously, the maker of such a book sought to provide the devout Christian with the opportunity to pray not only in the words of Scripture but in the words of his Master himself. The tendency of such a book is, of course, quite in keeping with the scripturalism of the time. But it would be a mistake to overemphasize this aspect. For the tendency to a freer treatment, already apparent in both the traditional and the contemporary handling of Scripture, was apparent here, too. *The Treasure of Gladnesse* presented what was substantially a new cursus in its, for this time, uncommon specialization in prayers of praise. And parable and scriptural episode were drawn upon with an eye to the controversies of the time as well as to devotion. Indeed, this freedom of handling of scriptural materials led presently to the creation of what were in essence mosaics of Scripture. In books like those of Thomas Becon and Henry Bull the scriptural theme, one of the timeless truths of the spiritual life, was developed with Biblical examples and illustrations so that something almost like a new piece of noncanonical Scripture resulted.

And in spite of the intention to keep as close to the Bible as possible, apparent among devotional writers in these years, and the widespread fear of any human addition to, or adornment of, that revelation, something like a combination of meditation and prayer based on biblical episodes and transactions appeared in the *Canticles or Balades of Salomon*. Apparently the temptation was too great for the pedagogical impulse so apparent in the sixteenth-century devotional writers. Such a combined meditation-prayer may properly be regarded as a connecting link between the old Passion prayers and the Ignatian type of meditation that was developing in the recusant books of the mid-century and that was to play so considerable a part in seventeenth-century Catholic literature, prose and poetry alike. There were various restraints on the development of this type in England, notably the reserve and inhibitions, already noted in the treatment of Christ's humanity. In England the development remained at a half-way stage as in works like Bradford's *Godly Meditations on the Lord's Prayer*. There is a good deal of homely vividness in Bradford's meditations, a vividness that dramatically assimilates the worlds of the Bible and of contemporary England, but Bradford scrupulously concentrated on Christ in his re-creation, and confined himself to the physical data of the transaction witnessed by the devout eye instead of trying to penetrate into the psychology of the experience. In other words, even in the fairly developed meditation the tendency was to adhere pretty closely and objectively, if not literally, to the data of Scripture. And where the editor essayed something of his own, he was more apt to concern himself with the drawing of the appropriate theological lesson or moral reminder than with any elaborate imaginative or emotional interpretation or re-creation of his own. This is one of the most important developments of the time for religious literature, both prose and poetry.

One of the obvious explanations of this reserve in the matter of meditation or even contemplation is to be found in the contemporary approach to the whole problem of devotion. That is perhaps most clearly revealed in the guides to the devout life, one of the staples of traditional devotional literature that had been carried over into the new period, simply because it filled a persistent need. Here as so often, the invention of printing and the resultant multiplication of books had made the satisfaction of this need more feasible, and had made it possible to reach further down in the social and economic scale than ever before. And again, here as elsewhere, the reformers were perhaps more resourceful in exploiting the possibilities of the new situation than were those who were still operating along traditional lines.

Not that the traditional devotional writers had by any means failed to appreciate the need. But they had envisaged the same audience as the editors of the Psalter and the Primer, the typical sinner without regard to class or position. One adaptation they had tried to make, and that was to the layman as distinct from the religious. But they still expected a good deal from the layman, as may be seen in the famous work of Maister Quentin so often found in the primers of the time. Maister Quentin did try to take the demands of secular business into consideration as he planned a schedule of prayer for the layman, but in his devotional provisions he still demanded a good deal of that usually untrained individual. For his technique was, as a rule, to suggest the theme and the objective of the needed prayer to the reader but leave the actual composition of the prayer itself to him. And in his suggestions he paid almost as much attention to meditation as to prayer. In all this Quentin is representative of a whole group of clerical or monastic writers who often displayed real psychological insight in writing for the beginner in meditation and devotion, but who still expected a good deal of resourcefulness from him in the way of making his own prayers. And this is true of even the greatest of the English writers of this genre, Richard Whitford.

Whitford showed plenty of imagination in his envisaging of the conditions of life of the layman for whom he was writing and in trying to provide for them. Indeed, he displayed a very lively familiarity with certain aspects of lay life, particularly as it was lived in the great households of the time, and he revealed very considerable pedagogical skill in his outlining of a course of devotion for men living under such conditions, but he still expected a good deal of his layman in the way of actual composition of prayers.

His contemporary in the Catholic reforming movement, Erasmus, and his junior, Vives, shared his concern for the layman, not surprisingly, for Vives was a layman, and Erasmus seems to have lived much like a layman a good part of his life. And they endeavored to minister to his devotional needs, Vives, in particular, trying to provide for his devotional routine. But they anticipated the Protestant devotional writers in providing detailed forms of prayer for specific occasions and needs. They seem to have grasped more clearly than Whitford and his monastic colleagues the limits of the untrained layman's capacities for devotional composition and to have tried to provide him with adequate forms of prayer for his specific needs and occasions. Consequently, their work not only exerted a great influence on English devotional writers but was used extensively in the sixteenth-century collections of prayers of all sides. In this way long-established traditions of type and form of prayer were adapted to new points of view and developed with greater explicitness and fullness of provision for the layman.

But one great change in orientation of this devotional literature should be noted. In the old books the question of social orientation had hardly arisen, the reader being envisaged as the typical erring and struggling generic human being without reference to class or place in

society. But in the middle of the century Thomas Becon undertook
to provide prayers for different social groups and classes, introducing
a degree both of specialization and adaptation of appeal that was to
have an important influence on the development of later sixteenth- and
seventeenth-century devotion. While most of the later books would not
specialize to the extent of some of Becon's prayers, the middle-class
orientation would become well established, especially in the most popular type of all, that offering help to "householders."

These various guides would, like the other types of devotional books
which we have been studying, draw from a wide area of the literature
of the past and the present for their materials, even including contemporary recusant work like Parsons' famous *Booke of Christian
Exercise*. But whatever their source, they would represent a very well-
considered and skillful effort to reach their prospective audiences where
they stood in their daily life, with a shrewd appraisal of their
interests and their aptitudes, both their potentialities and their limitations.

And yet in spite of this more specialized development, the old more
general and more universal type of primer-like collection of prayers
continued to hold its own. A very elementary type is to be seen in
The Queenes Praiers in which out of a very loose series of petitions
something like an order of logical progress gradually became apparent. The inspiration of the Psalms was quite obvious in the aspirations of this book as in so many of the Primer prayers, but there was an
almost colloquial simplicity and intimacy in the language in which the
theme was developed that recalled the tone and temper of ancient
prayers like the *Fifteen Oes*.

The traditional element was even more directly apparent in much
of the work of Thomas Becon, whom we have already met as one of
the leaders in some of the most striking innovations in this field. There
is no question of the reforming orientation of Becon. The survey of
Christian teachings on the Redemption in the group of meditations
found in some copies of his *Pomaunder of Prayer* put that beyond any
doubt. But the influence of the Primer is to be seen in the brevity of so
many of the individual prayers in that collection. Many of these prayers
were, in fact, taken from the old primers.

In the case of Bradford, with more of meditation added to the prayers
and perhaps a sharper concern about the pedagogical needs of a de-

votional book for the reënforcement of allegiance to a more recent position as well as for prayer, the traditional elements came mainly through the medium of Vives, upon whose devotions Bradford drew freely. And this Vives-Bradford material was taken over by the Bull-Middleton books of the middle of the century. But though there was no question of the loyalty of these books to the new order, from the first they drew very heavily and directly on traditional materials, printing a good many prayers, apparently straight from the Primer.

Even more strikingly traditional was Middleton's collection called significantly *A Godly Garden,* which in the fashion of the Marian primer of 1555 added to the usual reformed-primer materials daily prayers of a highly traditional character, and medieval devotional materials, like the famous Communion prayer of Saint Thomas Aquinas, not usually found in the Primer. Such books as these are one evidence of a very considerable revival of interest in ancient devotional literature in the third quarter of the sixteenth century, a revival in keeping with other contemporary manifestations of interest in the religious expression of the past.

That the Bull-Middleton books did not stand alone is made quite clear by the first of the Day prayer books which appeared in 1569. The very physical appearance of this book suggests a resurrection of the old Primer, for it went so far as to use a type of decoration with which we are already familiar in the old books. In its contents this first of the Day prayer books exhibited that tendency to recapitulation so characteristic of this literature. For it used not only a new version of the daily prayers of Vives which Bradford had already translated and the Bull-Middleton book had taken over from Bradford, but, also, a good many of Bradford's occasional prayers, with all their relations to tradition. And it took a number of prayers from the Primer, and a number of Primer elements such as the Seven Penitential Psalms and the litany and suffrages, with, of course, the appropriate modifications and substitutions. All in all, it was a Protestant book, but strikingly reminiscent in its pattern and even in its actual materials of the traditional primer.

Such a book would make one wonder as to its reception in the religious climate of the second half of the sixteenth century. Some hint may be found in the second edition that appeared in 1578. The use of the Pietà in the page decorations must have aroused official objection, for it was somewhat awkwardly expurgated, but so far as the contents were concerned, the traditional character of the whole work was enhanced in the extensive revisions. True, the editor was obviously concerned about the theological orientation of his reader, and anxious that he should not misconstrue the orthodox acceptance of predestination and make it an excuse for spiritual laziness. In the miscellaneous prayers he was careful to cover the fundamental religious positions of the Elizabethan Settlement in a fashion that indicates that he accepted them. But he took a good many of his prayers for the day's routine from Vives and Erasmus, and though there was much that seems, on the one hand, encyclopedic and, on the other, miscellaneous, in his actual choice of materials the great bulk of these prayers came either from the Primer or from more recent writers in that tradition. The popularity of such a book at this time gives impressive evidence both of the existence of a considerable public in the England of the day, for whom the traditional devotional literature had an enduring appeal, and the disposition of authority, once certain limits had been enforced as in the case of the Marian elements in the decorations, to be tolerant in the recognition of such an interest.

But striking as this traditional element was in the devotional books of the time, there was nothing antiquarian about the way it was handled. These materials were presented in the context of the inner life of the English church of the time. The editors from the first approached their traditional materials with a good deal of freedom, not hesitating to modify and adapt wherever they thought it necessary.

With some prayers, of course, there was no problem. In spite of all the changes of the intervening years, they still appealed to the basic preoccupations of the day. The pleading of the sinner in the *O bone Iesu* is a good example. The old audaciously intimate touch of arguing with the Lord might yield to the self-exhortation that was more in the mood of the sixteenth century, the taste of a latter-day prose writer might prompt revision in the interest of smoothness and grace, but there was surprisingly little change in the colorful old prayer of Saint Bernardine of Siena.

Usually there was more change. Apparently, the motives for such change varied. Very often it was pretty much a matter of rhetoric. Sometimes the later editor condensed the original in the interest of either economy or taste. More often he expanded it, developing and clarifying the implications, as was the wont of an age in which the reformer's need of defining and establishing his premises had made such explicitness habitual. Sometimes, of course, in such clarification a change of basic orientation became apparent as in certain adaptations of the prayers of Vives where the helplessness of man was underscored in keeping with current preaching on justification. And sometimes the change was one of mood and temper with all the resultant difficulty of distinguishing between adjustment to prevailing climate of opinion and personal taste and predilection. And this difficulty was not diminished by a certain teetering back and forth in the chronological aspect of the process.

This process of adaptation was, of course, characteristic of the whole area of devotional literature, not confined alone to prayers from Scripture or the Primer but found also in the handling of collections of prayers attributed to particular authors like Augustine.

Finally, it should be noted that here as in the expanded Psalter one comes every so often upon prayers not to be found in any of the more popular versions of the Primer, in all probability not primer prayers at all, but still sounding very much like the Primer. Some of the haunting sense of familiarity in such works may be easily explained, of course, by the fact that the ultimate source of the composition is to be found in the Bible. For, as cannot be overemphasized, the language of Scripture was always the common instrument of Christian devotion. In other cases, more prolonged attention will reveal that two or more old prayers have been run together. Sometimes portions rather than whole prayers were so blended, and then it is almost impossible to sort out what is in fact a mosaic of fragments of traditional works. For the writers of these books often used the Primer as they used the Psalter and the Bible as a whole, as a quarry out of which they might hew the raw materials to be shaped into their own fresh compositions. And even when for some continuing need of humanity the old prayer was rejected out of some scruple of changed premise, still there is more than a memory of the rejected old prayer in the substitute. It is this element of continuing influence even in the midst of revolutionary change that makes this whole process of adaptation so fascinating.

Nowhere is it better illustrated than in the history of the *Fifteen Oes* during these years. One should perhaps not be surprised at their power of survival, for they are a distillation of centuries of meditation on the Passion, the central and key event in Christian history. But the form which this cumulative meditation assumed in the work of Saint Bridget was one highly typical of the period of its composition, with an emphasis on the humanity of Christ and an emotional tenderness and intimacy of treatment, characteristic of late medieval devotion. One would hardly expect these prayers to appeal to an age in which the reformer's necessity of establishing his premises had led to an overwhelming preoccupation with theological concepts, and a fear of human contamination of divine revelation and human distraction from the divine primacy had rendered such a treatment and such an attitude suspect if not uncongenial. And yet these prayers did continue to enjoy a very high degree of popularity.

Something of this was due to the reserve and relative simplicity of Caxton's version, quite apparent when it is set beside the more elaborate one of the Regnault *Hore* of 1527. But still more was it due to a process of adaptation which found its culmination in the Day version of 1578. Those changes sum up what had happened in English devotion in the almost ninety years since Caxton made his translation. The most striking are, of course, the omissions. The sixth prayer, for instance, with its emphasis on the human comfort which Christ on the cross received from the presence of his mother went the way of all the Marian prayers. The sacramental emphasis of the eighth prayer on the Eucharist, would for the dominant commemorative view be regarded as an infringement on the unique redemptive potency of Christ's sufferings; so it, also, was omitted, and so was a reference to confession in the first prayer. On the other hand, a passage which had dropped out unaccountably in the Caxton version of the same prayer and had been restored in the Marian primer of 1555 was carried over, probably because it underscored the penitential motive.

But even more interesting are the slight modifications. A shift in emphasis from God the Son to God the Father in a number of the prayers may not seem much in itself and was probably not noticed. But taken in conjunction with the general shift in emphasis from the human implications of Christ's life on earth to the redemptive function it becomes significant of perhaps the most consequential change in the whole devotional approach of the time. It is interesting to recall that the emphasis on the human aspects of Christ's life was historically closely associated with the attention paid to his mother. This shift in the attitude toward Christ's life on earth is probably the key to the most significant differences between English devotion of the fifteenth century and the seventeenth.

Yet the fact that in spite of such major shifts in point of view and emphasis prayers of so humanly emotional a character could have enjoyed such obvious popularity is in itself evidence of the persistently cumulative character of the inner life of piety. It is evidence, too, that, in spite of the revolutionary character of many of the changes of the period, there were not wanting editors and publishers who sought to preserve and to disseminate as much as they could of the wealth of the tradition of private Christian devotion, nor a public to appreciate and make use of their efforts.

REFERENCES AND NOTES

INDEX

REFERENCES AND NOTES

The titles in the following list are mainly those to which repeated reference is made. Most of those referred to but once are not listed here; full bibliographical data are given in the notes where they occur. A few of the single citations, e.g., primers and psalters, are given here for the sake of complete listing of those documents.

SECONDARY MATERIALS

Althaus, D. Paul. *Zur Charakteristik der evangelischen Gebetsliteratur in Reformationsjahrhundert.* Leipzig, 1914.

Baudot, Jules. *The Breviary.* London, etc., 1929.

Bishop, Edmund. Introduction to Henry Littlehales (ed.), *The Prymer or Lay Folks' Prayer Book.* London: Early English Text Society, No. 109, 1897.

Brightman, F. E. *The English Rite.* London, 1915. 2 vols

Butler, Cuthbert. *Ways of Christian Life.* London, 1932.

————. *Western Mysticism.* London, 1927.

Butterworth, Charles C. *The Literary Lineage of the King James Bible 1340–1611.* Philadelphia, 1941.

Cabrol, Fernand. *The Books of the Latin Liturgy.* London and St. Louis, 1932.

————. *Liturgical Prayer, Its History and Spirit,* translated by a Benedictine of Stanbrook. London, 1922.

Chansou, J. *Étude de psychologie religieuse sur les sources et l'efficacité de la prière dans l'expérience chrétienne.* Toulouse, 1927.

Chew, Samuel C. "The Iconography of *A Book of Christian Prayers* (1578) Illustrated," *Huntington Library Quarterly,* VIII (May, 1945), 293–305.

Dugmore, C. W. *The Influence of the Synagogue upon the Divine Office.* Oxford, 1945.

Fortescue, Adrian, ed. *Pange Lingua, Breviary Hymns of Old Uses with an English Rendering,* by Alan G. McDougall. London, 1916.

Gasquet, Francis Aidan. "The Bibliography of Some Devotional Books Printed by the Earliest English Printers," *Transactions of the Bibliographical Society,* VII (London, 1904), 163–89.

————, and Edmund Bishop. *The Bosworth Psalter.* London, 1908.

Gasquet, Francis Aidan, and Edmund Bishop. *Edward VI and the Book of Common Prayer*. London, 1928.

Goodier, Alban. *An Introduction to the Study of Ascetical and Mystical Theology*. London, 1938.

Gougaud, Louis. *Dévotions et pratiques ascétiques du moyen âge*. Paris, 1925.

Guardini, Romano. *The Spirit of the Liturgy*, translated by Ada Lane. London, 1930.

Heiler, Friedrich. *Das Gebet, eine religionsgeschichtliche und religions-psychologische Untersuchung*. München, 1923.

Hoskins, Edgar, ed. *Horae Beatae Mariae Virginis, or Sarum and York Primers of the Reformed Roman Use*. London, etc., 1901.

Knowles, David. *The Benedictines*. New York, 1930.

———. *The Monastic Order in England*. Cambridge, 1940.

Morison, Stanley. *English Prayer Books: An Introduction to the Literature of Christian Public Worship*. Cambridge, 1945.

Pourrat, Pierre. *Christian Spirituality in the Middle Ages*, Vol. I translated by W. H. Mitchell and S. P. Jacques. London, 1922; Vol. II translated by S. P. Jacques, London, 1924.

Segond, J. *La Prière: Étude de psychologie religieuse*. Paris, 1911.

Simmons, Thomas Frederick, ed. *The Lay Folks' Mass Book*. London: The Early English Text Society, 1879.

Vernet, Félix. *La Spiritualité médiévale*. Paris, 1929.

Wilmart, A. *Auteurs spirituels et textes dévots du moyen âge latin*. Paris, 1932.

PRIMARY MATERIALS

Primers, Books of Hours

Enchiridion praeclare ecclesie Sarum. Parisiis: vi[due] Thielmanni Kerver expensis Alardi Plomier, 1528.

A Goodly Prymer in Englyshe. London: John Byddell for Wylliam Marshall, June 16, 1535.

A Goodly Prymer in Englysshe, newly corrected and prynted with Certeyne Godly Meditations and Prayers. London: J. Byddell for W. Marshall, [1537?].

[*Horae ad usum Sarum*]. Paris: Johannes Jehannot [for N. Lecomte], 1498.

Hore Beate Marie Virginis secundum usum Sarum. Paris: Thielman Kerver pro Johanne Ricardo Mercatore, 1497.

Hore Beatissime Virginis Marie ad legitimum Sarisburiensis Ecclesie ritum. Paris: à Francisco Regnault, 1527.

Hore Beatissime Virginis Marie secundum usum Sarum. Antwerp: Christopher of Endhoven for Francis Byrckman, 1525.

Hore Intemerate Virginis Marie secundum usum Romanum. [Paris]: Thielman Kerver, [1500].

Hore presentes ad usum Sarum. Paris: Philippe Pigouchet for Simon Vostre, 1502.

Littlehales, Henry, ed. *The Prymer or Lay Folks' Prayer Book.* With an Introduction by Edmund Bishop. London: Early English Text Society, No. 109, 1897.

————. *The Prymer or Prayer-book of the Lay People in the Middle Ages in English dating about 1400 A.D.* London, 1892.

The Manual of Prayers, or the Prymer in Englysh and Laten set forth by Jhon . . . Bysshoppe of Rochester. London: John Wayland, 1539.

The Primer in Englishe and Latyn, set foorth by the Kynges Majestie and his Clergie. London: Richard Grafton, 1545.

A Primer in Englysshe with Dyvers. Prayers and Godly Meditations. London: Thomas Godfray, n.d.

The Primer, set foorth by the Kynges Majestie and his Clergie. London: Richard Grafton, May 29, 1545.

A Prymer in Englyshe. London: Johan Byddell for Wyllyam Marshall, n.d.

The Prymer in Englyshe, and Latyn with the Epystles and Gospelles: of Everye Sonday, and Holye Daye in the Yere. London: Robert Toye, 1542.

The Prymer in Englysshe after the Use of Salysbury. Rowen: Nycholas le Roux for Franchoys Regnault, 1538.

This Primer of Salysbery Use, both in Englyshe and in Laten. London: Johan Gowghe, 1536.

This Prymer off Salysbury Use. Paris: Yolande Bonhomme, Widow of Thielman Kerver, for J. Growte, 1533.

Thys Prymer in Englyshe and in Laten. Rouen, 1536.

Thys Prymer in Englyshe and in Laten. Paris, 1538.

Thys Prymer in Englyshe, and in Laten. Rouen: [Nicholas le Roux], 1538.

Thys Prymer newly impryntyd. London: W. Rastell, 1532.

Thys Prymer of Salysburye Use. Rouen: pro Francisco Regnault, 1537.

An Uniforme and Catholyke Prymer in Latin and Englishe. London: John Waylande, 1555.

Scripture, Liturgy, The Psalter

Anglo-Saxon and Early English Psalter: Now first printed from MS in British Museum. London and Edinburgh: The Surtees Society, 1843.

Baldwin, William. *The Canticles or Balades of Salomon, phraselyke declared in Englysh Metres.* London: William Baldwin, servaunt with Edwarde Whitchurch, 1549.

Beza, Theodore. *Christian Meditations upon Eight Psalmes of the Prophet David,* translated by I. S. London: C. Barker, 1582.

The Boke of Psalmes. Geneva: Rouland Hall, 1559.

The Byble in Englyshe. [Paris: F. Regnault, and London]: R. Grafton and E. Whitchurch, 1539.

The Byble in Englyshe of the Largest and Greatest Volume. London: Rycharde Grafton, 1541.

Certaine Devout and Godly Petitions commonly called, Jesus Psalter. [Lon-
don? 1545?].

Hunnis, William. *Certayne Psalmes chosen out of the Psalter of David, and
drawen furth into Englyshe Meter.* London: Wydowe of Jhon Herforde
for Jhon Harrington, 1550.

Joye, George. *Davids Psalter . . . with Breif Arguments before Every
Psalme, declaringe Theffecte therof.* [Antwerp]: Martyne Emperour,
1534.

Psalmes or Prayers taken out of Holye Scripture. London: Thomas Berthelet,
1544.

*The Psalter of David in English . . . whereunto is annexed Certayne Godly
Prayers thoroweoute the Whole Yere, commenly called, Collettes.* London: Edwarde Whytchurch, [1542?].

*The Psalter of David in Englishe purely and faithfully Translated aftir the
Texte of Feline.* Argentine [Strassburg]: Francis Foxe, 1530.

*The Psalter, or Boke of the Psalmes, whereunto are added Certayne Other
Devout Prayers taken out of the Byble.* London: John Whyte, [1550?].

*The Psalter or Booke of the Psalmes, wherunto are added Other Devoute
Praiers taken out of the Byble.* [E. Whitchurch? 1540?].

*A Right Christian Treatise, entituled S. Augustines Praiers . . . Whereunto
is annexed Saint Augustines Psalter,* translated by T. R.   London: Henrie
Denham, 1581.

Rolle, Richard. English Psalter in *English Writings of Richard Rolle,
Hermit of Hampole,* edited by Hope Emily Allen. Oxford, 1931.

The Rosary of our Savyour Jesu. London: Pynson, [1526?].

*Six Spirituall Bookes . . . And First, Certaine Devout and Godlie Peti-
tions, commonlie called, The Jesus Psalter.* Doway: John Heigham, 1618.

Sternhold, Thomas, John Hopkins, and Others. *The Whole Booke of Psalmes,
collected into Englishe Meter.* London: John Day, 1567.

[Tyndale, William]. *The Newe Testament.* Antwerp: Marten Emperowr,
1534.

Prayer Books, Devotionary Books

Becon, Thomas. *The Flower of Godly Prayers,* in *The Seconde Part of the
Bokes, which Thomas Beacon hath made.* London: [John Day], 1560, etc.

————. *The Pathwai unto Prayer* in *The Bokes, which Thomas Beacon hath
made.* Part I. London: John Day, 1564.

————. *The Pomaunder of Prayer.* London: John Day, 1561.

————. *The Pommaunder of Prayers.* London: John Daye [1560?].

Bradford, John. *Godly Meditations on the Lord's Prayer, Belief, and Ten
Commandments, with other Exercises,* in *The Writings of John Bradford,*
edited by Aubrey Townsend. Cambridge: Parker Society, 1848.

———. *Godly Meditations uppon the Ten Commaundementes, the Articles of the Fayth, and the Lords Prayer.* London: William Seres, 1567.

———. *Private Prayers and Meditations, with Other Exercises,* in *The Writings of John Bradford,* edited by Aubrey Townsend. Cambridge: Parker Society, 1848.

Bull, Henry. *Christian Praiers and Holie Meditations.* London: Henrie Middleton, [1578].

Bunny, Edmund. *A Booke of Christian Exercise, appertaining to Resolution, by R. P. Perused, and Accompanied now with a Treatise tending to Pacification.* London: N. Newton and A. Hatfield for John Wight, 1584.

Clay, William Keatinge, ed. *Private Prayers, put forth by Authority during the Reign of Queen Elizabeth.* Cambridge, 1851.

Day, John. *Christian Prayers and Meditations in English, French, Italian, Spanish, Greeke, and Latin.* London: John Daye, 1569.

Day, Richard. *A Booke of Christian Prayers.* London: John Day, 1578.

[Dering, Edward]. *Godly Private Prayers for Housholders.* London, [1576?].

———. *A Shorte Catechisme for Housholders, with Prayers to the same adjoyning.* London: James Roberts, 1603.

A Dyurnall for Devoute Soules. London: Robert Wyer, n.d.

[Erasmus, Desiderius]. *The Prayers of Erasmus,* translated and edited by Charles Simeon Coldwell. London, 1872.

The Fifteen O's, and Other Prayers, Printed by . . . William Caxton, circa 1490. Reproduced in photo-lithography by Stephen Ayling. London, 1869.

A Godly Garden. London: H. Middleton, 1574.

Melanchthon, Phillip. *A Godlye Treatyse of Prayer,* translated by John Bradforde. London: John Wight, [1556–57?].

Parsons, Robert. *A Christian Directorie guiding Men to their Salvation.* N.p., 1585.

The Pomander of Prayer. London: Robert Coplande, 1530.

The Queenes Praiers or Meditations. London: H. Wykes, [1568?].

A Right Christian Treatise entituled S. Augustines Praiers, . . . translated by Thomas Rogers. London: H. Denham, 1581.

A Right Christian Treatise, entituled S. Augustines Praiers . . . Whereunto is annexed Saint Augustines Psalter, translated by T. R. London: Henrie Denham, 1581.

A Tablet for Gentlewomen. London: William Seres, 1574.

The Treasure of Gladnesse. London: W. Williamson for J. Charlewood, 1563. Another edition, 1568.

Whitford, Richard. *A Werke for Housholders.* London: Wynkyn de Worde, 1530.

NOTES TO CHAPTER I

1. Cabrol, *Liturgical Prayer*, pp. 1, 38.

2. Heiler, *Das Gebet*, pp. 53 ff.

3. Segond, *La Prière*, p. 350.

4. *Ibid.*, p. 93.

5. Chansou, *Étude de psychologie religieuse*, p. 3.

6. Guardini, *The Spirit of the Liturgy*, p. 69.

7. Saint Augustine, *Confessions*, trans. E. B. Pusey (London, etc., 1917), IX, XII, 32.

8. Cf. Edith L. Klotz, "A Subject Analysis of English Imprints for Every Tenth Year from 1480 to 1640," *Huntington Library Quarterly*, I (1937–38), 417–19.

9. Littlehales (ed.), *The Prymer or Prayer-Book of the Lay People in the Middle Ages*.

10. The *Ars moriendi* or *The Art of Dying Well* might be included in this group, but since it has already been very adequately treated as a "conduct book" by Sister Mary Catharine O'Connor, *The Art of Dying Well: The Development of the Ars moriendi* (New York, 1942), I have omitted it.

NOTES TO CHAPTER II

1. Cabrol, *Liturgical Prayer*, pp. 116 ff.

2. Heiler, *Das Gebet*, p. 241; Butler, *Western Mysticism*, pp. 23–24.

3. Segond, *La Prière*, pp. 237–38.

4. Goodier, *An Introduction to the Study of Ascetical and Mystical Theology*, p. 37.

5. Vernet, *La Spiritualité médiévale*, p. 8.

6. Goodier, *op. cit.*, pp. 41–42.

7. Cf. John Wyclif, *De Blasphemia, contra Fratres*, Pars III, in *Select English Works*, ed. Thomas Arnold (Oxford, 1871), III, 420–22.

8. Bishop, Introduction to *The Prymer or Lay Folks' Prayer Book*, Part II, xiii.

9. Cabrol, *op. cit.*, chap. xx.

10. *Ibid.*, chap. xxi.

11. Gustave Bardy, *Saint Augustin, l'homme et l'oeuvre* (Paris, 1948), pp. 145–46.

12. *Ibid.*, pp. 160–64.

13. *Ibid.*, pp. 86 ff.

14. *Ibid.*, pp. 102–3.

15. Cf. Knowles, *The Monastic Order in England*, pp. 139–42, and Pourrat, *Christian Spirituality*, II, 104–6, 253–56.

16. Baudot, *The Breviary*, pp. 89–92.

17. Cf. *The Saint Andrew Daily Missal* (St. Paul, 1925), pp. 86–87, 101.

18. Cf. Althaus, *Zur Charakteristik der evangelischen Gebetsliteratur in Reformationsjahrhundert*, pp. 19, 63.

19. Cf. Pourrat, *op. cit.*, II, 293 ff., and Wilmart, *Auteurs spirituels et textes dévots du moyen âge latin*, pp. 426 ff.

20. Butler, *Ways of Christian Life*, pp. 3–4.

21. Knowles, *The Monastic Order in England*, pp. 10–14; Pourrat, *op. cit.*, I, 243.

22. Goodier, *op. cit.*, p. 42.

23. Knowles, *The Benedictines*, pp. 16–18.

24. Vernet, *op. cit.*, p. 7.

25. Goodier, *op. cit.*, p. 42.

26. Butler, *Western Mysticism*, p. 137.

27. *Ibid.*, p. 138, and Pourrat, *op. cit.*, II, 33.

28. Pourrat, *op. cit.*, II, 38–51.

29. *Ibid.*, pp. 51–60.

30. Vernet, *op. cit.*, p. 85.

31. *Ibid.*, pp. 79, 95.

32. Goodier, *op. cit.*, p. 45.

33. Pourrat, *op. cit.*, II, 153 ff.

34. *Ibid.,* pp. 168 ff.
35. *Ibid.,* p. 153.
36. *Ibid.,* pp. 188–89.
37. Goodier, *op. cit.,* p. 47.
38. *Ibid.,* p. 53; Pourrat, *op. cit.,* II, 210 ff.
39. Pourrat, *op. cit.,* II, 198–99.
40. *Ibid.,* pp. 253 ff., and Vernet, *op. cit.,* p. 59.
41. Pourrat, *op. cit.,* II, 255.
42. *Ibid.,* pp. 260–61.
43. Vernet, *op. cit.,* p. 96.
44. Guardini, *The Spirit of the Liturgy,* p. 27 n.
45. Gougaud, *Dévotions et pratiques ascétiques du moyen âge,* pp. 75–89.
46. Wilmart, *op. cit.,* p. 426.
47. Saint Augustine, *An Introduction to the Love of God,* trans. R. Fletcher (London, T. Purfoote, 1574).
48. Saint Augustine, *An Introduction to the Love of God,* trans. R. Fletcher (London: T. Purfoote, [1581?]).
49. Saint Augustine, *The Glasse of Vaine-glorie,* trans. W. P[rid] (London: J. Windet, 1585).
50. *Certaine Select Prayers gathered out of S. Austines Meditations* (London: John Daye, 1574).
51. *S. Augustines Manuel,* trans. T. Rogers (London: H. Denham, 1581).
52. *A Right Christian Treatise entituled S. Augustines Praiers,* trans. Thomas Rogers (London: H. Denham, 1581).
53. S. Augustine, *A Pretious Booke of Heavenlie Meditations,* trans. T.

Rogers (London: Henrie Denham, 1581).
54. Becon, *The Pomaunder of Prayer,* sig. G6 ff.
55. Day, *A Booke of Christian Prayers,* and Clay, *Private Prayers, put forth by Authority during the Reign of Queen Elizabeth,* pp. 494, 501, 503, 528, 557, 574.
56. For the general bibliography of the *Imitation* see Augustin de Backer, *Essai bibliographique sur le livre de Imitatione Christi* (Liége, 1864).
57. Gasquet, "The Bibliography of some Devotional Books printed by the Earliest English Printers," p. 187.
58. *A Boke newely translated out of Laten in to Englysshe, called the Folowynge of Cryste* (London: R. Wyer, [1530?]).
59. *The Imitation or Following of Christ amended by S. Castalio,* trans. E. H[ake] (London: H. Denham, 1567).
60. Thomas à Kempis, *Of the Imitation of Christ,* trans. T. Rogers (London: H. Denham, the Assigne of W. Seres, 1580).
61. S. Augustine, *A Pretious Booke of Heavenlie Meditations,* sig. A8v–9v.
62. Thomas à Kempis, *The Imitation or Following of Christ,* trans. Edwarde Hake (London: Henry Denham, 1568).
63. Thomas à Kempis, *Of the Imitation of Christ,* trans. T. Rogers (London: R. Yardley and P. Short, 1592).
64. *Ibid.,* sig. A2v–4v.

NOTES TO CHAPTER III

1. Mark 15 : 34; Psalm 21 : 1 (Psalm 22 : 1).
2. Dugmore, *The Influence of the Synagogue upon the Divine Office,* pp. 60, 70.
3. Cabrol, *The Books of the Latin Liturgy,* p. 148.
4. Fortescue, Introduction to *Pange*

Lingua, Breviary Hymns of Old Uses, pp. xi–xii.
5. See, for example, Sternhold, Hopkins, and Others, *The Whole Booke of Psalmes,* sig. A2–4.
6. Fortescue, *op. cit.,* p. xiii.
7. Hoskins, *Horae Beatae Mariae Virginis,* pp. viii–ix.

8. Gasquet and Bishop, *The Bosworth Psalter*, pp. 5–6.

9. *Ibid.*, p. 126.

10. Hoskins, *op. cit.*, p. xi.

11. Butterworth, *The Literary Lineage of the King James Bible*, p. 23.

12. *Ibid.*

13. Hoskins, *op. cit.*, p. x.

14. Morison, *English Prayer Books*, p. 44.

15. *Anglo-Saxon and Early English Psalter*, I, 3.

16. Rolle, English Psalter, in *English Writings of Richard Rolle, Hermit of Hampole*, p. 1.

17. *Ibid.*

18. *Ibid.*, p. 4.

19. *Ibid.*, pp. 7–8.

20. *Ibid.*, p. 7.

21. *Ibid.*, p. 3.

22. Hoskins, *op. cit.*, pp. xii–xiii.

23. Butterworth, *op. cit.*, p. 64.

24. *Ibid.*

25. *Ibid.*, pp. 66–67.

26. *Ibid.*, pp. 66 ff.

27. Joye, *Davids Psalter . . . with Breif Arguments before Every Psalme*, sig. I4v.

28. Butterworth, *op. cit.*, p. 64.

29. *The Psalter in Englishe . . . aftir the Texte of Feline*, sig. A1v.

30. *Ibid.*, sig. C4r–v.

31. *Ibid.*, sig. BB1r–v.

32. *Praiers of Holi Fathers*, sig. G4v ff.

33. *Ibid.*, sig. I2v.

34. *Ibid.*, sig. N6v–8v.

35. *The Boke of Psalmes*, sig. *2v–7.

36. *Ibid.*, sig. ²F4.

37. Butterworth, *op. cit.*, p. 65.

38. *The Psalter of David in English . . . whereunto is annexed Certayne Godly Prayers*, sig. P3v ff.

39. *Ibid.*, sig. *1 ff.

40. *The Psalter or Booke of the Psalmes, wherunto are added Other Devoute Praiers taken out of the Byble* ([E. Whitchurch? 1540?]).

41. *The Psalter, or Boke of the Psalmes, wherunto are added Certayne Other Devout Prayers taken out of the Byble*, sig. R1 ff.

42. Hunnis, *Certayne Psalmes chosen out of the Psalter of David*, sig. [unsigned] 1v.

43. *Ibid.*, sig. [A]1r–v.

44. *Ibid.*, sigs. B1v, C1v.

45. Ernest Brennecke, *John Milton the Elder and His Music* (New York, 1938), p. 100.

46. *Ibid.*, pp. 100–1.

47. *Tessaradelphus, or the Foure Brothers*, etc., collected and translated by Thomas Harrap (n.p., 1616), sig. D2v.

48. Sternhold-Hopkins, *The Whole Booke of Psalmes*, sig. A2–4.

49. *Ibid.*, sig. A2–3.

50. *Ibid.*, sig. A4r–v.

51. *Ibid.*, sig. A5 ff.

52. *Ibid.*, sig. B2v ff.

53. *Ibid.*, sig. B5v ff.

54. *Ibid.*, sig. R1v–2.

55. *Ibid.*, sig. R1v–4.

56. *Ibid.*, sigs. R4–S1.

57. *Ibid.*, sig. S1–5v.

58. *Hore Beatissime Virginis Marie* (Regnault), sig. Y4v.

59. *A Right Christian Treatise, entituled S. Augustines Praiers . . . Whereunto is annexed Saint Augustines Psalter*, sig. K7.

60. For example, *Thys Prymer in Englyshe and in Laten* (Paris, 1538), sig. C2r–v.

61. *Hore Beatissime Virginis Marie* (Regnault), sigs. R8–S1.

62. *Psalmes or Prayers taken out of Holye Scripture*, sig. A2.

63. *The Byble in Englyshe* (1539), sig. CC3v.

64. *Ibid.*

65. *Psalmes or Prayers*, sig. G4v–5.

66. *The Byble in Englyshe* (1539), sig. AA5.

67. *Psalmes or Prayers*, sig. M7r–v.

68. Gasquet and Bishop, *The Bosworth Psalter*, p. 6.

69. Day, *Christian Prayers and Meditations,* sig. D2v.

70. *Ibid.,* sig. E1–2.

71. *The Queenes Praiers or Meditations,* sig. F2r–v.

72. *Ibid.,* sig. G4r–v.

73. Gasquet, "The Bibliography of Some Devotional Books," p. 187.

74. *Thys Prymer* (Paris, 1538), sigs. A1 ff., and C6 ff.

75. Beza, *Christian Meditations upon Eight Psalmes,* sig. A2.

NOTES TO CHAPTER IV

1. Cabrol, *Liturgical Prayer,* pp. 138–58.

2. Baudot, *The Breviary,* p. 4.

3. Bishop, Introduction to *The Prymer or Lay Folks' Prayer Book,* Part II, p. xiii.

4. Baudot, *op. cit.,* pp. 89–92.

5. Bishop, *op. cit.,* p. xvi.

6. *Ibid.,* p. xxv.

7. *Ibid.,* pp. xxvi–xxxvii.

8. Hoskins, *Horae Beatae Mariae Virginis,* p. xviii.

9. Bishop, *op. cit.,* p. xxxix.

10. *Ibid.*

11. *Ibid.,* p. ix.

12. Hoskins, *op. cit.,* p. xvii.

13. *Hore Beatissime Virginis Marie* (Regnault), sig. G7v ff.

14. *Ibid.,* for example, sig. S1v ff.

15. *Ibid.,* sigs. a2–10v, A1v–7v.

16. *Ibid.,* sigs. A8–B4.

17. *Ibid.,* sig. B4r–v.

18. *Ibid.,* sig. B4v–5v.

19. *Ibid.,* sig. B6.

20. *Ibid.,* sig. B4v.

21. *Ibid.,* sig. A8.

22. *Hore Intemerate Virginis Marie secundum usum Romanum,* sig. n1v ff.

23. *Ibid.,* sigs. o1v–4, p1–8v.

24. *Hore Beatissime Virginis Marie* (Regnault), sig. B7v–8.

25. *Ibid.,* sig. D6v ff.

26. *Ibid.,* sigs. B6–F8v.

27. *Ibid.,* sigs. G1–H6v.

28. *Ibid.,* sig. G1.

29. *Ibid.,* sig. H5v–6.

30. *Ibid.,* sig. H6.

31. *Ibid.,* sig. G3.

32. *Ibid.,* sig. G2.

33. *Ibid.,* sigs. G1v–2.

34. *Ibid.,* sig. G4v–6.

35. *Ibid.,* sig. G7v–8.

36. *Ibid.,* sig. H4–5.

37. *Ibid.,* sigs. H8v–I1.

38. *Ibid.,* sig. I1–4v.

39. *Ibid.,* sigs. I5–Q2.

40. *Ibid.,* sig. L6–7.

41. *Ibid.,* sigs. O8v–P1v.

42. *Ibid.,* sig. P2v–3.

43. *Ibid.,* sig. Q1r–v.

44. *Ibid.,* sig. N1r–v.

45. *Ibid.,* sig. N6 ff.

46. *Ibid.,* sigs. P4r–v, P5v–6, P6v–7, P8r–v.

47. *Ibid.,* sigs. I8v–Q2.

48. *Ibid.,* sigs. Q2v–R4.

49. *Ibid.,* sig. Q4.

50. *Ibid.,* sigs. R4–S1v.

51. *Ibid.,* sigs. R8–S1.

52. *Ibid.,* sigs. S2 ff., S8v–T1.

53. *Ibid.,* sig. V5.

54. *Ibid.,* sig. X5v.

55. *Ibid.,* sig. X6.

56. *Ibid.,* sigs. Y4–Z4.

57. *Ibid.,* sig. Z4v ff.

58. *Ibid.,* sig. &3 ff.

59. *Ibid.,* sig. Q4–5v.

60. *Ibid.,* sig. Q5v–8.

61. *Ibid.,* sig. Q8v.

62. *Ibid.,* sig. aa1–5v.

63. *Ibid.,* sig. aa5v–6v.

64. *Hore Beatissime Virginis Marie* (Christopher of Endhoven for Francis Byrckman), sig. T1 ff.

NOTES TO CHAPTER V

1. Littlehales (ed.), *The Prymer or Prayer-Book of the Lay People in the Middle Ages,* Part II, p. 2.

2. *Ibid.,* pp. 2–10.

3. *Ibid.,* p. xi.

4. *Ibid.,* pp. 2, 8.

5. *Ibid.,* p. 5.

6. *Ibid.,* pp. 7–8.

7. *Ibid.,* Part I, pp. 4, 11.

8. *Ibid.,* Part II, p. xvi.

9. *Ibid.,* p. xviii.

10. [*Horae ad usum Sarum*], sig. &1–8v.

11. *Hore Beatissime Virginis Marie* (Regnault), sigs. A8–B5v.

12. [*Horae ad usum Sarum*], sigs. I3v–K2.

13. *Hore Beate Marie Virginis* (Kerver pro Mercatore), sigs. i3v–k2.

14. *Hore presentes ad usum Sarum,* sigs. i6–k3v.

15. *Hore Beatissime Virginis Marie* (Christopher of Endhoven), sig. ✠8r–v.

16. *Ibid.,* sig. T1–5.

17. *Thys Prymer off Salysburye Use* (Yolande Bonhomme), sig. d4 ff.

18. *Ibid.,* sig. ✠1 ff.

19. *Ibid.,* sig. ✠✠3 ff.

20. *Ibid.,* sig. O3 ff.

21. *Ibid.,* sig. L6 ff.

22. *Ibid.,* sig. N2v ff.

23. Hoskins, *Horae Beatae Mariae Virginis,* p. 194.

24. *Ibid.*

25. *Thys Prymer* (Rouen, 1536), sig. A1.

26. *Ibid.,* sigs. N2r–v and K1–3v.

27. Hoskins, *op. cit.,* pp. 159–61.

28. Since writing the above, I have been able to examine the copy of the Rouen primer of 1536 now in the Bodleian Library. As I expected, the Calendar (sig. ✠1–4v), is, but for a few minor differences of no importance, the same as that of the 1538 edition,

quite traditional. The Litany (sigs. M8–N4), is the same down to the prayer for the king found in the 1538 primer but not in the 1536 version. And the reforming preface (sig. ✠5–7) is the preface of 1538.

29. *Thys Prymer* (1536), sigs. A1–B5.

30. *Ibid.,* sig. B5 ff.

31. *Ibid.,* sig. K4v ff.

32. *Ibid.,* sig. L1v ff.

33. *Ibid.,* sig. M8 ff.

34. *Ibid.,* sig. N7v ff.

35. *Ibid.,* sig. T6 ff.

36. *Ibid.,* sig. V7v ff.

37. *Ibid.,* sig. Y2 ff.

38. *Ibid.,* sig. D6.

39. *Hore Beatissime Virginis Marie* (Regnault), sig. D2r–v.

40. *Ibid.,* sigs. A8–B6, G1–H6v.

41. *Ibid.,* sig. V4r–v.

42. *Thys Prymer* (1536), sig. S1–3.

43. *Hore Beatissime Virginis Marie* (Regnault), sig. Q4v–5v.

44. *Thys Prymer* (1536), sig. Y3v–5v.

45. Butterworth, *The Literary Lineage of the King James Bible,* p. 105.

46. *Thys Prymer* (Rouen, 1538), sig. A1–2v.

47. *Hore Beatissime Virginis Marie* (Regnault), sigs. a2, a4, and *Thys Prymer* (Rouen, 1538), sigs. ✠2, ✠4.

48. *Hore Beatissime Virginis Marie* (Regnault), sig. a7v, and *Thys Prymer* (Rouen, 1538), sig. ✠7v.

49. *Thys Prymer* (Rouen, 1538), sig. ✠3.

50. *Ibid.,* sig. I2.

51. *Hore Beatissime Virginis Marie* (Regnault), sig. R4v, and *Thys Prymer* (Rouen, 1538), sig. I2v.

52. *Hore Beatissime Virginis Marie* (Regnault), sig. R5, and *Thys Prymer* (Rouen, 1538), sig. I3v.

53. *Ibid.*

54. *Hore Beatissime Virginis Marie*

(Regnault), sig. R6, and *Thys Prymer* (Rouen, 1538), sig. I4.

55. *Thys Prymer* (Rouen, 1538), sigs. B4 and C2.

56. *Ibid.*, sig. G4.

57. *Ibid.*, sig. I7.

58. *Thys Prymer* (1536), sig. T5v-6.

59. *Thys Prymer* (Rouen, 1538), sig. N5.

60. *Ibid.*, sig. I5v.

61. *An Exposycyon after the Maner of a Contemplacyon*, etc., with *Thys Prymer* (Rouen, 1538), sig. a1 ff.

62. Hoskins, *op. cit.*, p. 207.

63. Butterworth, *op. cit.*, pp. 47-48, and Simmons, *The Lay Folks' Mass Book*, pp. 47-48.

64. Cf. [Tyndale], *The Newe Testament*.

65. *Thys Prymer* (Paris, 1538), sig. N1, and *Thys Prymer* (1536), sig. I8; and, respectively, sig. P6v and sig. N7v; sig. C5 and sig. A4v; sig. E8v and sig. C7; sig. I1 and sig. F8v; sig. I5v and sig. G5; sig. K2 and sig. H1v; sig. K7 and sig. H8.

66. Butterworth, *op. cit.*, p. 105.

67. For example, *The Prymer in Englysshe* (Le Roux for Regnault) sig. P2, and *Thys Prymer* (Rouen, 1538), sig. M5v.

68. Further evidence of such a relationship is to be seen in a Latin primer, printed at Rouen for Regnault in 1537. A number of the smaller plates of the Paris English-Latin primer of 1538 are used in this volume, which is too small for the main plates, for example, *Thys Prymer* (Paris, 1538), sigs. F8-G4, and *Thys Prymer of Salysburye Use* (Rouen, 1537), sig. D2-5v.

69. Since writing the above I have found in the British Museum another version of the Paris English-Latin primer of 1538 (C52. f. 16). This has in place of Maister Quentin's guide the reforming preface of the Rouen primers of 1536 and 1538 (sig. B6v ff.),

further proof, if proof is needed, of the relations of these primers and of their general situation.

70. *Thys Prymer* (Paris, 1538), sig. A2v ff., and *Thys Prymer* (Rouen, 1538), sig. ✠2 ff., and, respectively, sig. O7 and sig. I2.

71. See above, note 28.

72. *Thys Prymer* (Paris, 1538), sig. B6v-8v.

73. Butterworth, *op. cit.*, p. 106.

74. *Ibid.*

75. *Thys Prymer newly imprynted*, sig. D4v.

76. *Thys Prymer* (1536), sig. F3.

77. *Thys Prymer off Salysburye Use* (Yolande Bonhomme), sig. i5v, etc.

78. Similar verses are found in the same places in a Latin primer with English headings which Regnault published at Paris in 1527: *Thys Prymer of Salysbury Use* (Paris: Franciscus Regnault, 1527), sig. D4 ff.

79. *A Primer in Englysshe with Dyvers Prayers and Godly Meditations*, sig. O2r-v, and *Thys Prymer* (Rouen, 1538), sig. N5.

80. *A Prymer in Englyshe*, sig. Q8v.

81. *Ibid.*, sig. I3, and *Thys Prymer* (1536), sig. E5.

82. *A Goodly Prymer in Englyshe*, sig. ²R4r-v, and *Thys Prymer* (1536), sig. Y2v.

83. Hoskins, *op. cit.*, p. 159. There is in the Bodleian Library (Tanner 278) a primer bearing the date of 1538 in a style uniform with that of two works bound up with it, a "Pystles and Gospels" which bears no date but Robert Redman's name, and "An Exposycyn after the Maner of a Contemplacion" which bears both Robert Redman's name and the date 1539. Except for some minor differences this is certainly the Rouen Primer of 1538.

84. *The Prymer in Englyshe, and Latyn* (Toye), sig. T2v.

NOTES TO CHAPTER VI

1. Butterworth, *The Literary Lineage of the King James Bible,* p. 67.

2. *A Primer in Englysshe* (Godfray), sig. [A]3, [A]4.

3. *Ibid.,* sigs. [A]8 ff., B1v ff.

4. *Ibid.,* sig. D4v ff.

5. Brightman, *The English Rite,* I, lii.

6. *A Primer in Englysshe* (Godfray), sig. E1.

7. *Ibid.,* sig. E3-4.

8. *Thys Prymer* (1536), sig. B7v.

9. *A Primer in Englysshe* (Godfray), sig. E7v-8v.

10. *Ibid.,* sig. G4 ff.

11. *Ibid.,* sig. N6v ff.

12. *Ibid.,* sig. O2v-3v.

13. *Ibid.,* sig. O4 ff.

14. *Ibid.,* sigs. P3v-Q6.

15. *Ibid.,* sigs. O2r-v, and *Thys Prymer* (Rouen, 1538), sig. N5.

16. *A Primer in Englysshe* (Godfray), sig. P3v.

17. *The Psalter of David in Englishe . . . aftir the Texte of Feline,* sig. BB1.

18. *A Goodly Prymer in Englyshe* (1535), sig. ²L2v.

19. *A Prymer in Englyshe* (Byddell-Marshall), sig. ✠2, ✠7r-v.

20. *Ibid.,* sig. F2, and *A Primer in Englysshe* (Godfray), sig. G4 ff.; and, respectively, sig. R1 ff. and sig. D4v ff.; sig. S2 and sig. O2v ff.

21. *A Prymer in Englyshe* (Byddell-Marshall), sig. I3, and *Thys Prymer* (1536), sig. E5.

22. Butterworth, *op. cit.,* p. 65.

23. *Ibid.,* p. 67.

24. *A Prymer in Englyshe* (Byddell-Marshall), sig. D6v-8.

25. *Ibid.,* sig. D7.

26. *A Goodly Prymer in Englyshe* (1535), sig. ²L2v.

27. *Ibid.,* sig. A1.

28. *Ibid.,* sig. A3v-4.

29. *Ibid.,* sigs. A4v-B1.

30. *Ibid.,* sig. A3v.

31. *Ibid.,* sig. C3v.

32. *Ibid.,* sig. C1v.

33. *Ibid.,* sig. B3.

34. *Ibid.,* sigs. D1v-²D1v.

35. *Ibid.,* sigs. F4-²A4v, ²B1-²C4, ²C4v-²D1v.

36. *Ibid.,* ²E1.

37. *Hore Beatissime Virginis Marie* (Regnault), sig. B7v-8.

38. *A Goodly Prymer in Englyshe* (1535), sig. ²E1v, and *Hore Beatissime Virginis Marie* (Regnault), sig. B8.

39. *A Goodly Prymer in Englyshe* (1535), sig. ²E3v, and *Hore Beatissime Virginis Marie* (Regnault), sig. C1v.

40. *A Goodly Prymer in Englyshe* (1535), sigs. ²E3v-²F1, and *Hore Beatissime Virginis Marie* (Regnault), sig. C1v-2.

41. *A Goodly Prymer in Englyshe* (1535), sig. ²G2, and *Hore Beatissime Virginis Marie* (Regnault), sig. C7.

42. *A Goodly Prymer in Englyshe* (1535), sig. ²I3r-v, and *Hore Beatissime Virginis Marie* (Regnault), sig. F4v-5.

43. *A Goodly Prymer in Englyshe* (1535), sig. ²K2v.

44. *Ibid.,* sigs. ²L2v-²M2.

45. Brightman, *op. cit.,* p. lii.

46. *A Goodly Prymer in Englyshe* (1535), sig. ²L2v-3.

47. *Ibid.,* sigs. ²M3-²R4.

48. *Hore Beatissime Virginis Marie* (Regnault), sig. A1v-7v.

49. *Thys Prymer* (Paris, 1538), sigs. C3-D3v.

50. *A Goodly Prymer in Englyshe* (1535), sigs. ³A-³E3v.

51. *Ibid.,* sig. ³E1v.

52. *Ibid.,* sig. ³E4v.

53. *Ibid.,* sig. ³F1-2.

54. *Ibid.,* sig. ³E4v.

55. *Ibid.,* sigs. ³G3v-³H2v, ³H3-³I1v.

56. *Ibid.*, sig. ³K4.

57. *Hore Beatissime Virginis Marie* (Regnault), sig. F4v–5v.

58. *A Goodly Prymer in Englyshe* (1535), sig. ³M1.

59. *Thys Prymer* (1536), sig. Y2v, and *A Goodly Prymer in Englyshe* (1535), sig. ²R4r–v.

60. *Ibid.*, sig. ³I2r–v.

61. *Ibid.*, sig. ²D4.

62. *Ibid.*

63. *A Goodly Prymer in Englysshe, newly corrected* (1537?), sig. C1.

64. *Ibid.*, sig. ²V1 ff.

65. *Ibid.*, sig. ²T4v.

66. Butterworth, *op. cit.*, p. 105.

67. *This Primer of Salysbery Use, both in Englyshe and in Laten*, sig. T8.

68. *Ibid.*, sig. V6.

69. *Ibid.*, sig. ⧣⧣1 ff.

NOTES TO CHAPTER VII

1. *The Manual of Prayers, or the Prymer in Englysh and Laten*, sigs. Vv2–4v.

2. *Ibid.*, sig. Ff3v ff.

3. *Ibid.*, [unsigned]2.

4. *Ibid.*, sig. [A]A4v.

5. *Ibid.*, sig. BB1.

6. *Ibid.*, sig. EE2r–v.

7. *Ibid.*, sig. ✠1–2.

8. Butterworth, *The Literary Lineage of the King James Bible*, p. 147.

9. *The Manual of Prayers*, sig. BB1r–v.

10. *Ibid.*, sigs. X1v–Z1, and *Thys Prymer* (Paris, 1538), sig. M3 ff.

11. *Hore Beatissime Virginis Marie* (Regnault), sig. I1.

12. *Thys Prymer* (Rouen, 1538), sig. X1v–2.

13. *The Manual of Prayers*, sigs. F1–G1; *Thys Prymer* (Paris, 1538), sigs. F7–G7.

14. *The Manual of Prayers*, sig. Z2ff.; *Thys Prymer* (Paris, 1538), sig. N1 ff.; *A Goodly Prymer in Englyshe* (1535), sig. ²K2v.

15. *The Manual of Prayers*, sigs. Ee4v–Ff3; *A Goodly Prymer in Englyshe* (1535), sig. ²M2r–v; *Thys Prymer* (Paris, 1538), sig. P3v–5.

16. *A Goodly Prymer in Englyshe* (1535), sigs. ²L3v–²M2; *The Manual of Prayers*, sigs. Dd4v–E1v.

17. *The Primer, set foorth by the Kynges Majestie and his Clergie*, sig. *2–3v.

18. *Ibid.*, sig. ***2v–8.

19. *Ibid.*, sigs. A1–H3v; I1–L1; L2–M4; N1–Q2; Q3–S4v; T1–V3v; AA1–BB2v; BB3–CC2.

20. *Ibid.*, sig. ³K4.

21. *Hore Beatissime Virginis Marie* (Regnault), sigs. S2–V4v; *Thys Prymer* (Paris, 1538), sigs, P6v–T8v; *The Primer, set foorth by the Kynges Majestie*, sigs. N1–O2.

22. *Thys Prymer* (Paris, 1538), sig. T6v, and *The Primer, set foorth by the Kynges Majestie*, sig. P2.

23. *Thys Prymer* (Paris, 1538), sig. T6v; *Hore Beatissime Virginis Marie*, sig. V4.

24. *The Primer, set foorth by the Kynges Majestie*, sig. P2.

25. *Ibid.*, sig. Q2v.

26. *Hore Beatissime Virginis Marie*, sig. X4–5v, and *Thys Prymer* (Paris, 1538), sig. X3r–v.

27. *The Primer, set foorth by the Kynges Majestie*, sigs. T1–U4v; *Hore Beatissime Virginis Marie* (Regnault), sigs. X5v–Y4v; *Thys Prymer* (Paris, 1538), sigs. X3v–Y4v.

28. *The Primer, set foorth by the Kynges Majestie*, sigs. AA1–BB2v; *Hore Beatissime Virginis Marie* (Regnault), sig. A3v–7v.

29. *The Primer, set foorth by the Kynges Majestie*, sigs. BB3–CC2.

30. See above, p. 97.

31. *Thys Prymer* (Paris, 1538), sig. E1.

32. A Goodly Prymer in Englyshe (1535), sig. ²E1v.

33. *The Primer, set foorth by the Kynges Majestie*, sig. A2r–v.

34. *Hore Beatissime Virginis Marie* (Regnault), sig. C1v–2; *A Goodly Prymer in Englyshe* (1535), sigs. ²E3v–²F1.

35. *The Primer, set foorth by the Kynges Majestie*, sig. B1–2v.

36. *Ibid.*, sig. B4.

37. *A Goodly Prymer in Englyshe* (1535), sig. ²F2–3.

38. *Ibid.*, sig. E2v–3v, and *Hore Beatissime Virginis Marie* (Regnault), sig. E3–5.

39. *The Primer, set foorth by the Kynges Majestie*, sig. L2r–v.

40. *Ibid.*, sig. L2v.

41. *Ibid.*, sig. M3–4.

42. *Hore Beatissime Virginis Marie* (Regnault), sig. R7–8, and *Thys Prymer* (Paris, 1538), sig. P3v–5.

43. *A Goodly Prymer in Englyshe* (1535), sig. ²M2r–v.

44. See, for instance, *The Primer, set foorth by the Kynges Majestie*, sig. M4.

45. *Thys Prymer* (Paris, 1538), sig. N5.

46. *The Primer, set foorth by the Kynges Majestie*, sig. K1v–3.

47. *Ibid.*, sigs. CC2–LL1v.

48. *Ibid.*, sigs. CC4v, DD1–2, FF3r–v.

49. *Ibid.*, sig. DD2r–v.

50. *Ibid.*, sigs. CC2, KK4, LL1r–v.

51. *Ibid.*, sigs. CC3v, HH1, HH1v–2, HH3–4, HH4–II1, KK1v–4.

52. *Ibid.*, sig. II3–4.

53. From Erasmus, *Precationes aliquot;* see Clay, *Private Prayers*, pp. 98–103.

54. *The Primer, set foorth by the Kynges Majestie*, sigs. FF3v, FF4.

55. *Ibid.*, sig. GG2.

56. *Ibid.*, sig. GG3.

57. *Ibid.*, sig. GG3v–4.

58. Clay, *op. cit.*, p. 102 *n.*

NOTES TO CHAPTER VIII

1. *The Primer, set foorth by the Kynges Majestie*, sig. L1v.

2. Hoskins, *Horae Beatae Mariae Virginis*, p. 289.

3. *Ibid.*, p. 290.

4. *Ibid.*

5. *Ibid.*, p. 292.

6. *Ibid.*

7. *Ibid.*

8. *Ibid.*, p. 294.

9. *Ibid.*, pp. 292–95.

10. *An Uniforme and Catholyke Prymer in Latin and Englishe.*

11. *Ibid.*, sigs. ¶4–( )2v; ( )3–(2)1v.

12. *Ibid.*, sigs. P2–Q4v.

13. *Ibid.*, sig. A1.

14. *The Manual of Prayers*, sigs. Ff1r–v.

15. *An Uniforme and Catholyke Prymer*, sig. d3.

16. *Ibid.*, sigs. *1–¶3v.

17. Cf. [*Horae ad usum Sarum*], sig. &1v, and *Hore Beatissime Virginis Marie* (Regnault), sig. A8r–v.

18. *An Uniforme and Catholyke Prymer*, sig. *3.

19. *Hore Beatissime Virginis Marie* (Regnault), sig. A8r–v.

20. *An Uniforme and Catholyke Prymer*, sig. *3.

21. *The Primer in Englishe and Latyn, set foorth by the Kynges Majestie*, sig. O4v ff.

22. *An Uniforme and Catholyke Prymer*, sig. ¶2–3v.

23. *Ibid.*, sigs. X4–Dd2.

24. *The Primer, set foorth by the Kynges Majestie*, sig. CC2 ff.

25. *An Uniforme and Catholyke Prymer*, sig. Dd4.

26. Cf., *ibid.*, sig. y1v–2v.

27. *Ibid.*, sigs. Aa3v–Bb1.

28. *Ibid.*, sig. z1v–z2.

29. *Ibid.*, sigs. Cc1v, z2v.

30. *Ibid.*, sigs. &4r-v, Aa1r-v.

31. *Ibid.*, sig. Bb3r-v.

32. *Ibid.*, sig. Cc3-4v.

33. *Ibid.*, sig. Cc2-r-v.

34. *Ibid.*, sig. Dd2-3v.

35. *Ibid.*, sig. Dd2; *Hore Beatissime Virginis Marie* (Regnault), sig. Q5.

36. *The Primer, set foorth by the Kynges Majestie*, sigs. CC4v-DD1, and *An Uniforme and Catholyke Prymer*, sig. y4v.

37. *The Primer, set foorth by the Kynges Majestie*, sig. CC3v-4, and *An Uniforme and Catholyke Prymer*, sig. y4; and, respectively, sigs. DD4v-EE1v and sig. z1; sig. LL1r-v and sig. &2v.

38. *Thys Prymer* (Paris, 1538), sig. Z8.

39. *The Primer, set foorth by the Kynges Majestie*, sig. II3.

40. *An Uniforme and Catholyke Prymer*, sig. Aa1.

41. *The Primer, set foorth by the Kynges Majestie*, sig. II1v-2v.

42. Clay, *Private Prayers*, pp. 107, 201.

43. *The Primer, set foorth by the Kynges Majestie*, sig. II2v.

44. *An Uniforme and Catholyke Prymer*, sig. &2v.

45. *The Primer, set foorth by the Kynges Majestie*, sigs. FF3v-GG4v; Clay, *op. cit.*, p. 98.

46. *The Primer, set foorth by the Kynges Majestie*, sigs. KK4-LL1v; Clay, *op. cit.*, p. 206.

47. *An Uniforme and Catholyke Prymer*, sigs. Bb3v, &2v.

48. Becon, *The Flower of Godly Prayers*, sig. EEE5.

49. *An Uniforme and Catholyke Prymer*, sig. *3v.

50. Clay, *op. cit.*, p. 1.

51. Hoskins, *op. cit.*, pp. 248-50.

52. Clay, *op. cit.*, pp. 10-11.

53. Hoskins, *op. cit.*, p. 250.

54. Clay, *op. cit.*, p. 13; Hoskins, *op. cit.*, p. 251.

55. Clay, *op. cit.*, pp. 15-18.

56. *Ibid.*, p. 19.

57. See for instance, *The Primer, set foorth by the Kynges Majestie*, sig. B2v, and Clay, *op. cit.*, pp. 27-28.

58. Clay, *op. cit.*, p. 51.

59. *The Primer, set foorth by the Kynges Majestie*, sig. L2 ff.

60. According to Hoskins, *op. cit.*, pp. 252, 66.

61. *The Primer, set foorth by the Kynges Majestie*, sig. N1 ff., and Clay, *op. cit.*, pp. 57 ff.; and, respectively, sig. Q2v ff. and pp. 68 ff.; sig. T1 ff., and pp. 75 ff.; sig. BB3 ff., and pp. 85 ff.; sig. CC2 ff., and pp. 88 ff.

62. Hoskins, *op. cit.*, pp. 250-57.

63. *Ibid.*, p. 289 ff.

64. *Ibid.*, pp. 299, 300.

65. *Ibid.*, p. 300.

NOTES TO CHAPTER IX

1. *Praiers of Holi Fathers, Patryarches, Prophetes, Judges, Kynges, and Renowmed Men and Women of Eyther Testamente*, sig. A1.

2. *Ibid.*, sigs. B2v, B8v, C6v, E1v, F1.

3. *Ibid.*, sig. C1.

4. *Ibid.*, sig. D5v.

5. See above, Chapter III, p. 41.

6. *Praiers of Holi Fathers*, sig. K1.

7. *Ibid.*, sigs. O4v-P4v.

8. *Hore Beatissime Virginis Marie* (Regnault), sigs. M1v-Q2v.

9. *Ibid.*, O8v, Q1.

10. *Ibid.*, sigs. O8v-P1v.

11. *Praiers of Holi Fathers*, sig. A1.

12. *Ibid.*, sigs. E1v-2v.

13. *Hore Beatissime Virginis Marie* (Regnault), sig. P2v-3.

14. *Ibid.*, sigs. P3v-Q1, and *Praiers of Holi Fathers*, sigs. C2v-D6.

15. *Hore Beatissime Virginis Marie* (Regnault), sig. P8v.

16. *Praiers of Holi Fathers,* sig. D4v.

17. *Hore Beatissime Virginis Marie* (Regnault), sig. P3v–4.

18. *The Byble in Englyshe of the Largest and Greatest Volume,* sig. Ggg3v.

19. *Praiers of Holi Fathers,* sig. C3r–v.

20. *Hore Beatissime Virginis Marie* (Regnault), sig. P8r–v.

21. *Praiers of Holi Fathers,* sig. D4v.

22. *Ibid.,* sig. F3v–4v.

23. Cf. *Hore Beatissime Virginis Marie* (Regnault), sig. C2r–v.

24. *Thys Prymer* (Paris, 1538), sig. E6–7.

25. James Nicolson printed two editions of the Coverdale Bible in 1537.

26. *The Psalter, or Boke of the Psalmes, whereunto are added Certayne Other Devout Prayers,* sig. R1.

27. *Praiers of Holi Fathers,* sig. A1.

28. *The Psalter . . . whereunto are added Certayne Other Devout Prayers,* sig. R1.

29. *Ibid.,* sig. R2v ff.

30. *Ibid.,* sigs. T6v–7v, V2v–3.

31. *Ibid.,* sig. V3r–v.

32. *The Treasure of Gladnesse* (London: W. Williamson for J. Charlewood, 1563).

33. *The Treasure of Gladnesse* (London, 1568).

34. *Ibid.,* sigs. N7–P2.

35. *The Queenes Praiers or Meditations,* sigs. F3v–G8v.

36. *The Treasure of Gladnesse* (1568), sig. A2–6.

37. *Ibid.,* sigs. B1v–8v, C1–8.

38. *Ibid.,* sig. C8.

39. *Ibid.,* D3r–v.

40. *An Uniforme and Catholyke Prymer,* sig. &2.

41. *The Treasure of Gladnesse* (1568), sig. F2v–3.

42. *Ibid.,* sig. F5–7v.

43. Cf. Whitford, *A Werke for Housholders,* sig. B2v–3.

44. *The Treasure of Gladnesse* (1568), sig. F8 ff.

45. *Ibid.,* sig. G4v–5v.

46. *Ibid.,* sigs. M4–N6v.

47. Becon, *The Flower of Godly Prayers,* sig. HHH1r–v.

48. Bull, *Christian Praiers and Holie Meditations,* sig. Y5v–7v.

49. *The Byble in Englyshe* (1539), sig. Ddd1v.

50. Baldwin, *The Canticles or Balades of Salomon,* sig. A1v.

51. *Ibid.,* sig. f4v.

52. See, for instance, *Thys Prymer* (Paris, 1538), sig. C1–2.

53. *Ibid.,* sig. M3 ff.

54. *The Rosary of our Savyour Jesu,* sigs. C3, D3.

55. See above, p. 97.

56. *Certaine Devout and Godly Petitions commonly called, Jesus Psalter,* sig. A3–4.

57. *Ibid.,* sigs. A4, A5, A7v, A8v, B1v, D1, D2v–3v.

58. *Sixe Spirituall Bookes . . . And First, Certaine Devout and Godlie Petitions, commonlie called, The Jesus Psalter,* sig. A3r–v.

59. *Ibid.,* sig. A6v.

60. *Ibid.,* sigs. A10v, B1v, B4v, B10v, C10v.

61. See above, p. 97.

62. For example, *Thys Prymer* (Paris, 1538), sig. C1–2.

63. Bradford, *Godly Meditations on the Lord's Prayer,* p. 199.

64. *Ibid.*

65. See above, p. 97.

NOTES TO CHAPTER X

1. Gasquet, "The Bibliography of Some Devotional Books," p. 186.

2. *Thys Prymer* (Paris, 1538), B6v–8v.

3. *Ibid.,* sig. B6v.

4. *Ibid.,* sig. B7.

5. *Ibid.,* sig. B7r–v.

6. *Ibid.,* sig. B8.

7. *Ibid.*

8. *Ibid.*, sig. B8v.

9. *Ibid.*

10. *The Pomander of Prayer* (Coplande), [unsigned]2.

11. *Ibid.*, sig. A2.

12. *Ibid.*, sig. A1r–v.

13. *Ibid.*, sig. G2v.

14. *Ibid.*, sig. D2 ff.

15. *A Dyurnall for Devoute Soules*, sig. a2.

16. *Ibid.*, sigs. a2–c2.

17. *Ibid.*, sig. a2r–v.

18. *Ibid.*, sig. a2v–3.

19. *Ibid.*, sig. b2v.

20. *Ibid.*, sig. b3v.

21. See p. 160, below.

22. Edward J. Klein, Introduction to *The Imitation of Christ from the First Edition of an English Translation made by Richard Whitford* (New York and London, 1941), p. xiv.

23. Whitford, *A Werke for Housholders*, sig. B1v.

24. *Ibid.*, sig. A3.

25. *Ibid.*, sig. B2v–3.

26. *Ibid.*, sigs. B3v–C1.

27. *Ibid.*, sig. C1.

28. *Ibid.*, sigs. C1–F4v.

29. *Ibid.*, sig. C2.

30. *Ibid.*, sigs. C3v–D1v.

31. *Ibid.*, sig. D4.

32. *Ibid.*, sig. D4r–v.

33. *Ibid.*, sig. D4v.

34. *Ibid.*, sig. G1–4.

35. *Ibid.*, sig. H1v.

36. *Ibid.*, sig. H2v–3.

37. *Ibid.*, sig. H3v.

38. Pourrat, *Christian Spirituality*, II, 252 ff.

39. Hoskins, *Horae Beatae Mariae Virginis*, pp. 242–43, 257–70.

40. *The Prayers of Erasmus*, p. vii.

41. Bradford, *Private Prayers and Meditations*, pp. 224–29.

42. *Ibid.*, p. 232.

43. *Ibid.*, pp. 233–34.

44. *Ibid.*

45. *Ibid.*, pp. 242–47.

46. Becon, *The Pommaunder of Prayers*, sigs. B4v–E5.

47. Becon, *The Flower of Godly Prayers*, sig. DDD5.

48. *Ibid.*, sig. DDD5v. See also Becon, *The Early Works* (Parker Society, 1848), p. x.

49. Becon, *The Flower of Godly Prayers*, sigs. FFF3–HHH2v.

50. *Ibid.*, sig. HHH3v–5.

51. *A Tablet for Gentlewomen*, sig. F2.

52. Dering, *A Shorte Catechisme for Housholders*, sig. E5 ff.

53. *Ibid.*, sigs. F7v–8v, I6v–K2.

54. *Ibid.*, sig. F5–6.

55. Dering, *A Sermon preached before the Queenes Majestie, the .25. Day of February . . . Anno 1569* (n.p., n.d.).

56. Parsons, *A Christian Directorie guiding Men to their Salvation*, pp. 20–21.

57. Bunny, *A Booke of Christian Exercise, appertaining to Resolution*, sig. *2r–v.

58. See Helen C. White, *English Devotional Literature (Prose) 1600–1640* (Madison, Wisconsin, 1931), pp. 143–47.

59. Richard Baxter, *Reliquiae Baxterianae: Or, Mr. Richard Buxter's Narrative of the Most Memorable Passages of his Life and Times*, ed. Matthew Sylvester (London: for T. Parkhurst, F. Robinson, F. Lawrence and F. Dunton, 1696), p. 3.

NOTES TO CHAPTER XI

1. Becon, *The Pathwai unto Prayer*, sig. L4v.

2. Melanchthon, *A Godlye Treatyse of Prayer*, sig. A5.

3. *Ibid.*, sig. F6v.

4. *The Queenes Praiers or Meditations*, sigs. A7v–8, B6v–8v.

5. *Ibid.*, sigs. A2, B3v.

6. Becon, *The Pommaunder of Prayers*, sigs. A3–5, A7–B4v.

7. *Ibid.*, sigs. E7, E8v, F2v, F4, F5, F6v, F7v.

8. *Ibid.*, sigs. H3v, H5.

9. *Ibid.*, sigs. I5v, I7, I8.

10. *Ibid.*, sig. K1–6.

11. *Ibid.*, sigs. L4–M1, M5v ff., P4 ff.

12. Becon, *The Pomaunder of Prayer* (1561), sigs. G6v–I3v.

13. *Ibid.*, sigs. I4–L2.

14. Bradford, *Godly Meditations uppon the Ten Commaundementes*, sig. A3.

15. Whitford, *A Werke for Housholders*, sig. B2v ff.

16. Bradford, *Godly Meditations on the Lord's Prayer*, pp. 118–39.

17. *Ibid.*, pp. 173 ff., 185 ff., 188 ff., 193 ff., 196 ff.

18. *Ibid.*, p. 173.

19. *The Primer, set foorth by the Kynges Majestie*, sig. LL1r–v.

20. Clay, *Private Prayers*, pp. 556–57.

21. *Ibid.*

22. Bradford, *Writings* (Parker Society), p. 273.

23. Bull, *Christian Praiers and Holie Meditations*, sigs. B1–C8v.

24. *Ibid.*, sigs. D1–E2v.

25. *Ibid.*, sigs. I2v–L2v.

26. Bradford, *Writings* (Parker Society), p. 233, and Bull, *op. cit.*, sigs. I2v–L2.

27. Bull, *op. cit.*, sigs. M5–R2.

28. *Ibid.*, sigs. O4, O7v, P7v, Q5, R2.

29. *Ibid.*, sigs. L3–5, L5–M4, M5, N3, N4–6v, N7–O4.

30. *Ibid.*, sigs. R2, R8.

31. *Ibid.*, sigs. S1v, T6.

32. *Ibid.*, sig. S6v, T3v, T7v, X2–4, Y1–3v.

33. *Ibid.*, sigs. Z5v–Cc4v.

34. *Ibid.*, sigs. Aa3v, Aa8.

35. *Ibid.*, sig. Z5v.

36. *Ibid.*, sigs. Bb2–3.

37. *Ibid.*, sig. Bb3.

38. *Ibid.*, sigs. Cc5–Dd7v.

39. *Ibid.*, sigs. Dd8–Ee4v.

40. *A Godly Garden* (H. Middleton, 1574), sig. B6.

41. *Ibid.*, sig. C3v.

42. *Ibid.*, sigs. C7v–8v, D1 ff.

43. *Ibid.*, sig. E7.

44. *Ibid.*, sig. H6.

45. *Ibid.*, sig. F7v ff.

46. *Ibid.*, sig. I8v–Z1.

47. *Ibid.*, sig. K4; [*Horae ad usum Sarum*], sig. &1v; *Hore Beatissime Virginis Marie* (Regnault), sig. A8r–v.

48. *A Godly Garden*, sig. L5v; Bradford, *Writings* (Parker Society), p. 231; *An Uniforme and Catholyke Prymer*, sig. *2v.

49. Bull, *op. cit.*, sig. I3v; Day, *Christian Prayers and Meditations*, sig. a3.

50. *A Godly Garden*, sig. N3v ff.

51. *The Roman Missal in Latin and English*, ed. F. Cabrol (Tours, [1922?]), pp. xl–xli.

52. *Ibid.*, p. lx.

53. *A Godly Garden*, sig. R4v–5.

54. Abbot Ælfric, *A Testimonie of Antiquitie* (London: John Day, 1567).

55. *The Treasure of Gladnesse* (London, 1568).

56. Day, *Christian Prayers and Meditations*, sig. [hand]1v.

57. *Ibid.*, sig. pp2v–3.

58. Cf. *ibid.*, sig. k3v.

59. Chew, "The Iconography of *A Book of Christian Prayers* (1578) Illustrated," pp. 294–95.

60. *Ibid.*, p. 300.

61. Day, *Christian Prayers and Meditations*, sigs. a2–c4v.

62. Clay, *op. cit.*, p. 440.

63. Day, *Christian Prayers and Meditations*, sigs. d1–p2v.

64. *Ibid.*, sigs. d1–e2v.

65. Bull, *op. cit.*, sigs. S1v, S4.

66. *Ibid.*, sig. O4, and Day, *Christian Prayers and Meditations*, sig. e2v; and, respectively, sig. O7v and sig. f3; sig. P7v and sig. i2v.

67. Day, *Christian Prayers and Meditations*, sigs. k2, m2; Bradford, *Writ-*

ings (Parker Society), pp. 187–91, 194–95.

68. Day, *Christian Prayers and Meditations,* sig. p2v; cf. *Thys Prymer* (Paris, 1538), sig. &3v.

69. Day, *Christian Prayers and Meditations,* sigs. A1–F4v.

70. Cf. *ibid.,* sigs. A2r–v.

71. *Ibid.,* sigs. G1–N2.

72. *Ibid.,* sigs. Aa1–Gg4v.

73. Cf. *ibid.,* sig. k1r–v.

74. Cf. Day, *A Booke of Christian Prayers,* sigs. F1, L2.

75. Chew, *op. cit.,* p. 299.

76. Day, *A Booke of Christian Prayers,* sig. M1 ff., and Chew, *op. cit.,* p. 300.

77. Day, *A Booke of Christian Prayers,* sigs. R2, Q1v.

78. Day, *Christian Prayers and Meditations,* sig. a2; Day, *A Booke of Christian Prayers,* sigs. [hand]2–A2v, and Clay, *op. cit.,* p. 437.

79. Day, *A Booke of Christian Prayers,* sigs. [hand]2v–A2.

80. *Ibid.,* sig. A3 ff.; Clay, *op. cit.,* p. 440.

81. Day, *A Booke of Christian Prayers,* sig. B3r–v; Clay, *op. cit.,* pp. 441–42.

82. Day, *A Booke of Christian Prayers,* sigs. D4–F3, F4, G2–L3v, L3v–O3, O3–P3v, P3v–V4, V4–Aa1, Aa1v–3v.

83. *Ibid.,* sigs. Aa4v–Bb1, Bb1v–Cc2v, Cc2v–Dd1v.

84. *Ibid.,* sig. Ff2 ff.

85. *Ibid.,* sigs. Ll2 ff., Nn3v ff., Oo2v.

86. *Ibid.,* sig. Ee1, and Clay, *op. cit.,* p. 526.

87. Day, *A Booke of Christian Prayers,* sig. G2; Clay, *op. cit.,* pp. 458–59.

88. Day, *A Booke of Christian Prayers,* sig. P3v; Clay, *op. cit.,* p. 488.

89. Day, *A Booke of Christian Prayers,* sig. Bb1v; Clay, *op. cit.,* p. 517.

90. Day, *A Booke of Christian Prayers,* sig. H1v.

NOTES TO CHAPTER XII

1. *Hore Beatissime Virginis Marie* (Regnault), sig. L6r–v.

2. *Ibid.,* sig. L6–7; *Thys Prymer* (Paris, 1538), sigs. Z8–&1.

3. *The Manual of Prayers,* sig. V2–3v; *The Prymer in Englyshe, and Latyn* (Toye), sig. N6r–v; *An Uniforme and Catholyke Prymer,* sig. Aa1r–v; *A Goodly Prymer in Englyshe* (1535), sig. R4r–v; *The Primer, set foorth by the Kynges Majestie,* sig. II3–4; Day, *A Booke of Christian Prayers,* sig. R2–3; Bull, *Christian Praiers and Holie Meditations,* sig. Bb3–4v.

4. Day, *A Booke of Christian Prayers,* sig. R2–3.

5. Bull, *op. cit.,* sig. Bb3–4v.

6. *Enchiridion praeclare ecclesie Sarum,* sig. B1v–2; Bull, *op. cit.,* sig. L2r–v; Day, *Christian Prayers and Meditations,* sigs. c4, D2v.

7. *The Primer, set foorth by the Kynges Majestie,* sigs. KK4v–LL1.

8. Clay, *Private Prayers,* p. 206.

9. *An Uniforme and Catholyke Prymer,* sig. Bb3v.

10. Day, *A Booke of Christian Prayers,* sig. Ii4r–v.

11. Clay, *op. cit.,* p. 183; *The Primer, set foorth by the Kynges Majestie,* sig. CC3v–4; *An Uniforme and Catholyke Prymer,* sig. y4; Day, *A Booke of Christian Prayers,* sigs. Cc4v–Dd1.

12. Hoskins, *Horae Beatae Mariae Virginis,* p. 243.

13. *The Prymer in Englyshe, and Latyn* (Toye), sig. N8; *The Primer, set foorth by the Kynges Majestie,* sig. II4r–v.

14. Becon, *The Pommaunder of Prayers,* sig. L4–8v; Bull, *op. cit.,* sig. Y2–3v; Day, *A Booke of Christian Prayers,* sigs. Ff4v–Gg2.

15. *Thys Prymer* (Paris, 1538), sig. &3.

16. *The Prymer in Englyshe, and Latyn* (Toye), sig. O1r–v; *The Primer, set foorth by the Kynges Majestie*, sig. EE4r–v; *An Uniforme and Catholyke Prymer*, sig. Aa2v; *Praiers of Holi Fathers*, sig. F6v–7; Day, *Christian Prayers and Meditations*, sig. Gg3v–4v.

17. [*Horae ad usum Sarum*], sig. &1v.

18. *Hore Beatissime Virginis Marie* (Regnault), sig. A8r–v; *The Manual of Prayers*, sig. DD4r–v.

19. *An Uniforme and Catholyke Prymer*, sig. *3.

20. Bull, *op. cit.*, sig. L7–8.

21. Day, *A Booke of Christian Prayers*, sig. B3r–v.

22. *A Right Christian Treatise, entituled S. Augustines Praiers*, sig. h8v; Day, *A Booke of Christian Prayers*, sig. Aa1v.

23. [*Horae ad usum Sarum*], sig. &1v; Bull, *op. cit.*, sigs. L7–8, I2v; Clay, *op. cit.*, p. 441; Becon, *The Pommaunder of Prayers* sig. A3–4.

24. [Dering], *Godly Private Prayers for Housholders*, sig. G1.

25. Hoskins, *op. cit.*, p. 242; *The Primer, set foorth by the Kynges Majestie*, sig. CC2v.

26. *Hore Beatissime Virginis Marie* (Regnault), sig. O6v–7.

27. Becon, *The Flower of Godly Prayers*, sig. GGG3r–v.

28. Clay, *op. cit.*, p. 544.

29. Bull, *op. cit.*, sig. Y4–5.

30. Day, *A Booke of Christian Prayers*, sig. Kk1v–2.

31. *Hore Beatissime Virginis Marie* (Regnault), sig. C6v.

32. *Thys Prymer* (Paris, 1538), sig. P2.

33. *Ibid.*, sig. P3v–4v.

34. *Ibid.*, sig. &3v.

35. *Thys Prymer* (Rouen, 1538), sig. I5v.

36. *The Primer, set foorth by the Kynges Majestie*, sigs. L3v–M4.

37. *An Uniforme and Catholyke Prymer*, sig. d3r–v.

38. *Psalmes or Prayers taken out of Holie Scripture*, sig. N5r–v.

39. Becon, *The Pommaunder of Prayers*, sig. O3v–5.

40. *The Queenes Praiers or Meditations*, sig. G5v; Bull, *op. cit.*, sig. Dd2v; Day, *Christian Prayers and Meditations*, sig. I1r–v; and Day, *A Booke of Christian Prayers*, sig. M3v–4.

41. Day, *A Booke of Christian Prayers*, sigs. L3v–N3.

42. Becon, *The Flower of Godly Prayers*, sig. FFF3.

43. Day, *Christian Prayers and Meditations*, sig. p2v–3.

NOTES TO CHAPTER XIII

1. *The Fifteen O's, and Other Prayers*, prefatory note.

2. *Ibid.*

3. *Hore Beatissime Virginis Marie* (Regnault), sig. I1.

4. *The Manual of Prayers*, sig. X1v–2.

5. *The Fifteen O's*, sig. a2.

6. *Ibid.*, sigs. a3, a3v, a4, a4v.

7. *Ibid.*, sig. a4r–v.

8. *Ibid.*, sig. a7.

9. [*Horae ad usum Sarum*], sig. G5v ff.; *Hore Beatissime Virginis Marie* (Christopher of Endhoven), Latin, sig. I3 ff., English, sig. S8v ff.; *Hore Beatissime Virginis Marie* (Regnault), Latin, sig. I1v ff., English, sig. aa1 ff.; *Thys Prymer* (1536), sig. K5; *Thys Prymer* (Rouen, 1538), sig. G4 ff.; *Thys Prymer* (Paris, 1538), sig. M3 ff.; *The Manual of Prayers*, sig. X1v ff.; *The Prymer in Englyshe* (Toye), sig. F3 ff.; *An Uniforme and Catholyke Prymer*, sig. P2 ff.

10. *Thys Prymer* (Paris, 1538), sig. M5r–v.

11. *The Fifteen O's*, sig. a4r–v.

12. [*Horae ad usum Sarum*], sig. G7v–8; *Hore Beatissime Virginis Marie* (Christopher of Endhoven), sig. I4v–5; *Hore Beatissime Virginis Marie* (Regnault), sig. I2v–3.

13. *Hore Beatissime Virginis Marie* (Christopher of Endhoven), sig. T2v–3; *Hore Beatissime Virginis Marie* (Regnault), sig. aa2v–3.

14. *Thys Prymer* (1536), sig. K5v–6; *Thys Prymer* (Rouen, 1538), sig. G5v–6.

15. *The Manual of Prayers*, sig. Y1r–v; *The Prymer in Englyshe, and Latyn* (Toye), sig. F4–5; *An Uniforme and Catholyke Prymer*, sig. Q1r–v.

16. *The Fifteen O's*, sig. a3; *Hore Beatissime Virginis Marie* (Regnault), sig. [a]a2.

17. *The Fifteen O's*, sig. a5; *Hore Beatissime Virginis Marie* (Regnault), sig. aa3v.

18. *Thys Prymer* (Paris, 1538), sigs. M4, M6.

19. *An Uniforme and Catholyke Prymer*, sigs. P2–Q4v.

20. *Ibid.*, sig. P2.

21. *Ibid.*, sig. P2v.

22. *Hore Beatissime Virginis Marie* (Regnault), sigs. I1v, aa1.

23. Cf. the twelfth prayer, *An Uni-forme and Catholyke Prymer*, sig. Q3r–v, and *The Fifteen O's*, sig. a6r–v.

24. Day, *A Booke of Christian Prayers*, sig. V4r–v.

25. *The Fifteen O's*, sig. a4.

26. *Ibid.*, sig. a4r–v.

27. *Ibid.*, sig. a5; Day, *A Booke of Christian Prayers*, Y2v.

28. *The Fifteen O's*, sig. a4v.

29. *Ibid.*, sig. a5.

30. *Ibid.*, sig. a6v–7.

31. *Ibid.*, sig. a2; *An Uniforme and Catholyke Prymer*, sig. P2; and Day, *A Booke of Christian Prayers*, sig. X3r–v.

32. *An Uniforme and Catholyke Prymer*, sig. P2v.

33. *Hore Beatissime Virginis Marie* (Regnault), sig. I1v; *Thys Prymer* (Paris, 1538), sig. M3.

34. Day, *A Booke of Christian Prayers*, sig. X3v.

35. *Ibid.*, sig. X4r–v.

36. *The Fifteen O's*, sig. a2v–3.

37. *An Uniforme and Catholyke Prymer*, sig. P3.

38. Day, *A Booke of Christian Prayers*, sig. Y1.

39. *The Fifteen O's*, sig. a6; Day, *A Booke of Christian Prayers*, sig. Y3.

40. *The Fifteen O's*, sig. a7v–8; Day, *A Booke of Christian Prayers*, sig. Y3v.

41. Day, *A Booke of Christian Prayers*, sig. Aa1.

INDEX

Active and contemplative life, 12

Adaptation of traditional materials, 196-215; to needs of time, 197; according to methods of time, 197; purging of blemishes of past, 197-98; some prayers relatively unchanged, 197-201; rhetorical changes, condensation, 201-2; expansion, 202-3; adjustment to new theological orientation, 203-6; changes in mood and temper, 206; no fixed chronological order in changes, 206-7; process applied to other types of prayers, 207-8; free adaptations difficult to trace, 208-9; combination of prayers, 209-10; mosaic of traditional elements, 210-11; traditional elements substituted for rejected prayer, 211-15; summary, 244-46

Aelfric, Abbot, *A Testimonie of Antiquitie,* 187

Aleph, Johan, 39

Alfred, King, 34

Ambrose, Saint, 8, 47, 55. *See also Canticum Ambrosii et Augustini*

Ancren Riwle, The, 35

Anselm, Saint, 59

Antiquarian interest, 187

Aquinas, Thomas, Saint, influence of, 6, 26, 127; Communion prayer, 186-87, 243

Ars moriendi, discussion of, omitted, 256

Asceticism, 128

Athanasius, Saint, guide to the use of the Psalms, 32, 44-45; mentioned, 55

Atkinson, William, 28

Augustine, Saint, 6-7, 17-19, 21-22, 47, 55, 59, 62, 178, 230-31, 245
— *Certaine Select Prayers gathered out of S. Austines Meditations,* 27; *Confessions,* 8, 12, 17, 27; *Glasse of Vaineglorie,* trans. W. P[rid]. 27; *Meditations and Prayers,* 28, 29; *His Private Talke with God; A Pretious Booke of Heavenlie Meditations,* trans. T. Rogers, 27-28, 29-30; *Right Christian Treatise, entituled S. Augustines Praiers . . . Whereunto is annexed Saint Augustines Psalter,* trans. Thomas Rogers, 27, 47, 208; *S. Augustine's Manuel,* trans. T. Rogers, 27. *See also Canticum Ambrosii et Augustini*

Ayling, Stephen, 216

Backer, Augustin de, on *Imitation of Christ,* 257

Baldwin, William, *Canticles or Balades of Salomon,* 143-44, 239

Basil, Saint, 55

Baxter, Richard, influenced by Bunny's *A Booke of Christian Exercise,* 171

Bayfield, Richard, 71

Beauty, awareness of, in Saint Augustine, 16; in Saint Bernard of Clairvaux, 20

Becon, Thomas, 153, 161, 166-67, 176, 182, 183, 237, 239, 242
— *Flower of Godly Prayers,* 129-30, 166, 167-68, 211-14; *Pathwai unto Prayer,* 174; *Pomander of Prayer* (1558), 176-77; *Pomaunder of Prayer* (1561),